Jane Christmas

WHAT THE
psychic
TOLD THE
pilgrim

GREYSTONE BOOKS

Douglas & McIntyre Publishing Group

Vancouver/Toronto/Berkeley

Greystone Books
A division of Douglas & McIntyre Ltd.
2323 Quebec Street, Suite 201
Vancouver, British Columbia
Canada V5T 4S7
www.greystonebooks.com

Library and Archives Canada Cataloguing in Publication
Christmas, Jane
What the psychic told the pilgrim : a midlife misadventure on Spain's
Camino de Santiago de Compostela / Jane Christmas.
ISBN 978-1-55365-240-3
1. Christmas, Jane—Travel—Spain, Northern.
2. Santiago de Compostela (Spain). 3. Spain, Northern—Description and travel.
4. Self-actualization (Psychology). I. Title.
DP285.C47 2007   914.6′10483   C2007-902417-3

Editing by Nancy Flight
Copy editing by Iva Cheung
Cover and text design by Jessica Sullivan
Cover map by The Bridgeman Art Library/Getty Images
Interior map by C. Stuart Daniel/Starshell Maps
Printed and bound in Canada by Friesens
Printed on acid-free paper that is forest friendly (100% post-consumer
recycled paper) and has been processed chlorine free.
Distributed in the U.S. by Publishers Group West

We gratefully acknowledge the financial support of the Canada Council for the Arts,
the British Columbia Arts Council, the Province of British Columbia through the Book
Publishing Tax Credit, and the Government of Canada through the Book Publishing
Industry Development Program (BPIDP) for our publishing activities.

WHAT

THE

{ PSYCHIC }

TOLD

THE

PILGRIM

*A Midlife Misadventure
on Spain's Camino
de Santiago de Compostela*

For Adam, Matthew, and Zoë

AUTHOR'S NOTE

ALL the events related here actually happened, though many of the names have been changed to spare embarrassment and lawsuits.

I am grateful to those who, wittingly or unwittingly, encouraged me in this endeavor: Valeria Grimshaw, Paulah Dauns, Allan and Trudi McGirr, Marianne Perry, Jennifer Grover, Agnes Bongers, Mike Ulmer, Lorna Shibley, Georgina Haig, Susan Meiras, Judy Birthelmer, Stephanie MacKendrick, the Algar twins, Susan and Liza, the late Fred Omstead, and most especially, the Englishman.

My appreciation extends to those who assisted in my research: Biblioteca de Estella, the Confraternity of St. James, the Canadian Company of Pilgrims, and Muriel at the Locke Street Libary.

Rob Sanders and Nancy Flight at Greystone Books patiently shepherded me through the writing process with sharp-eyed counsel and unfailing good humor.

Finally, to the many pilgrims on the Camino de Santiago de Compostela with whom I walked or met, who shared their stories, and who urged me on step by step: thank you. It was an unforgettable journey and the memory of it will last a lifetime.

THE CAMINO
FRANCÉS

100   200   300 km

Bay of Biscay

Bordeaux

Saint-Jean-Pied-
de-Port

Santiago de Compostela   San Juan de
                                Ortega
Portomarin   León   PYRENEES
       Ponferrada   Estella
              Castrojeriz   Logroño

Porto

P O R T U G A L

Madrid

Valencia

Lisbon

S P A I N

Cartagena

Granada

Cádiz

Mediterranean Sea

FRANCE

I

IMPULSE is intuition on crack.

If Intuition is the prudent angel who carefully directs your spirit, Impulse is its mischief-making twin, the "imp" in "impulse."

Impulse scoffs at the notion of second thoughts. Before you can apply a smidgen of rationale to your actions, Impulse has dragged you to the launch pad of adventure, where you find yourself staring bug-eyed at the bungee cord around your waist and asking, "How did I get here?"

In the same way that a change in temperature by a mere degree or two can cataclysmically alter the precarious balance of nature, so too can an impulsive act set off an unexpected chain reaction. You barely have time to gather your wits when the dominos start collapsing.

It was Impulse, disguised as a small bottle of wine, who knocked over the first domino and hurtled me toward an eight-hundred-kilometer pilgrimage.

A pilgrimage was the furthest thing from my mind when I boarded an airplane in Hamilton, Ontario, bound for Vancouver,

British Columbia. I was on a promotional tour for my first book, a memoir about escaping urban life, and I was focused on simply getting to my destination, delivering a coherent interview on a national TV talk show, and flying back home. It was a steel-gray December afternoon as the airplane taxied down the runway, an entirely unremarkable day that would have remained so had it not been for the tiny bottle of wine tucked in my purse, its genie itching to get out and commit a crime.

I was traveling on one of those cut-rate airlines that serve neither food nor beverages, or so I was explicitly told by a reservation clerk when I booked my flight. The information was partially incorrect; how could it have been otherwise? The communication of incorrect information that stirred Impulse and knocked over the first domino.

When I spied a liquor store on the way to the airport, Impulse implored me to pull out of the traffic and into the parking lot so that I could buy a little bottle of wine to quaff during my no-frills flight. The flight that had no bar service, or so I was told.

I belong to that rare species that adores airplane food. I love the giddy anticipation of not knowing what will be served and being handed a meal I have not had to lift a finger to prepare. The tidy bento box–like compartments, the perfectly sized proportions hidden beneath a layer of shiny tinfoil, are, quite simply, a treat.

However, I sacrificed the thrill of an in-flight meal service when I opted to fly on a discount airline out of the small and relatively uncomplicated John C. Munro International Airport in Hamilton rather than on a full-service airline out of the labyrinthine circus that is Lester B. Pearson International Airport in Toronto. (It is no coincidence that airports are named after politicians, the masters of confusion and distraction.)

An hour into the flight, I unpacked my brown-bag dinner (purchased at a deli also en route to the airport) and pulled the bottle of wine from my purse. I unscrewed the bottle cap, took a swig, and settled back into my seat. The drone of the airplane's engine pushed the clatter of daily life to the background and made conditions ripe for dreaming.

I started thinking about how I might mark my fiftieth birthday, a milestone that lay on the fast-approaching horizon. I craved something unusual and experiential to celebrate the occasion, but no matter how often or how hard I thought about it, only dull, predictable ideas came to mind: A party. A week at a spa. Buying a painting, a piece of antique furniture, an exquisite bauble. The usual tepid fare. I knew there had to be something better, something remarkable, adventurous, exotic, but not extravagant. OK, maybe a little extravagant.

I took another polite sip from my bottle of wine and stared out the window, waiting for inspiration to flow through my veins and deliver the eureka moment.

"Hi there!"

I turned my head to find a tall, bald, mustachioed steward looking down at me. He promptly took the empty seat next to mine.

Well, I thought to myself, aren't these flight attendants nice? I mean, when was the last time one of them paid an iota of attention to you during a flight?

"How are you doing?" His tone was friendly but concerned.

"I'm very well," I said brightly, raising my little bottle of wine in a sign of "cheers."

He looked serious, as if he were about to deliver bad news.

"You're not supposed to open your own wine on a flight," he said gravely.

"Oh, it's OK," I assured him. "This is just a screw top. I can manage..."

"No," he interjected. "Corked or not, you're not allowed to bring wine on board a flight and consume it. There's a fine."

Silence.

"The fine," he leaned over to whisper, "is ten thousand dollars."

Great! Was this how I was to spend my fiftieth birthday—paying off a fat fine for the heinous act of opening a small bottle of cheap wine on an airplane?

I told the steward about the reservation clerk's explicit warning that there was no in-flight food service and no in-flight bar service.

"But we do have a bar on board," the steward said. As if on cue the unmistakable tinkle of glass against glass began to fill the cabin as the drinks trolley jiggled to life and started its slow, jerky journey down the aisle.

I could have argued my case, but to what end? The fingerprints were already on the opened bottle. So I did what any self-respecting Canadian would do: I apologized. Profusely and genuinely.

"I'll be right back," the steward said seriously. He got up from his seat and disappeared.

This cannot be happening to me, I thought. How will I explain this to my children, and how will I ever be able to pay the fine? Was the fine merely the beginning? Did it come with a jail term or community service?

Seconds later, the steward returned, sat down and slipped me a small plastic wine glass.

"Don't tell anyone," he said with a wink, thus turning me into a lifelong fan of Westjet Airlines.

After I gasped my heartfelt thanks, we started to chat about things of greater importance than silly airline regulations with fines and jail sentences attached. Our conversation shifted to the subject of holidays and unusual destinations, and Barry—we were now on a first-name basis—told me that he and his wife—there always seems to be a wife—had spent a recent vacation walking Spain's Camino de Santiago de Compostela. It was a mouthful of a name that heightened its exoticism. I pressed him for details.

The Camino, he explained, is a thousand-year-old pilgrimage route that pays homage to St. James, one of Christ's apostles. The trail is eight hundred kilometers long and wends its way through the quaint medieval towns, cities, farms, and fields of northern Spain.

"History, art, religion, and architecture all rolled into gorgeous scenery," said Barry. "There are pilgrim hostels along the way, but if you get tired of staying at them there are some really nice old inns."

"You walked eight hundred kilometers?" I asked.

"Yup," he answered proudly. "Worked out to about twenty-five kilometers a day."

That sounded doable even to someone who had never walked twenty-five kilometers in a day.

"How long did it take?"

"About a month," he answered. "It was great exercise, totally laid-back, and pretty inexpensive, too. But it was also the most spiritually meaningful holiday we had ever taken."

Goose bumps erupted on my body. At that precise moment I knew the Camino was the fiftieth birthday present I craved: spiritual, challenging, unstructured, nomadic, something that would quiet the mind, give me a little quality time with God, and let my gypsy spirit out for a run.

I must come clean here. The Great Outdoors and I had only a fleeting acquaintance. I had never backpacked, never owned hiking boots, never done any long-distance walking. Furthermore, I had never had a positive outdoor experience.

My only foray into the outdoors involved a few years of summer camp as a youngster, an experience for which I am still receiving therapy. The regimentation, the fly-infested doorless outhouses, the bunk beds, the early-morning trumpet call heralding a sprint to the lake for a wash, the clamorous meal times, the snakes—I hated it. Most of all, I hated the cliques of girls. Their effortless social skills, their astonishing knowledge about menstrual periods and sex (my parents had excluded this information from my education), their squeals and sorority-type covens—all completely intimidated me. The mere thought of being stranded in that milieu for a two-week stint stirred something deep in my bowels, something that sent a warning to my brain to stay very close to a washroom. Every year, I begged my parents to allow me to stay home, and every year they ignored my request.

Over time I developed an ingenious coping mechanism. The moment the bus arrived at camp and the campers' luggage was being unloaded, I would position myself beside the hunkiest counselor, inhale the scent of pine needles, and drop to the ground. The shocked counselor would sweep me into his arms and carry my limp-but-very-conscious body to the infirmary. I was slipped between crisp, white linens with hospital-tucked corners, and there I remained for the two-week duration of camp. The cause of my fainting spell perplexed the kind, fretting nurses who kept me supplied with lots of pillows and comic books and delivered meals to my bedside. It was heaven. Two days before the end of camp, I would stage a miraculous recovery. I joined the other campers who, predictably, had forged iron-clad exclusivity pacts with each other that did not permit fraternizing with "the new kid." I happily wandered off alone to tame yards of gimp into a woven bracelet or stick pine cones on a picture frame crafted from Popsicle sticks or haul a bow and a quiver of arrows to the archery field for a little target practice.

When camp was over and the bus returned us from the tree line to the heat-saturated asphalt of a shopping mall parking lot, my father would be waiting for me.

"How was the infirmary this year?" he'd ask with a knowing smile. I suppose we both got what we wanted. He and my mother got two weeks without parental responsibilities; I got two weeks of rest and room service.

As I grew older, I gravitated toward the kind of vacations in which "roughing it" meant going without a blow dryer for twenty-four hours. I avoided everything that wasn't neatly mowed or encased in concrete or didn't come with the words "all-inclusive."

Around my mid-forties, something changed. Midlife crises can be godsends, and I will always be grateful to my ex-husband for his. Had he not bolted, leaving me with three children, I might never have become sufficiently stressed and overworked to flee to Lake Erie's tiny and remote Pelee Island, population 120. There I spent three months one winter captivated by sunrises, sunsets, and a life removed from the noise of modern life. My inner nature nymph stirred.

The Camino seemed a logical, albeit extreme, next step in my reconciliation with Mother Nature. All I needed was a backpack of belongings, strong legs, and boundless enthusiasm. Check. Check. Check.

The idea of a pilgrimage—it has such a Chaucerian ring—was irresistible. It evokes a noble challenge, a test of one's faith on a harsh, unknown, ancient path, the sort of pursuit that taps the primal urge to wander with intense curiosity.

Pilgrimage. When the word first entered my consciousness, in grade school history class, it sparked a dormant gene to life. I acquired a passion for all things medieval that, curiously, I never thought to integrate into a career. In later years, if I stumbled across the word "pilgrimage" in a book or in a newspaper article, the spark would fire up again and then smolder until, lacking the continuous stoking it required, it all but extinguished itself. Until Barry the Steward's account reawakened it.

There were, of course, other, less easily admitted reasons that a pilgrimage seemed like a grand idea at this point in my life. The holy trinity of parental burnout, job dissatisfaction, and a broken relationship were the prime catalysts, and there seemed no better way to deal with them all than to walk them off.

Of the three, parenting was the most worrying, though not because of the usual teenage dramas that every parent endures, for I knew that stage would pass (and I hoped soon). No, the part that worried me was that unlike other mothers in my circle, I was not wracked by the prospect of empty-nest syndrome.

Here's a truism about being a parent that parenting manuals never teach you: a child trips into adulthood around the same time that a parent rediscovers rebellion; one that's almost spiritual in its midlife incarnation.

It's not a graceful period—for either party. It is rather like driving a standard-transmission vehicle for the first time: frustration and impatience overload the senses as you attempt a smooth transition between gears.

Then courage takes hold. You get an urge to test-drive your individualism, buried all those years ago when you learned how to bite your lip. You're ready to cross the line. You want to take a little risk, until that killjoy, Resistance, creeps in, and you end up shaking your head saying, "Nah, what am I thinking? I can't do that!" But then the Little Voice Inside pipes up: *"Oh yes you can."*

If nothing else, age and experience teach you that opportunities can melt as quickly as they appear. The only thing that trumps fear is regret. I ached for an adventure, a bona fide expedition to wake up my senses and astonish my jaded middle-aged eyes.

I had a million questions to ask the steward, but the plane was preparing to land, and he had to take his leave. We said good-bye, and I was left to ponder the goose bumps.

I flipped open my notepad and scribbled down the name: Camino de Compostela de Santiago. Was that it, or was it Santiago Camino de Compostela? I also wrote "800 kilometers," and underlined it three times. The spark was lit.

"This will be perfect," I beamed with immense satisfaction as I leaned back in my seat.

A YEAR AND a half after that chance encounter on one airplane, I stood in line to board another. This one was going to Spain. Lined up behind me was a posse of middle-aged women hauling backpacks. A word of advice: never divulge your intentions to the national media.

Allow me to explain.

Immediately after my conversation with Barry the Steward on that serendipitous flight to Vancouver, I headed off to do the TV interview. At the end of it, the genial host asked, "So, what's your next adventure going to be?"

Without pausing or thinking through the consequences, I blurted, "I've decided to walk the Camino de Santiago." It was a rather presumptuous and brazen declaration; I had only heard about the Camino a few hours earlier from Barry the Steward and would not have been able to point out the Camino's route had you handed me a map of Spain. No matter. The studio audience applauded as they do for all lunatics on talk shows, and I said thank you and returned home.

Pandora's Box opened just a crack, initially.

My friend Georgina was the first to get in touch. She shares my penchant for embracing an idea with a staggering amount of naïveté.

"I've always wanted to do the Camino," she enthused via e-mail. "Would you like company?"

Would I like company? Would I want someone to share the torture of an extremely long hike through a country I knew nothing about?

"Sure!" I wrote back. The idea of having Georgina along as a companion was rather appealing. She's a cautious but jolly sort, a good counterweight to my madcap-but-moody personality. I figured I could stand her for an entire month. Besides, she's a priest, and to say no to a priest at the start of a spiritual pilgrimage was just inviting bad karma.

I originally intended to walk the Camino alone only because I assumed—incorrectly, as it turned out—that it would be difficult to find people willing to leave their loved ones and jobs for four weeks to walk a distance most people nowadays do by plane. Apparently there are more people than you might think who want to do this.

E-mails began arriving from people from across Canada, the United States, Britain, and Europe, all eager to come on a walk with me. I cleared their requests with Georgina and then said yes to them, too. Within a month I had a yes list of forty-five women. Somewhere in there was a hard lesson about knowing when to say no. That lesson came, as lessons do, much later.

We established from the beginning a very short list of criteria for our Camino trek. You had to be female, and you had to be within spitting distance of fifty years of age. No perky twenty-year-olds with designer water bottles and sleek blonde ponytails pulled neatly through their pink and white baseball caps. And no men, gay or straight. Men would change the dynamic of the group, we reasoned. Again, this was another lesson waiting to be learned. From the cruel vantage point of hindsight, sprinkling some men into the mix might have been a good thing.

We made our introductions via e-mail and maintained a cyber correspondence for the better part of a year. Some of us arranged to meet in person under the guise of sharing ideas and plotting our route but really to size each other up in person. Some of the husbands wanted to meet me to make sure I wasn't a cult leader or a crazy person (I managed to fool them on both counts). Thankfully, not one of the women was a marathoner or a triathlete or an Olympic medalist. We were a pretty average-looking group, a bit doughy around the midsection and with higher-than-average expectations about our physical capabilities.

Our group proved to be highly efficient and resourceful. Like they say, if you want something done, hire a woman.

We sought out people who had walked the Camino, interrogated them, and relayed our findings to the rest of the group. We questioned experienced hikers about gear and maps and about how to train for a long hike. We scoured the Internet, grateful that God gave us Google, and hunted for cheap airfares and information about weather conditions, currency rates, and essential gear. A mild addiction to all things Camino began to take hold. A few books about the Camino were recommended, but I resisted wholesale immersion in the subject; too much research can kill an adventure.

We pored over the glossy catalogs of Mountain Equipment Co-op, scouted out practical clothing, compared prices, and made careful purchases, only to rethink our transactions and return the goods the following day.

For months we talked of nothing but hiking boots. High boots or short boots? Merrells or Salomons? Orthotics? Insoles? Types of socks? The chatter was amusing coming from women who, generally speaking, had never pulled on hiking boots, let alone darkened the door of a hiking store. "Do they carry them at Holt Renfrew?" one asked.

Outfitters and their largely knowledgeable staff became our new best friends. They counseled us on what we would need and what was superfluous. We became obsessed with the weight of each item, knowing we would have to schlep it on our backs for eight hundred kilometers. Everything we packed into our knapsacks had to be practical and durable and serve a multitude of uses. A fleece jacket could double as the stuffing of a pillowcase; a bottle of Campsuds could serve as shampoo, body soap, and laundry detergent.

When you embark on a hike of some consequence, you quickly become acquainted with the mountains of merchandise available in outdoor-adventure stores. Some of it is ingenious, and some of it is just plain idiotic.

In one store I stood transfixed as a young sales clerk explained the workings of a small retractable shovel for burying my poop. He also tried to tempt me with a headlamp (similar to those worn by miners) for hiking at night and a titanium omnifuel stove. It was the word "cooking" that snapped me out of my trance and sent my wallet back into the depths of my purse. I informed the clerk that I do not poop in the woods and that I would never walk through dark, unfamiliar territory, with or without a headlamp.

As for the portable cooker, I would not under any circumstances be preparing meals. This might be a pilgrimage, but this pilgrim was not going near a stove.

But what was really on the minds of some of the women was whether we could get through the pilgrimage without biting off each other's heads.

Theresa was the first to raise the thorny subject.

"What if we get cranky or bitchy?" she asked.

"What if we do?" I replied breezily. "Being unstable and bitchy is part of my charm."

Theresa was not placated. She wanted an emblem to communicate the various colors that swing through a woman's hormonal landscape. Thus was born the hag flag, a small, laminated card depicting a witch on a broom. On grumpy days, it could be conveniently pinned to our backpacks as an early-warning signal to the others.

One member of our group found herself in France on business the summer before our departure to Spain, and she took a quick side trip to size up Saint-Jean-Pied-de-Port, our agreed-upon starting point of the Camino.

"Have you actually *seen* the Pyrenees?" she e-mailed me. "You might want to start training really hard. Now! And you might want to consider starting in Roncesvalles [the Spanish starting gate of the Camino] instead of Saint-Jean."

I considered her advice and then promptly parked it in the far reaches of my brain, where I forgot about it until it was too late. I did, however, heed her advice about training and stumbled upon the perfect training ground.

The Bruce Trail is a rugged 850-kilometer footpath that follows the Niagara Escarpment, a million-year-old limestone spine that starts around Niagara Falls in southern Ontario and stretches north to Tobermory on the shores of Georgian Bay, almost halfway through the province. People from around the world visit Canada expressly to hike the Bruce—it is a true, natural gem that bears UNESCO's stamp of approval.

It was ironic and a little sad that it took training for a hike three thousand kilometers away in Spain to acquaint me with the Bruce Trail, a portion of which lies about three blocks from my home.

As part of my training, I also climbed the steep stairs that scale a portion of the Niagara Escarpment that runs through Hamilton. When Hamilton's incline railway was dismantled in the 1930s, a set of metal stairs was constructed to connect the city's downtown community to its suburban alter ego at the top of the escarpment. Today the Stairs, as they are known locally, offer a great cardio workout through a lovely, quiet stretch of forest. Initially, I did my stair training alone in the early evening, after work, until someone mentioned that a body had recently been found hanging from a tree in the vicinity. I promptly switched to daylight workouts on the Bruce Trail with lots of company.

By chance, a friend who had hiked the entire Bruce Trail and had a badge to prove it invited me to join her hiking group. She was concerned that I wasn't quite grasping the rigorous nature of a long-distance hike, but between you and me I think she wanted me in her group so that she could listen to me wax on about the Camino. Two months before we left for Spain, Beth decided to join our pilgrimage.

Although physical training was the primary reason I joined her group of weekend hikers, I had an ulterior motive: to get some practice hanging out with a group of women.

Large groups of women frighten me. Women are complicated and unpredictable. The alpha-chick pecking order, the social machinations, the exclusionary tactics, the nuances—some conveyed by the mere raising of an eyebrow—tie my stomach in knots. I tend to speak my mind (not always loudly enough) and to wear my mood swings on my sleeve. It's not an ideal personality, but it's easy to read. Many women operate on a more subtle level. A wide open smile and squeal-like "Hi! How are you!?" momentarily distract you from the knife concealed in their right hand. The one destined for your back.

The other thing about groups of women is that they have a way of tamping down my bohemian spirit. On too many occasions I have set aside my desires and opinions and acquiesced to the wishes of others, figuring it was better to be an approval whore than a social misfit. As you age, however, conformity loses both appeal and potency; the payoff never quite ratchets up a measurable degree of satisfaction. It's easier to shed people who dampen your spirit than to barter away your sense of self.

The hiking itself was liberating. I'm not particularly athletic: I distinguished myself in school by the number of excuses I managed to concoct to get out of gym class. In nature I found my stride. Walking through the woods, negotiating rocky passageways, and scrambling up steep, timber-strewn hills were far more appealing than walking into a loud, smelly gym. My first hike was seven kilometers; the second, fifteen; the third, eighteen; and the fourth, twenty-four. People cautioned me against attempting longer, more arduous hikes so early in my training, but moderation is not my strong suit, especially when I embrace an idea. I don't believe in warming up (surely the mere act of getting out of bed each morning and putting on the kettle is warm-up enough), and I've never been good at locating my pulse, much less checking it (standing and breathing is sufficient evidence that my system is functioning).

Training continued over several months, during which time the size of our Camino cohort expanded and, mercifully, contracted. The original list of forty-five dwindled to nine for various reasons. Some came to their senses and fled, some had doubts about their ability to take on the Camino, and others simply lost their enthusiasm. A few bowed out for family reasons. Inexplicably, three weeks before our departure six more women signed on. No training. No prior experience. They just felt called to walk the Camino.

THAT'S HOW I ended up at Pearson International Airport on April 29, 2004, with ten middle-aged women. We were to meet four others in Saint-Jean-Pied-de-Port. All of us came from various parts of Canada, and most of us were strangers to one another.

I watched them all kiss their husbands and children goodbye. A pang of regret shot through me; no one from my family was there to bid a teary farewell. Hardly surprising. My children had at first been ecstatic about my pilgrimage and constantly asked me the precise day and time of my departure. But when I accepted my mother's generous offer to move into my home and take care of things in my absence, the children suddenly stopped talking to me.

I sulked through security, boarded the plane, and found myself seated beside the only woman in our group who had apparently forgotten to pack her personality. Most women, out of politeness, will maintain a brief conversation just to establish a comfort level. Not this one. She smiled tightly at my efforts to draw her into conversation, preferring to keep her eyes fixed on reading material—the newspaper, the in-flight magazine, the safety instruction card, the air-sickness bag—anything to avoid talking to me.

Eventually, I gave up. I turned toward the window, made a little nest for myself, stared into the inky sky as twilight gave way to night, and began pondering the predictions of a psychic I had visited a few weeks earlier.

Ah yes, the psychic. You might be interested to know what she had to say about this little adventure.

2

"WHOA! What the hell are you doing in May?"

Thus spaketh the psychic, definitely not the type who holds her tarot cards close to her vest.

She had done a couple of readings for me in the past, and I decided to visit her just weeks before my pilgrimage—part due diligence and part perverse desire to see whether her psychic powers were still sharp.

Lori is a youthful, slim, pretty woman with long brown hair and green eyes that freak you out a bit because they look like lizard eyes. She wears faded jeans, a pink off-the-shoulder sweatshirt, and bare feet. She looks more like a pole dancer than a psychic.

Tarot may well be her specialty, but subtlety is not her strong suit. "Whoa!" was the tip-off.

So, just what was I doing in May?

"Well," I began tentatively, "I'm going to Spain in May. I'm walking the Camino de Santiago de Compostela. It's an ancient pilgrimage route that runs through northern Spain. About eight hundred kilometers long."

My speech began to speed up, gaining momentum like a horse off the rein. I was excited about the Camino, and I wanted her to be excited, too.

"It's not an organized trip," I continued. "You have maps, and you just follow the signs and arrows along the way. You start off crossing the Pyrenees; that's the mountain range that divides France from Spain. You carry a pilgrim passport with you, and it gets stamped in each town you stop at the end of the day. When you reach the end—in Santiago—you present your pilgrim passport and receive a parchment certifying that you completed the journey."

Lori stared at me. Her lizard eyes flashed. I half expected a tongue to fly out and slap me.

"But you're not going alone," she said matter-of-factly. Her brow furrowed as she puzzled over the tarot cards laid out before her.

"No," I replied brightly. "I'm leading a group of fourteen other women."

Lori raised her head and gave me a look of profound incredulity. "*Fourteen* other women?" She said this in a tone of voice that indicated that I should know better. She rolled her lizard eyes and let out an exasperated sigh. I sat chastened, my eyes downcast.

"No!" the Little Voice Inside urged. "*Don't you dare shrink. Don't let anyone screw your dreams.*"

I raised my eyes and looked defiantly at Lori. Come on, Lizard Eyes, I dared her. I can take it. I leaned in a little to show her I was unafraid of what she had to dish about the fourteen women.

Instead, she gathered up her cards and changed the subject.

"How much hiking have you done?" she asked tauntingly, glancing at my long skirt and pointy-toed stilettos. I might not look like a hiker, but, damn it, she didn't look like a psychic either. I refused to let her stare me down.

"Actually, I've been hiking the Bruce Trail and the Hamilton Waterfront Trail," I answered haughtily. "Been hiking for, oh, let's see, about seven months."

A sarcastic smile crept over her lips. Now it was her turn to lean toward me. "Have you ever been camping?"

The word "camping" caused my body to jerk.

"No, I haven't camped," I said, stiffening my resolve. "We won't be camping anyway; we'll be staying in *refugios*—pilgrim hostels."

Lori shuffled the deck and peeled off one card at a time, dramatically snapping each one face up against the shiny surface of her dining room table.

"You might find that this experience is a bit more... *rustic* than you want," she said with forced diplomacy. She began flipping the cards faster. I watched her and wondered whether I had wasted my money coming here just to be scolded.

"Watch your money," she blurted. "There's the possibility you may overspend."

I'm paying fifty dollars to hear *that*? There's *always* the possibility of my overspending. It's in my DNA.

"Be frugal," she added, narrowing her eyes on me. My cheeks flushed; I hoped she wasn't a mind reader.

She arranged a new round of cards in a semicircle, studied them, gathered them up, and reshuffled.

"Don't take jewelry."

Reflexively, I fingered my necklace that held a few personal totems—a silver cross, a gold pendant in the shape of Pelee Island, a small filigreed gold heart with the words "#1 Mom" (a gift from one of my sons), and a tiny gold shell, the Camino's universal emblem, given by a friend as a token of pre-Camino courage.

"I wear this everywhere," I told Lori. "I almost never take it off. And these earrings"—my hands moved to touch the gold hoops and diamond studs that decorated my ears. The hoops were a gift to myself when I was downsized out of a job and barely had money for groceries; the studs were a gift from a man who later downsized our relationship.

"If they're important, don't take them. You'll definitely lose something."

Lori dealt the cards again and pondered their message. I could almost hear the wheels turning in her brain.

Finally, she exhaled audibly. "Well, this trip may not be awful, but it won't be fabulous. You might write a book about it. You'll meet two celebrities."

My ears pricked up. "Like Harrison Ford?" I asked eagerly. "Or Robert Redford?" I hastily added Redford's name because in my excitement I forgot that I had removed Ford from my Hot Men list when he dumped his wife and kids for Calista Stick-woman. Now visions of hiking with movie stars raced into my mind. There I was with Redford, walking along a moonlit path as we murmured to each other about spiritual destinies...

"Not men," said Lori, interrupting my reverie. "Two women."

Crap.

"It won't be the trip you hoped it would be," she continued, "but oddly enough..."—she paused to double check her dog-eared cards as if disbelieving their message—"yup, looks like you'll do this sort of thing again."

She was silent for a moment, stunned by her own words. Then she continued.

"The group will be a bit of a problem," she said, nodding her head thoughtfully. "They'll be overanalyzing things and trying to be profound. You can't stand that sort of thing. They'll be going on and on about how magical everything is, reading stuff into everything they see, and you'll be saying 'Hey, I just like pizza.'"

What? I just like pizza?

"And beer."

Was this woman on medication?

She regarded the puzzled look on my face.

"You know what I mean," she sighed with exasperation. "Some days you see a formation of stones and it looks like the Virgin Mary. Other days it just looks like a pile of stones. That's what this trip will be. Everyone's looking for deep meaning, for a spiritual epiphany. Even you're looking for it. But you're not going to discover anything profound, and you'll understand that right from the start."

Gee thanks. I mentally calculated the cost of my grand adventure. Perhaps I should have chosen a spa vacation instead.

"Another thing about the women," she added cautiously. "Besides overanalyzing every aspect of this trip, they're going to expect you to be their leader. They're going to expect a lot from you. They're going to drive you crazy. I see cat fights. Lots of cat fights."

She looked back down at her cards and started flipping them again.

"There won't be cat fights," I assured her with a nervous laugh. "We're all around fifty years of age. We're beyond cat fights."

She raised her eyebrows and stifled a laugh. She could not believe my naïveté.

She shuffled the deck yet again and fanned out the cards. She asked me to select eight. I could sense her watching me as if she had something else to tell me but was debating whether I could handle it. Perhaps she was waiting for me to change my mind about going on the Camino. A psychic ought to know better: I am a spirited woman, and if nothing else I am resolute in my spiritedness. Even when I'm wrong.

"You're going to experience a death while you're away," she said abruptly.

Yeah, the spa vacation might have been a safer bet.

"This doesn't necessarily mean you or someone you're traveling with will die," she added quickly. "But you might witness a death or learn about a death. Sometimes this Death card means lots of things. You might see a dead animal, or you'll squish a bug, or maybe 'death' will signify a feeling of emptiness, or the death of a way of thinking and the birth of another, or putting an unresolved issue or relationship to rest."

Hmm. Was she trying to sugarcoat this?

"On the good side," she continued, "the weather will be great. You're going to be tanned and fit by the end of it."

Well, let's see, Madame Einstein: an eight-hundred-kilometer hike through the sunniest country in Europe—who wouldn't be tanned and fit after that?

I placed fifty dollars on the table and made cheerful small talk while I gathered my things and headed for the door. I tried to appear unconcerned about her cautionary messages, tried to show her that I wasn't going to take a psychic's words to heart, that this was just entertainment. A fluffy little sideshow.

Instead, I concentrated on her more uplifting predictions. The summer would be fun, there was a positive change for me on the job front, and I would remarry. (She'd been telling me that for the past three years. This time she mentioned a fair-haired man who was distant from me: "There's another home for you, but it doesn't necessarily mean you'll move.")

It would be untruthful to say I did not feel a pang of disappointment. In spite of my cavalier attitude toward the psychic, her predictions had been bang-on before. Now I wanted her to be wrong about the Camino.

I had already walked the Camino in my mind. I had polished the entire experience into a gleaming tale of camaraderie and accomplishment. Perhaps my expectations were too high. "And Jane," I reminded myself in an admonishing voice, "you are the Queen of High Expectations."

I got into my car, turned the key in the ignition, and drove off searching for a thread in her predictions that would link them to a couple of recurring dreams I had been having: one pleasant, one frightening. The dreams were so frequent that they had fused into one.

In the first dream, I am tired and alone (this is actually the pleasant dream). I am also wet, though I can't tell whether it is perspiration or rain dripping off me. I am trudging along the narrow, deserted street of a Spanish town when I spy a café. Dying of thirst, I enter the café and there, sitting alone at a table, is a tall, fair-haired man. He has a backpack beside him. Like me, he is a pilgrim. Our eyes meet, but being shy I look away and walk past him toward the bar.

At this point, I usually wake up from the dream and puzzle over why I am so shy (or maybe gun-shy) when it comes to meeting people, particularly men. Would someone honestly assume I was trying to pick them up if I simply asked, "Hey, mind if I join you?" And what if they did? I'm nearly fifty years old. I'm allowed to be bold.

The second dream was more worrisome. In fact, it was terrifying. If there were a case to be made against traveling solo, this was it.

In the dream, I am walking through a forest with a group of women. Somehow I get ahead of the group until I am so much farther ahead that I no longer see them behind me. The path eventually leads out of the forest into a huge field filled with tall yellow flowers. I start wading through them. The day is bright, and the sun emits a powerful and close heat. In the distance, I hear a car and, as it gets closer, loud music throbbing from it. The car—it's black—streaks past on the road about sixty yards from where I'm walking. The car windows are rolled down, and there is the unmistakable sound of boisterously drunk young men. I forge ahead through the mass of flowers. A few minutes later the black car returns. This time it stops. The young men get out and walk toward me. There are five of them. I keep walking, wondering why they are approaching me, and I am seized by fear.

"*Peregrina! ¿Cómo estás?*" Pilgrim! How's it going?

I feign a smile. They don't care how I'm doing. I wonder why they would rob a pilgrim, since pilgrims do not carry lots of money.

Robbery, however, is not on the minds of these young men. A knife flicks open, and my heart plummets. The men descend on me, knocking me to the ground, ripping open my clothes, pulling my legs apart. I have no time to react or put up a struggle because each man has seized one of my limbs while the fifth unzips his pants and dives into me. The terror paralyzes me, but I manage to reach inside myself, grab my soul, and tear it from my body, placing it outside this hideous scene. It is the only part of me I am able to protect. From its safe perch, my soul hovers in a silent vigil, praying that my life will be spared. When the young men are finished with me, one or two spit on me, and a third relieves himself on my face. They saunter away, laughing and talking to one another with an air of bravura. A minute later, their car starts up, and the pounding bass line of the music resumes as they speed off.

At this point, the dream has two endings:

1. I hear the laughing voices of the women in my Camino tribe. They are singing show tunes. I raise my walking stick so that it is visible above the yellow flowers. The women come running to my aid and immediately set about helping me.

2. I hear the swishing of grass. Someone is coming. It's a man. The same fair-haired man I had seen in the café in the first dream. He bends over me, tells me not to worry, that he will look after me.

"I wish I had spoken to you when I saw you in the café," he says with an English accent, as he tenderly examines the bruises that have started forming on my wrists, arms, and legs. "We would have walked together, and this would not have happened. I'm so sorry."

A cry rises in my throat but emerges guttural and weak. I turn my head away from the man and stare into the grass. I am overcome with shame.

"Don't worry," he says soothingly. "I'll look after you now."

A rape fantasy with a happy ending? What is it about women that forces dreams like these out of our subconscious? Are they intuitive warnings or a desire to be rescued?

In the days leading up to the pilgrimage, I would frequently revisit the dreams, trying to understand their meaning. I derive a sense of comfort in confronting the ugly thoughts, because by acknowledging them and preparing for them, I figure they likely won't come true. A kind of psychic insurance against the odds (or gods). It's when you aren't prepared or haven't faced your fear that calamity sneaks up behind you.

Dreams are often more metaphor than literal, or so I told myself. So what did five men represent? Do I feel pinned down or trapped in my life? Do I feel compromised? Violated in an intellectual or emotional sense? Do I feel that my independence or my self-esteem is threatened? And the rescue aspect of it: Was that about a search for self-expression?

As I drove home, the dreams and the psychic's predictions churned in my head: The group's expectation for me to be their leader. The cat fights. The politics of women. Lost jewelry. Celebrities. The group's spiritual overanalysis. The spectre of Death. The recurring dreams. The fair-haired man. Would any of it come to pass on the Camino?

3

HAD it not been for a mad, insecure king in the Holy Land, the Camino de Santiago de Compostela might never have happened.

King Herod Agrippa came from a highly dysfunctional family whose menfolk were frighteningly adept at blending barbarism with sycophancy. To wit: Agrippa's grandfather was responsible for the Slaughter of the Innocents as well as the execution of a few of his wives and sons (one of whom was Agrippa's own father).

In the Herod clan, brother plotted against brother, wives were swapped or beheaded, and all of them took delight in terrorizing the citizenry over which they ruled. Agrippa maintained this fine tradition and chose as his best buddy and confidante the Roman emperor Caligula.

It's a shame really, because the Herods were visionaries when it came to engineering. Their accomplishments included the magnificent harbor of Caesarea and the restoration of the Temple of Jerusalem. They are also credited with a number of stunning architectural marvels erected in the wake of a devastating earthquake that struck Jerusalem in 31 BC, killing thousands of people and reducing the city to little more than a rock farm.

Agrippa is acknowledged for bringing order and civility to his kingdom (no doubt aided by a heavy hand), and when it came to writing the laws of the land, he was said to be a rather bright bulb. Still, the Herods could not escape their tragic flaw of insecurity.

Agrippa inherited a debilitating inferiority complex. He was an Edomite (at the lower end of the tribal social scale of the day) desperate to curry favor with the Roman regime and to pump up the pride level among his Jewish subjects. It was a psychological juggling act that fed his hair-trigger temper and lowered his tolerance for anyone whose ideas ran counter to his. One group that earned his wrath was a little sect from Galilee known as the Christians, whose leader, a fellow named Jesus, had recently been crucified by the Roman-appointed governor Pontius Pilate. After the Crucifixion, Herod relentlessly hounded the Christians, notably Jesus's apostles, until some of them hightailed it out of Jerusalem.

One escapee, James, ended up in the far reaches of northwestern Spain, where he hoped to try his hand at converting the Basques, the Moors—anyone, really, who showed the slightest interest in embracing the Christian brand.

He did not meet with great success. All known reports about him say he was tactless and a consummate brownnoser. He also had an explosive temper, as we learn from the *Gospel According to Matthew*, where Jesus nicknames James and his brother, John, the "sons of thunder."

You have to wonder what Jesus was thinking when he brought James and John into his fold. It's hard to imagine a more ill-fitting pair in a love-thine-enemies religion, but then Jesus was a magnet for such people. Still is. James and John proved particularly dimwitted. When Jesus and his disciples were rebuffed by the people of a Samaritan village, the brothers brilliantly suggested torching the place to avenge Jesus's honor. Jesus patiently explained that such actions didn't quite reflect his mission statement. On another occasion, James and John, in a moment of shameless sucking up, asked Jesus if they could be placed on his left and right side in the Kingdom of Heaven. In recounting the incident in his gospel, Mark writes that the other disciples, upon learning of the request, "were indignant." No kidding. The ensuing squabble reached such a pitch that Jesus was compelled to proffer a rather elegant challenge, according to Mark 10:23: "Whoever wants to be a leader among you must be your servant, and whoever wants to be first must be the slave of all."

Although James and John were part of Jesus's inner circle and were often with Jesus at key moments in his ministry, the gospels portray the duo as the Beavis and Butt-Head of the group. You get the sense that Jesus spent a fair bit of time smacking his forehead in exasperation whenever he had to deal with their antics.

The brothers' behavior really hit a low point in the Garden of Gethsemane, where Jesus had brought James and John, along with Simon Peter, for moral support. As Jesus agonized over his fate, sobbing and begging God to spare his life, he turned for reassurance from his buddies, only to find them sleeping. Sleeping! Even when Jesus roused them and asked them to stay awake with him, they nodded off again and again. That behavior hardly deserves front-row seats in the Kingdom of Heaven.

Maybe it was an attempt to atone for his sycophantic sins that drove James to Spain after the Crucifixion. Whatever his motivation, he seems to have done everything to make the sojourn unremarkable. He felt no compunction to chronicle his travels; nor was he moved to write letters, sermons, or even a memoir of his years with the Son of God. After ten years in Spain, James simply folded his tent and shuffled back to Jerusalem.

Meanwhile, his crafty old nemesis, Agrippa, had been tipped off about James's homecoming and was waiting for him at the city gates. James was seized, arrested, and beheaded, earning the distinction of being the first of Jesus's apostles to be martyred.

James's coterie gathered their master's remains and placed them in a stone boat that was transported, according to legend, by angels back to Spain. There James was laid to rest on a vast, empty plain.

Our tale fast-forwards eight hundred years. A Spanish hermit named Paio stood on that same empty plain one evening, mesmerized by a stellar extravaganza occurring in the night sky. The ray of one star in particular appeared to point to a specific place, and Paio, because he had nothing better to do, followed it. He stumbled upon an ancient tomb containing three bodies and immediately rushed to the local authorities to report his discovery.

The authorities—the governor, the bishop, and other clergy are all mentioned in various versions of the story—concluded that the site was the grave of James and his disciples Athanasius and Theodore, based on the fact that one of the bodies had a severed head, with a name tag saying: "Here lies James, son of Zebedee and Salome."

The authorities couldn't believe their good fortune: the remains of a real, honest-to-goodness apostle of Christ had been found on Spanish soil. Before you could say "Holy souvenirs!" the site was proclaimed sacred, and Alphonse the Chaste, king of Asturias and Galicia, ordered that a simple church be constructed as a more fitting memorial for Spain's newly minted adopted son.

A town sprouted up around the new church, and by the tenth century the burgeoning burg began to appear in records as Santiago de Compostela (Iago is Spanish for James; compostela derives from *campus stellae*—field of stars).

The timing of these events could not have been better. Christian Spain was locked in a protracted war with the Muslim Moors, and Spain's powers that be figured that if they could stake out an area and claim it as having religious significance, it might keep the Moors at bay. It didn't. The Moors breached the line of defense in 997 and destroyed Santiago de Compostela. Undeterred, the Christians began reconstruction immediately.

War was not the sole reason for wanting to build a shrine to James.

Nothing was stronger to the medieval mind than the cult of the dead, and religious relics were potent currency. For the population at large, beholding the body parts of a saint was as good as beholding God; for the Church, the bones of a major religious figure were tantamount to a lottery win. James was swiftly elevated to the rank of patron saint of Spain, and his massive rehabilitation was underway.

As word spread about the discovery, the Old World made a beeline for Santiago de Compostela. Trails were blazed through Europe, converging at the small French town of Saint-Jean-Pied-de-Port. From there, the route snaked over the Pyrenees and moved through northern Spain to its western coast. A new pilgrimage route was born, and for a time, the Camino de Santiago de Compostela (literally, the Way of St. James in the Field of Stars) outranked the other two Christian meccas, Jerusalem and Rome, in popularity.

So you can credit King Herod Agrippa for tipping the first domino, James for his personal sacrifice, and the Catholic Church for cranking up the cult of James. But the Camino is nothing without pilgrims.

PARIS WAS RUBBING the sleep from its eyes when our plane touched down. My intrepid group of pilgrims-in-training wearily lugged its gear off the baggage carousel. Jet-lagged and trying to come to terms with the unpleasant sensation of unbrushed teeth—a first-time experience for a few of them—they shuffled toward me and looked at me expectantly.

We had four hours to kill before our connecting flight to Biarritz. A few of the women suggested we throw caution to the wind and take a bus to the Champs d'Elysées to hang in a café and people-watch; another bunch grumbled that the idea not only was reckless and a waste of money but could also cause us to miss our connecting flight. The minority browbeat the adventurous into submission, and we settled on trolling Charles de Gaulle Airport in search of coffee and croissants.

The group moved through the airport like a school of fish on Prozac. Being the type of person who darts off unexpectedly in the direction of bright, exotic colors, I am perhaps not the best candidate to lead anyone. I ended up creating more havoc than a travel-weary group deserved, but I couldn't help myself. I veered to the right toward a rather dainty cosmetics store, and the obedient conga line swarmed into formation behind me, lumbering with their bulging backpacks and thick hiking boots through narrow aisles as I followed the siren call of lipstick and perfume testers. Even while wearing a backpack, I cannot resist a tube of lipstick. The shop clerks held their collective breath. Exquisite bottles perched precariously on the edges of glass shelves shuddered as we passed; a sudden stop or a less-than-graceful turn would have taken out an entire display.

In the lineup for the flight to Biarritz, we shrank self-consciously into the background to gape at the parade of women in pencil-slim skirts and high heels. Even the men seemed like a new breed to us—nary a baseball cap or sloppy T-shirt in sight. One young chap was clad in red- and white-striped leather soccer-styled runners and a matching sweater worn over a pair of dark blue jeans. Stylish and casual.

Less than an hour after boarding our connecting flight and watching Paris's impressively varied skyline give way to a countryside of red-tiled roofs and secluded chateaux with azure swimming pools, the plane landed and taxied toward Biarritz's terminal.

Biarritz's airport is compact and uncomplicated. It is not, however, close to Saint-Jean-Pied-de-Port. Ten middle-aged faces again looked at me, waiting for direction.

"Well," I said with a chuckle, "I hadn't actually looked into how we would get from Biarritz to Saint-Jean. Did anyone else? Who speaks French?"

"Don't *you* speak French?" one of the women barked incredulously. She was a social worker, and pardon me, but I thought
social workers were more forgiving.

"A few words, but I'm not fluent," I replied.

"Jesus, you brought us all this way and you can't speak French!"
she snapped, looking to the others for support.

Her name was Colleen, and she was a fiery sort with a raspy
voice and a cackling laugh. Her ruddy complexion hinted at an
explosive temper and some serious alcohol issues. She was a late-
comer to our group, and though I had tried to talk her out of
coming—she had never hiked—she would not be dissuaded. "I'm
almost fifty and I've never even had lunch alone in a restaurant
let alone flown to France to walk across Spain," she had told me
at the time. "I have no idea why I'm doing this; I just know I need
to do it."

I spied a sign that read "Info" at the far end of the terminal
and started walking. At the very least, it would offer sanctuary
from Colleen's criticism about my linguistic deficiencies; at the
most, it would provide a map. I was wrong on both counts.

Colleen enlisted a few allies based on her admonishing mantra—"I can't believe she doesn't speak French"—and they were
at my heels like a pack of terriers. The rest of the group wisely
hung back at the luggage carousel. Upon reaching the information kiosk—*quelle surprise!*—there was not a stick of information
to be had.

An indifferent young woman behind the desk barely tolerated
my rudimentary command of her language. Colleen monitored
the conversation like a UN-appointed observer.

I had recently completed a French course, but French courses
never teach you snappy phrases for real situations. I could tell
this woman that "I would like to buy a green blanket for my aunt"
or that "my brother lives in St. Denis," but I could not immediately find the words to ask, "How do I get to Saint-Jean-Pied-de-
Port?" or more correctly, "Whom do I have to pay to get us to
Saint-Jean-Pied-de-Port?"

Through vocal and sign language, facial expressions, drawings, and head nods, I amassed the following information: We had to take a cab to Saint-Jean, and the cabs were located outside the terminal.

Well, that was a waste of time.

Meanwhile, Colleen began backpedaling.

"You *do* speak French!" she smiled with satisfaction. "I figured you were just teasing us."

Turning to the others, she gave the all-clear that they could resume liking me again. "It's OK. She speaks French really well." Then, continuing the conversation with me, she lowered her voice and asked, "By the way, what does *'Parlez lentement'* mean? You seemed to say that to the lady fairly often."

Outside the terminal, the snap of my fingers brought three Mercedeses to attention. I negotiated the cab fare *en français*, much to my surprise, and herded everyone into the waiting cars, ignoring the grumblings from a few of the women that this was an unexpected expense for which they had evidently not been prepared.

En route to Saint-Jean-Pied-de-Port, I cheerfully translated the driver's patter about the impressive cheese farms we were passing, the lay of the land, and a bit of the local history. I had a sneaking suspicion he was taking advantage of the fact that he had a car full of strict Anglophones. As we passed a herd of Limousin cattle, I could have sworn he said they were *"Vaches, comme vous."* ("Cows, like you.")

Saint-Jean-Pied-de-Port is a picturesque border town nestled in the protective crook of the mighty Pyrenees. Arching stone bridges, steep, narrow cobblestone roads, white stucco-and-timber buildings, and pretty shops make it look more Swiss than French. It is the hub of the Camino—three of the four European pilgrim routes converge here—and has enjoyed this distinction for the better part of a thousand years.

I looked toward the Pyrenees. The cautionary e-mail I had received several months earlier flashed to the fore: "You might

want to consider starting in Roncesvalles instead of Saint-Jean."
Had I really trained enough for this excursion?

When we finally reached our hotel, two more women—
Theresa and Lucy—were waiting for us, having arrived in France
a few days earlier for a bit of pre-Camino sightseeing. Theresa
was fluent in French and to my relief took over our registration at
the front desk, teasing and flirting with the handsome desk clerk,
who was also the owner of the establishment.

Our chattering group collected room keys and dragged its
gear up a wide-planked pine staircase that was hundreds of years
old. Pretty red-and-white heavy linen curtains framed a large
window on the landing that overlooked a gorge of the river Nive.

We regrouped in the lobby an hour later and set out to find
the pilgrims' office in order to register our intentions to walk
the Camino de Santiago de Compostela. Theresa had already
scouted out this detail and efficiently led the rest of us across
the street from the hotel and up a precariously steep cobblestone
road. My forehead broke out in a sweat, and I wondered how the
elderly of Saint-Jean-Pied-de-Port managed such roads every day.

There was a sense of trepidation about visiting the pilgrim
office. For decades, the office had been presided over by the fear-
some Madame Debril. According to some accounts, the first
obstacle on the Camino was not crossing the Pyrenees but securing a passport and stamp from Mme. Debril. She was known to
shame pilgrims into believing they were not worthy enough to
lick the mud off the boots of St. James himself, let alone walk the
Camino de Santiago. Mme. Debril had died a few years earlier,
but now the question was, who or what had replaced her?

Steadying ourselves on the threshold of Accueil Saint Jacques
on rue de la Citadelle, we took a deep breath, then bravely pushed
open the door.

We could not have had a nicer reception. A gracious older
couple gave us a welcoming smile as they dispensed information
and encouragement to other pilgrims. When our turn came, we

were each given a *carnet,* a white, accordion-pleated card about
the size of a postcard when folded. A large cockle shell decorated
the front of the card with the official words above it: *Carnet de
Pèlerin de Saint-Jacques: Credencial del Peregrino.*

We received our first stamp—a green marking depicting St.
James and the coat of arms of Saint-Jean-Pied-de-Port set against
a mountain range. The woman who served us carefully wrote the
date—30/04/04—beneath the stamp in each *carnet.* We would
have to collect similar stamps from clerics or town officials at the
end of each day we were on the Camino to validate our journey,
she said, pressing the *carnets* into our waiting palms.

"Don't lose this passport," she told us, with such seriousness
that we didn't dare ask what would happen if we did. "This will
be your most important document on the Camino. Keep it close
to you always."

She was like Glinda, the gentle Witch of the North, coun-
seling Dorothy to never let go of the ruby slippers, and she was
patient with all our questions. When you consider that at least
fifty to a hundred pilgrims pass through that office each day in
high season, burnout is a distinct occupational possibility. Here it
was nearly the end of the day, and she was as generous and smiling as she no doubt had been with the first pilgrim that day.

"Do you think we'll make it?" we all asked.

"Ah yes, of course you will!" she replied enthusiastically. "It
is very hard at times, but you will do it. And when you reach the
end, you will give Santiago a hug for me, yes?"

We nodded, but not very convincingly.

Back at the hotel, I had a few moments alone to absorb the
enormity of the journey ahead. I had become so wrapped up
in planning the pilgrimage, so concerned about everyone else's
preparations, that I had parked my own joys and fears. I hadn't
even given myself time to consider backing out. Now here I was
thousands of kilometers from home with the Pyrenees looming
like a salivating monster outside my window. Was I insane? How

had I managed to convince fourteen other women they could climb the Pyrenees and walk the Camino in thirty days?

But the bigger question was how I would cope with these women for an entire month. In the last eighteen hours, close to a dozen sets of eyeballs had bored into me each time a decision had to be made or a question was asked. Who was I? Answer Woman? Their mother? It was exhausting.

I moved toward the open window, lifted my eyes to a vast, nearly cloudless sky, and prayed. Really hard.

"Thank you, God, for leading me here. Thank you for putting all those people in my path, for all the seemingly random encounters and events that have brought me to this moment and to this beautiful place. But God, this was meant to be a solo journey, and I've ended up with fourteen cling-ons. I don't know whether I can be a leader or be the type of person they expect me to be. Is there a reason we have been brought together? Are we meant to kill each other, or will this actually be fun?"

Oh, it was selfish to want or expect a comfortable pilgrimage. I felt ashamed for asking, so I reframed my prayers. I drew a deep breath and focused on the bright blue sky above and the rushing torrent thundering through the river gorge below. I lifted my eyes again, filled my heart with compassionate thoughts, and opened my mouth to speak to God...

"Hey! Jane! Over here! Whaahooo!"

My prayers evaporated. I looked down from where I stood and saw Georgina and Theresa waving wildly on the bridge across from my hotel window. One of them raised a camera and snapped my picture, and like the good sport I sometimes pretend to be, I grabbed my camera and returned the favor.

The three of us were sharing a room, and I knew they would be back in minutes. I made my apologies to God and put Him on hold.

When they arrived, Georgina took me aside, as is her priestly way.

"Sorry we disturbed you; you were praying, weren't you?"

"Well, trying to," I said. "I'm so grateful about being here, and I had this urge to say 'thanks.'"

"I figured that's what you were doing," she whispered. "I didn't think we should bug you but—" she nodded in Theresa's direction—"she started it."

THAT NIGHT AT dinner, the tablecloth was cream colored, and the amber glow cast by candlelight baptized fifteen relative strangers gathered in the hotel's dining room. The menu was in French, which upset a few of the women. There really are people who don't expect to be handed a French menu in a French town in France.

They seemed like a happy, chatty, thoroughly white-bread collection of middle-class, middle-aged women, but you know what happens when objects of similar composition are put together.

I scanned the group for wildcards and for those who looked doubtful about their ability to trek twenty-five kilometers a day (that pretty much included all of us.) A few were on the heavy side; another was missing a leg. Oh dear. A couple of women were overly enthusiastic and gregarious, a sign of high maintenance and dependency. One or two looked like they had actually hiked before.

The bonding ritual had already begun; it was all so reminiscent of the first day of summer camp.

Out of everyone in our group two of them—Georgina and Beth—were friends of longstanding; two others—Serena and Theresa—were women I knew reasonably well.

Georgina was a sincere, fun-loving woman with short, spiky hair and a puckish grin. You just knew that not everything was starched beneath that clerical collar of hers, which she never wears, by the way. She had never done any serious hiking but always wanted to walk the Camino as an expression of faith, even if it meant spending a month away from her husband and two teenage children.

Between her initial gung-ho desire to walk the Camino and our departure for Spain, tragedy struck. One cold January day, she had flown to the tiny community of Pelee Island to conduct the twice-monthly church service. The short flight from the mainland had been a white-knuckle one but had managed to reach Pelee without incident. As the plane unloaded its cargo and prepared for the return flight to the mainland, Georgina stood on the tarmac chatting with several men who had spent a few days hunting pheasant and were about to fly back with their catch. When the plane was ready to go, the hunters waved good-bye to Georgina and boarded. It had no sooner lifted off the runway when something happened that caused the plane to career back to Earth, plunging through the thick layer of ice coating Lake Erie. It took two weeks for divers to recover the bodies. The incident so traumatized Georgina that it shook her faith, and she stepped away from the priesthood. She was not certain she had the courage to face daily life, let alone the Camino. But she decided to come anyway and hoped the journey would aid her healing.

Like Georgina, Beth was a married mother of two. She was also a newly minted grandmother, though you'd never know it by looking at her. She was petite yet sturdy with thick black hair that time had lightly streaked with gray and which she wore in a sporty chin-length bob neatly tucked behind her ears. She worked as a professor of nursing, but her strength and spiritual sustenance came from the outdoors. She lived and breathed hiking. When life got out of hand, she would often say, "I need the trail." Or if you were going through a tough patch, she would conclude, "You need the trail" and would then suggest a time and place. For her, a walk in the woods cured what ailed you.

Beth had hiked the Bruce Trail, and her vast knowledge and insights about gear and training were invaluable during the planning stages of our adventure. She wasn't a snob about it; she steered us in the correct direction in the gentlest way possible, always with a smile and always after her penetrating brown eyes

had fully absorbed our arguments. She was demure and diplomatic to a fault, and this was as much her strength as it was her
weakness, for she struggled to get people, even those closest to
her, to pay attention to her. Her husband, a commanding presence, was always the center of attention, and Beth lived quietly
and patiently in his shadow. Now, well into middle age, Beth was
ready to raise her voice. The Camino was her chance to chalk up
an adventure she could call her own.

Serena was a former neighbor of mine with whom I would
share casual conversations over the garden fence. We didn't have
a lot in common—she and her husband were newlyweds, whereas
my then-husband and I had a raucous houseful of children—but
I found peace in listening to Serena's soft, singsong voice as she
talked to me about what she was growing in her garden. When
each of us moved out of the neighborhood, we lost touch.

In the intervening years, Serena and her husband had taken a
belated honeymoon to South America. During a boat ride down
the Amazon River, Serena was bitten by a mosquito. By the time
she and her husband returned to Canada, a virus—the dreaded
West Nile version—had taken hold, and within days Serena had
lapsed into a coma. When she emerged from it a week later, a
chunk of her memory had been erased and she no longer recognized her husband or many of her friends. As a sort of cruel con-
solation, however, the coma left her with a gift of clairvoyance
(more on that later) and a burst of artistic expression that she
deftly spun into a flourishing business of garden sculptures that
she cast from concrete—praying angels, perched griffins, plump
hearts, massive leaves, chubby little birds, crosses, bird baths, and
garden borders. Serena's well-intentioned friends rallied to her
side to help her rebuild her life, but after a few years she found
their constant vigilance suffocating.

What brought Serena and me back together was an article in
our local newspaper about the plans Beth and I had to walk the
Camino. Serena was gripped by the idea immediately. While

rooting around in her basement that afternoon to see if she owned any hiking gear, she came across a small wooden box.

"You used to keep your favorite things in there," her husband explained when she asked what it held.

She reached into the darkness of the box and groped around, and the first thing she drew out was a small newspaper clipping— a birth announcement. She no longer recognized the name of the baby in the announcement, so her husband enlightened her.

"That's the daughter of the woman who is walking the Camino. They used to be our neighbors."

"I took that as a sign that I had to call you," she said to me on the phone that evening as she softly but insistently begged to be included in the pilgrimage. I could picture her slightly tremulous smile, her small happy eyes, and her gentle and flawless face that possessed a childlike, ethereal quality. "Please let me come. I want the chance to prove to people that I can do something on my own, without anyone's help. My sense of direction isn't the greatest, but all you have to do is yell if you see me going the wrong way."

Well, who could say no to a story like that? It made the hair on the back of my neck stand up.

The other woman I knew in the group was Theresa. Well, I sort of knew her. She had e-mailed me not long after I had opened my big mouth on the TV show, and we had clicked quickly. In preparation for the Camino, she immediately adopted a strict training regimen that included a twenty-kilometer-a-day walk to work during a particularly harsh Prairie winter.

Trim and tall, with a chic and spunky cap of white-gray hair, she was a ball of energy. She had a rollicking sense of humor and a big, dramatic laugh that made you laugh, too. She had three grown children and worked alongside her husband in a bakery business that sold its products to an international market. It was a roller coaster business, she said—the type of work that kept you awake at night with worry and ate away at your stomach lining.

Her husband was a risk taker and made good decisions, she confided, but at times the nail-biting intensity of it all was too much, and she needed a break.

She was a lapsed Catholic in that she no longer attended church every week, but her belief in God remained strong. Still, she had accumulated a considerable amount of residual "Catholic guilt."

"That's something we'll discuss on the Camino," she would say. We were saving a lot of topics for the Camino, as it appeared we would be spending a lot of time walking together.

Those were the women I knew; the others—Cathy, Sally, Lucy, Colleen, Joanna, Kate, Trish, Susie, Greta, and June—I had a month to get to know.

"What do you mean there's wine on the Camino!" one woman at our table said loudly and indignantly above the din of a dozen conversations as she poured herself a glass of wine.

"She's an alcoholic," someone whispered to me. "She told me on the plane."

Oh dear. Oh dear, oh dear, oh dear.

I tapped my wine glass with a fork and stood up to say a few words.

"It's great to meet all of you and to finally be gathered around the table as a group," I said. "This is going to be a lot of fun and a great adventure."

No one laughed or seconded the statement.

"Perhaps we should go around the table, introduce ourselves, and explain what drew each of us to this walk."

A handful gave their name, rank, and serial number and a throwaway line about their intentions. One or two gave their entire life history, warts and all. The rest were guardedly forthcoming and for the most part kept it short and sweet.

None of the women revealed any desperate desires or motivations; no one said that she was walking to ask St. James to intercede on her behalf, forgive a sin, provide enlightenment to a problem, or grant a miracle.

Most pilgrims don't know why they're walking. It was ever thus. A thousand years ago, pilgrims took to the open road as a form of penance, an expression of gratitude, or a way of coming to terms with a vexing problem. Sometimes a pilgrimage was a chance to spice up a mundane life with an adventure; it was most certainly as close as most people got to a holiday.

Over the centuries the material trappings have changed, but the concept of paring life down to its basic form has remained.

When you go on a pilgrimage, you put yourself on the margins of society. You escape its rules, but by the same token you put yourself at the mercy of a rather lawless frontier. In medieval times, setting foot in another country was not without its perils. Rape, murder, thievery, abduction were common on the road. Papal edicts and threats of excommunication had little effect, and pilgrims only had their faith and their wits to sustain them.

Then again, no one said a pilgrimage was a walk in the park; it was and still is a hard, punishing journey, a rigorous test for the soft Christian soul.

Fifteen women were about to find that out.

4

GUIDEBOOKS use words like "tough" and "hard" to describe the leg of the Camino that crosses the Pyrenees from Saint-Jean-Pied-de-Port to Roncesvalles. People who have walked it fix you with a faraway gaze and carefully choose words like "challenging" and "arduous," as if they can't quite reconcile memory with reality. Their comments are tempered by time, and you know what they say about time being a great healer. The "challenging" experience gets polished with each recounting of the tale into a smooth nugget of accomplishment and pride.

Gather round, boys and girls, while I tell you in the clearest, bluntest language what it's really like. Crossing the Pyrenees is torture; imagine Hell under sunny skies.

"Unbearable, brutal, wicked, hideous" doesn't describe it by half. Never has my body or my spirit been pushed or crushed so hard. It was the sort of pain that makes you weep, except that you cannot weep, because crying requires energy and you have to conserve every drop for the next step. At some point you're practically begging Death to wave his scythe over you and end the suffering.

The Camino is often described as a metaphorical journey through your lifetime. If that's the case, then the section from Saint-Jean, over the Pyrenees, and into Roncesvalles is a metaphor for one's struggle through the birth canal. No wonder we all emerge screaming.

The Pyrenees were a staggering challenge to our little group. Had one of us perished, it would not have surprised me. We were in over our heads. Several times during the climb I contemplated curling up into the fetal position by the side of the path just to rest, but the nice lady at the pilgrim office we had visited the day before had told us about a pilgrim who had done precisely that only weeks earlier. He was found dead.

It was understandable, then, that we were all skittish that first day on the Camino simply because of the Pyrenees. We insisted on starting in Saint-Jean, partly because we were purists and partly because we were vain; women rarely turn down anything described as a "calorie killer."

On May 1, we rose before dawn. Theresa, Georgina, and I conducted our morning ablutions with feigned confidence while struggling silently with our own levels of disorientation and jet lag. I know I wasn't the only one asking herself, "What the hell am I doing here?" I could see Georgina's lips moving as she placed her toothbrush and toothpaste in her toiletry bag, and I was pretty certain she was saying a prayer.

We laid out our clothing, some of which still had price tags attached. Theresa, spunky Prairie gal that she was, was slipping into a pair of fuchsia-colored pants she had borrowed from a friend. I had never seen anything like them—where do you buy fuchsia hiking pants?—and for a few seconds I experienced a case of gear envy. We dressed slowly, deliberately, as if girding for a crusade. Snaps, buckles, zippers, buttons were checked and double-checked. Hands slid firmly over trouser legs, smoothing out creases. Then the inevitable comments:

"I don't think khaki is a good color on me."

"Do these pants make my ass look big?"

"Whoa, these clothes fit fine in the store; what happened?"

"Nothing I brought matches!"

We filled our water bottles, joking that we should fill them with gin or wine. Like many of the women, I had brought a water pack—a large, clear plastic contraption that looks like a hot-water bottle with a tube that threads through the top of your backpack and allows quick access to water while you walk. There are two downsides to the water pack: when filled, it instantly adds three pounds to the weight of your backpack, and the exposed tube near your mouth looks as if you're receiving oxygen therapy.

The night before, we had dashed into *une épicerie* to stock up on bread, cheese, chocolate, paté, and oranges. Being women, we each purchased enough to feed six people. We had packed most of our provisions in plastic bags and tied them to the outside of our packs, but what do you do with a two-foot-long baguette? In the early morning darkness, Theresa, Georgina, and I stared at our backpacks, stymied by this challenge.

In a fit of pique, Theresa grabbed the baguette, ripped it in half, and stuffed both parts into one of the plastic bags.

"There," she said, brushing her hands together.

Georgina and I exchanged quick looks.

"Works for me," said Georgina as she ran a hand through her spiky hair and turned to finish tying her pack.

Finally, we were set. After sixteen months of planning, this was it. We left our hotel room and marched downstairs.

To say I was bright-eyed and bushy-tailed does not begin to capture how pumped I felt that morning. I took a deep breath and exhaled with gusto, and the three of us walked out the dark wooden front doors of our hotel—and smack-dab into a crisis of conscience.

Four members of our group were huddled around a car. Georgina quietly slid over to join them.

"What are you guys doing?" I asked, knowing full well what they were doing; they were negotiating with a taxi driver.

"I can't make it up the Pyrenees," said Joanna defiantly, refusing to make eye contact. "And I'm not going to wreck myself on the first day." She was a teacher, and her cranky manner sent a signal to me that she didn't like having her decisions contradicted.

"Me neither," said June.

I had already decided to cut Georgina some slack; she hadn't done much hiking and wasn't as fit as some of the others. Joanna and June, however, were both athletic-looking types, and both had bragged about hiking the entire Bruce Trail; June said she had hiked it three times.

If I were looking for an opportunity to shake off the mantle of leadership, this was it.

Rule number one in the *How Not to Be a Leader* handbook is "Don't get involved."

I considered standing around and trying to allay their fears and boost their confidence, but in the end I thought, "Screw it." I wasn't up to coddling anyone.

I wished them luck and gravitated toward another small group of women—Theresa, Sally, Trish, Cathy, and Lucy—who had already made up their minds to make the journey on foot, as planned. Off we went.

Pyrenees, Schmyrenees, I chuckled to myself.

We weaved through the narrow streets of a still-sleeping Saint-Jean-Pied-de-Port, the silence broken by the sound of our walking sticks clicking on the cobblestones. We eyed the illuminated shop windows. Naturally, all the merchandise looked attractive because the shops were closed. Even if they hadn't been, it would have been impossible to cram another thing into our packs or even *onto* our packs.

Every pilgrim negotiates a philosophical limbo at the start of a pilgrimage. You are part tourist, part pilgrim, but every step taken is an incremental shift away from the life you know, moving toward a parallel universe where the material world is of no consequence, where you put your trust in miracles, not in MasterCard.

We walked under the fourteenth-century gothic Porte d'Espagne—its clock tower read 6:45—and onto the Pont d'Espagne, a small stone bridge spanning the river Nive, and left the walled city of Saint-Jean-Pied-de-Port.

We were officially on the Camino. There was no fanfare, no signs reading "Thank you for visiting Saint-Jean-Pied-de-Port. Have a Nice Day," no arrow declaring "Santiago: 760 kilometers"—just a narrow, meandering band of asphalt, so nondescript that it compelled you to question whether you were on the correct path.

I stopped to inhale my surroundings and watched puffs of my breath disappear into the ether. I'm really here, I thought.

There are more than a hundred routes—stretching north beyond Oslo and east to Budapest—all of them aimed toward Santiago. It's surprising to learn that about a dozen more are currently under development.

Of the four traditional routes—Tours, Vézelay, Le Puy-en-Velay, and Arles—that originated during the formative years of the Camino de Santiago, three feed into Saint-Jean-Pied-de-Port, converging to create the Camino Francés. (The fourth bypasses Saint-Jean and winds through the Somport Pass.)

The Camino Francés was the route we were taking. It is the most traveled, best known, longest, and, as we were to discover, the most rigorous of more than twenty routes in Spain that carry pilgrims to Santiago.

We proceeded along a paved lane bordered by trees whose impossibly glossy leaves dazzled in the bright sun. Everything shimmered. I was beginning to relax and pay attention to the small details of life—the way dew glinted off a blade of grass, the gradations of color on a bird's wing, the emergence of buds on a tree's limb, the way the sun danced like sparks off an ember on Trish's auburn hair. A satisfied smile crept across my lips, knowing that a month's worth of such visual treats lay ahead.

At first the road climbed gradually, almost imperceptibly, but within five or ten minutes we were breaking a sweat. Being Type

A personalities, we continued to chat as though nothing were out of the ordinary, as if talking while panting heavily were normal behavior. Had anyone breathed a word about exertion it would have revealed a lax training regimen, and we all wanted to prove that we were fit for the task ahead.

I stopped to catch my breath on the pretext of adjusting my backpack. I looked up, up, up at mountains that were almost on top of us and spotted a small white building on the peak of one of them. It was about two galaxies away.

"At least we don't have to climb *that* high." I said, pointing to the building. "Who would think of putting a home way up there?"

We looked at the winding road ahead of us and then back up at the little white building. No, there appeared to be no connection between the two. We started up again.

A cab sped by stuffed to capacity with our comrades. We waved magnanimously, as those in a sisterhood are wont to do, but inwardly we muttered about the slackers in the car.

Eventually it became impossible to climb and talk at the same time. Our little band of pilgrims began to separate. The steepness was horrendous. I could not fathom how a road at such an incline could be paved, much less driven up. I half expected to see the tiny cab roll past in reverse.

I'm not sure how much time elapsed—perhaps twenty minutes—but the cab did reappear, empty, on its return trip to Saint-Jean. That gave me hope. The journey to Roncesvalles would be mighty difficult, but it wouldn't be long.

The road switched back and forth up the mountain at an incline of about seventy degrees. On either side, verdant pastures in varying shades of green stretched for miles like a crazy quilt across deep chasms gouged from the mountainside, the colors brightening and darkening as sunlight ebbed and flowed over the landscape. Occasionally the sun's rays cast a spotlight on one of the white stucco homes with red-tiled roofs scattered across the landscape. You can't help but be impressed at how an entire

country can subscribe to a single housing style and color scheme—
a welcome change from the restlessly competitive North American housing market where people fret over five hundred shades
of paint and an endless variety of building materials.

But it was the air that quite literally took my breath away. It
was so bracing you could have served it in a tall glass with a twist
of lime.

Still, it could not compensate for the intense physical exertion
that was slowly crushing my body.

My legs went rubbery. I kept my head down and my thoughts
focused solely on my inner core, because I could no longer take
in the scenery and breathe at the same time. I walked ten paces,
then stopped to take ten breaths, leaning heavily on my walking
stick as I struggled to modulate my breathing. I looked behind
me. Far below I saw Sally with her hop-skip gait, her two crutches
pounding the pavement. How on Earth was that poor woman
managing?

Sally was a wisp of a woman, but her body was muscular and
her hands strong. She wore a hiking skirt over black leggings that
covered the stump of her amputated leg, and her shoulder-length
sandy brown hair was covered with a red patterned bandana. Several of us wondered how long she'd last on the Camino, but no
one dared to lay a bet. She was made of stronger stuff than most
of us.

At the fragile age of thirteen she had lost her leg when a drunk
driver knocked her off her bicycle. Sally didn't let the accident
slow her down. She continued to compete in sports throughout high school and became the first amputee to scale Mount
McKinley. She had weathered a painful divorce and was raising
her children alone. A new partner held the promise of better days
ahead. She said her reason for walking the Camino was to test a
set of crutches she had designed—she was an occupational therapist—but you couldn't help wondering whether she also wanted
to test herself.

As I looked down at her moving steadily up the incline, I could not imagine how she would get through the entire trek, much less this first day.

I considered my own predicament. For the first time in my life, I felt like an entirely physical being without a modicum of intellect. (Had I possessed a modicum of intellect, I would have chosen the spa holiday.) My brain was incapable of thinking of anything beyond the pain I felt and the desperate urge to keep moving. I was operating on pure instinct.

"Oh. Fuhhhhck," I finally gasped as I moved slowly and painfully, step by step.

A cow in a pasture abutting the road raised its head, looked at me vacantly, and resumed grazing.

It was a startling sight. How can a cow live up here? How can anyone live up here? I peeked over a rickety split-rail fence and into the chasm below, a height I had previously only experienced from the inside of an airplane.

From a distant farmhouse, a light plume of smoke curled from a chimney. I closed my eyes and imagined the smells and sensations of lazing in front of a roaring fire, cozy and content. Yes, I decided, in my next life I would come back as a dog or a cat, some life-form that doesn't require challenges to spice up its existence.

I returned my gaze to the road, focused on the nearest fence post, and set myself the goal of reaching it. I was now walking in five-pace intervals. Walk five steps. Stop. Take five breaths. Walk five steps. Stop. Take five breaths. My heart hammered in triple time.

I dragged my exhausted body past a small inn at Untto. I knew two things about Untto: it was a mere five kilometers from Saint-Jean-Pied-de-Port and, worse, at least fifteen kilometers from Roncesvalles.

The path continued in its perpendicular fashion. Each time I thought I had reached the summit, the trail would turn a corner and there would be another incline, and another, and another.

Just when I could stand the pain no longer, when I prepared to collapse in a heap and let the elements do what they wished with me, the shadow of another pilgrim appeared on my right side. I lacked the energy to turn my head and make eye contact, but I could feel the person and hear him or her breathing. I bit back my tears—no one likes a crybaby on the trail—and forced myself to keep going.

Occasionally, I glanced down at the shadow and at once understood that the pilgrim was using me as a marker. Hadn't I done the same thing earlier, using a pilgrim as inspiration and motivation to keep moving forward?

On this desolate terrain, someone was now relying on me. It was the only thing that kept me going. I could sense the person telepathically encouraging me, and I sent back encouraging thoughts to him or her. "*We will make it over this hurdle together,*" I muttered defiantly. "*We will succeed!*"

The shadow kept pace with me, hanging back a bit but always within sight. Suddenly, it got longer and longer. The person was gaining on me. I looked up to make eye contact—only to discover with crushing humiliation that there was no one there. The shadow was mine.

I continued to pant my way up the Pyrenees as rivulets of sweat dribbled down my face. My breathing was so rapid it scared me, speeding up my breathing even more. If ever I were to have a heart attack, it would be here. My heart was reverberating so hard and so loudly that it was giving me an earache.

From time to time, a car passed, and I looked at its driver with imploring eyes, hoping someone would take pity, roll down the window, and ask, "Wanna lift?" Had Jeffrey Dahmer been behind the wheel, I would have climbed in and willingly offered him my left arm as a snack.

Farther ahead, a loose string of people shuffled silently, heads bowed. They walked as if they were all recovering from caesarean sections. A few had stopped for a smoke. A smoke!

While catching my breath for the umpteenth time, I caught the eye of a woman a few feet away from me.

"Are you American?" she panted.

"Canadian," I gasped back, too exhausted to berate her for mistaking me for an American.

"Australian?" I asked. She nodded, gasping for breath.

"You've come a long way," I said in a ludicrous attempt to make chitchat while panting like a crazed animal.

"We're on our honeymoon," she replied.

"Did you have any idea it would be like this?" I asked, curious as to whether there had been a miscommunication with her fiancé concerning heavy breathing on a honeymoon.

She shook her head. "We stayed at Untto because we were told it would make the climb easier. Did you start in Saint-Jean?"

I nodded.

"God, I don't know how you're managing," she said.

With our breathing sufficiently upgraded from "stand by for a stroke" to "at death's door" we pushed on.

I felt utterly out of shape. I was certain I had prepared adequately for the pilgrimage. I had done three complete laps three times a week on the James Street steps near my Hamilton home. Why was this so difficult?

"It's difficult because you didn't count on a real mountain, you moron," the Critic Within sneered. *"Hamilton Mountain is no more a mountain than a blade of grass is a meadow."*

The Critic Within had a point.

The other difficulty was the absurd incline, which placed my nose very close to the pavement.

Then there was the altitude. I had forgotten to factor in that little detail during my training. So, let's see: a killer incline, high altitude, and jet lag. Oh yeah, and a fifty-year-old body.

As I glanced around to get my bearings, I passed a small white house—the same small white house I had pointed out to the others way down below on the road just outside Saint-Jean-Pied-de-

Port, the house I jokingly said we would not have to pass. I was almost hysterical. It didn't help that we weren't even remotely near the top of the mountain, either. There was still more climbing.

A yellow arrow pointed away from the asphalt road to a muddy path up yet another steep hill. Lemminglike, the pilgrim horde turned en masse.

"*Please God! Not another steep climb,*" I screamed silently. Just then, someone called my name.

"Jane! How's it going?"

It was Cathy, one of the women in our group whom I had met briefly the night before. She was from British Columbia and was one of those blonde, bubbly types. She was as infuriatingly perky as she had been when we set out that morning.

She quickly moved beside me and began talking. Incessantly. I looked at her in amazement. How did she do it? I was so winded from walking I could barely utter a word, but Cathy was gabbing a mile a minute, peppering me with a million questions.

Under normal circumstances I gamely chatter to people even when I don't feel like it. That rule was now gone, my friend. I kept walking, stone-faced, as Cathy blathered. All I could muster was, "Can't. Talk. While. Climbing."

"Oh, ok," she said brightly. "Maybe when we get to Roncesvalles and we all get settled at our *refugio* we can go out for dinner and bond! Boy, I hope it's a good dinner! I'll be really hungry by then! Won't you? Aren't you just dying for a glass of wine?! Yum!! Red wine, eh? I hear the wine in this part of Europe is amazing! This is so much fun. I can't wait to get to know all the women better! They're sooo amazing! This is amazing! The next time I . . ."

And on she went. If she had talked about how bone-wearing this trek was, I could have offered sympathy and gasped out some conversation. But cheerful talk? That was beyond me. I was miserable, and I wanted only miserable company. I made a mental note of her light blue jacket so as to avoid running into her again.

I blocked out Cathy and pushed on, determined to manage the ascent of yet another steep hill. If nothing else, I had to outpace her to escape her nonstop yammering. Just then Sally appeared on my left flank like a stealth fighter and vaulted ahead of me. I was floored.

"The one-legged woman isn't going to get ahead of me," I snarled.

I pushed myself harder until I overtook her, clawing with ruthless determination over boulders and through muddy culverts to reach the top. This spiritual pilgrimage was turning me into an animal.

The hill delivered us to a paved road that shot across a vast, unforgiving plain toward the horizon. This was Charlemagne territory. Now there was a leader.

From the time he became king of the Franks in 771, Charlemagne presided over the Holy Roman Empire, which comprised every nook and cranny from the Atlantic Ocean to the Vistula River in Poland and from the Pyrenees north to the Baltic Sea. Perhaps "presided" is too fine a word for a fellow who gave his pagan POWs the choice of Christian baptism or death and who beheaded 4,500 Saxons in a single day. He personally led about fifty campaigns—brought the Saxons to their knees in 785, forced back the Slavs in 789, crushed the Avars from 790 to 805—you know, all in a reign's work.

Yet history has applied a sanitizing gloss to Charlemagne's reputation, suggesting that he preferred his role as an administrator to that of a warrior. He certainly demonstrated exceptional prowess in this area. Religion, politics, land deeds, military service, even marital problems and taming his own barbaric tribe—Charlemagne touched every facet of Germanic life. He was both a politician and a tactician, and perhaps his biggest success was how he managed to hold together his disparate and far-flung empire by sheer force of his charismatic personality. The mere mention of his name was enough to make men quake at the knees.

Charlemagne's own family was a mess. So fond was he of his daughters that he forbade them to marry (some historians have hinted at incest), yet he turned a blind eye to their voracious sexual appetites and welcomed the offspring of their libidinous labors.

Not that Charlemagne was a paragon of chastity or domestic loyalty. He had an eye for the ladies—four wives and five mistresses—and they had an eye for him. Women threw themselves at him, begging to be part of his harem rather than settling down with one of the town mopes. Of the twenty children he sired, only eight were legitimate.

But enough about Charlemagne's sex life. The reason for mentioning Charlemagne is that he has a pivotal role in the Camino legend (of which there are many, with erratic variations on the theme).

The most popular tale begins with Charlemagne's recurring dream about the Milky Way. Obsessed with what it meant, he finally received an explanation from none other than St. James himself, who appeared to the emperor one night in a vision. James told Charlemagne that it wasn't the Milky Way he was dreaming about exactly but a metaphor for the route that led to James's tomb in northern Spain. (If you superimpose the Milky Way on a map of the Camino, the stars closely match the route.) There was one problem, James pointed out—those nasty Moors were blocking the road. Would Charlemagne be so kind as to open it up?

Charlemagne didn't have to be asked twice. The Camino became his personal crusade, and he plowed and murdered his way through the barricades and became a hero to pilgrims everywhere. It's a curious and rather jingoistic tale that makes a German-French warrior the father of Spain's Camino. I don't know how the Spanish let that one slip by.

Charlemagne's fanaticism was tested one day on the very spot where I now stood. A pivotal but disastrous battle took place in 778, a battle that resonates nearly a millennium and a half after the last sword was swung. The rearguard of Charlemagne's army was ambushed and slaughtered to the last man by the Basques or the Moors, depending on who's telling the story. Among the dead was Charlemagne's majordomo, Roland, the legendary knight immortalized in *Chanson de Roland*, the epic paean to chivalry and courtly love that remains France's most famous poem.

Today people say that Charlemagne's anguished cries when he was told of Roland's death can still be heard in the wind that pounds this desolate terrain.

EXHAUSTED, BEATEN, and desperate for a little victory of my own, I marched on. Just ahead, I spied a lone pilgrim lumbering on the trail. New prey, I slyly thought. Overtaking other pilgrims had become a survival sport, entertainment for my idling brain. This particular pilgrim was wearing a Tilley hat (which is always fun to refer to as a "silly hat").

As I motored passed the pilgrim, it struck me how much she looked like Georgina—same build, same gait, same goofy Tilley hat. But it couldn't be; Georgina had taken a taxi over the Pyrenees.

I took a closer look: It was indeed the spiky-haired vicar. She didn't look too happy.

"Oh God, Jane, this is brutal," she wailed.

"What are you doing here? I thought you took a cab."

"We did," she sputtered. "The driver dropped us at Untto."

"Untto? That's miles back? Why didn't you take it all the way to Roncesvalles?"

"None of us knew enough French to tell the driver," she said fighting back tears. "He just dumped us there, and we had no choice but to walk. I'm not going to make it."

"What are you doing with that?" I asked, referring to the small tape recorder she held to her mouth.

"I'm going to die here," she said without emotion. "But in case I don't, I'm going to have a recording of my thoughts to replay at home when I think I'm having a bad day. No day could be worse than this."

I tried to boost her spirits, but it was hard when my own were dragging like a ball and chain.

I wanted to tell her, "Look, this was a crazy idea. We've made a huge mistake. Let's flag down a car and quit right now." The very thought made my eyes sting. I wanted to do the Camino so badly, and yet here I was, barely halfway through the first day, and already I wanted to bail.

I tried slowing my pace to match Georgina's, but after a few minutes my legs rebelled, and relief came only from moving quickly.

"Hang in" was the best I could offer. "We'll gather just around that bend, and then we'll sit down and have our lunch."

A hundred or so meters ahead, I recognized Theresa's long stride and her fuchsia hiking pants beneath her overstuffed backpack. I struggled to catch up to her and told her about Georgina and the other taxi-hags being dumped in Untto.

The news stopped her in her tracks.

"They're *walking?*"

I nodded. "We need to stop somewhere and take a break. Everyone's wiped." And then apologetically: "They must be cursing me for suggesting this expedition."

"Oh, how could they? Look at this," she exclaimed, with a wide sweep of her walking stick. "This is breathtaking. We're on the top of the fucking Pyrenees, Janie! How many of us imagined this three days ago? We did it! I'll bet everyone is completely *grateful* to you for letting them experience this."

The grateful part was a stretch, but Theresa was right about the view. It was spectacular. We *were* on top of the world. What's more, the weather gods had bestowed brilliant conditions—bright blue skies and cool air.

We met up with Cathy, Beth, Joanna, Colleen, and Susie and immediately embarked on that inane exercise women do of trying to find *a good spot* for lunch. High in the mountains, on a treeless windswept plateau, women will still insist on searching for *a good spot* to eat.

Perhaps it wasn't about finding the best spot but about waiting until someone claimed an area as *a good enough spot*. As soon as I stretched out on the grass, my legs began to throb from the shock of not moving.

We saw Lucy limping slightly, and we waved her over. When she reached our picnic, she collapsed and started groping at her water hose, sucking on it madly to get a drink.

"Are you having trouble with that?" asked Beth with nurscly concern.

"I can never seem to get enough water up this tube," said Lucy. "It's as if there's an obstruction. I was sucking on that thing all the way up the mountain and couldn't get more than a trickle."

"I'm having the same trouble with mine," I said. "I'm practically getting a hernia from sucking on that hose."

Beth mulled this over.

"Open your packs," Beth ordered. We untied our backpacks and lifted the flaps. Within seconds Beth deduced the problem.

"I'm surprised you got any water at all," Beth said shaking her head with a mix of humor and exasperation. "You've put them in upside down."

Lucy and I burst out laughing.

"Well, that's hardly a surprise," I said. "I've never even been camping, so what do I know about water packs?"

"You've never been camping?" Colleen the social worker glared with incredulity. "And you expect to walk across Spain?"

"We're not camping across Spain; we're walking," I reminded her. "But if we had to camp, I bet I could do it."

Colleen rolled her eyes and looked away, wondering how she was going to get across Spain with a hopeless leader who didn't speak French (or Spanish—I hadn't told her that yet) and who had never camped. I couldn't seem to win with her.

We unwrapped our huge picnic and shared an orgy of food.

Joanna ripped off a chunk of baguette that was passed to her. I decided against asking her about her cab ride up the Pyrenees.

"Did you see that French couple back there," she said, brushing her short, wavy blonde hair from her eyes and then leaning back, propped up by her elbows. "They actually had a tablecloth laid out and a bottle of wine."

"The wine will dehydrate them," Colleen knowingly retorted with an admonishing shake of her head.

"I think I'm developing tendonitis," Lucy said, rubbing her hip. "My hip is killing me."

I had no idea what to do in the case of injuries such as tendonitis of the hip, but I wasn't about to say anything; no point giving Colleen more ammunition about my growing list of deficiencies.

Lucy was a hardy, happy gal. I didn't know her well, but she struck me as the type that wouldn't wimp out at the first sign of a painful twitch. Her pretty face had kindness written all over it, but her impish grin and the twinkle in her eyes let you know that she wasn't above going out with friends to engage in juvenile pranks aimed at disreputable ex-husbands and ex-boyfriends. Definitely a fun-loving soul. I hoped we'd get a chance to walk together. But at that moment, her normally happy face bore the trace of concern for her hip.

Georgina was the next to arrive.

"What the hell was that?" she gasped, referring to the mountain we just climbed.

"We're all in shock, Georgie," I said. "Here, have some chocolate. At least we're now at the top—touch wood."

"We still have to get down," muttered Susie. "Going down is harder than climbing."

Like Colleen, Susie seemed to reside on the gloomy side of the street. She was an odd little thing—thin build and long, frizzy, sandy hair. She had a habit of screwing up her face and squinting at you through her granny glasses as if she were trying to place you somewhere on the idiot scale. It wasn't likely that we'd be walking together.

"Is anyone going to take their shoes off?" asked Theresa. "The guidebooks all say we should. Stretch your toes, massage your soles, that sort of thing."

None of us did. We weren't sure we would ever get them back on. Instead, we passed around chocolate, cheese, paté, and bread and did our best to ignore how worn-out we were by marveling at the view.

We sat close to a hideously dangerous drop. Beyond lay a wide-screen panorama of a lofty mountain range cascading endlessly into the horizon. The sky was a *Simpsons* sky—a surreal tableau of fat, cumulus clouds painted on a baby-blue canvas. It was an awesome sight.

With lunch over, we hoisted our backpacks in place and almost toppled from the weight.

"Maybe this is the worst part of the pilgrimage, so we should be grateful that we're getting it over with early on," I said, hoping to mitigate the strain of the Pyrenees.

"Nope," said Theresa. "There's O Cebreiro, or whatever it's called. That's supposed to be worse."

Worse seemed impossible.

I HAD BEEN trudging along lost in thought when who should suddenly appear beside me but chatty Cathy. She was still going full tilt. Talking, that is. I gave her a look of astonishment, which she misread as interest in her conversation. I would be hard pressed to remember what exactly she was talking about, but it had nothing to do with climbing or pain. I think she was talking about her family, one of her kids' school projects, the cost of groceries, or maybe her job.

Suddenly, a gust of wind tore into us, nearly blowing us off our feet. I struggled to stay upright, but it proved difficult even with a heavy backpack anchoring me. The wind shifted into higher gear. I steadied my feet and scrambled together a mish-mash of instincts and muscles I had never used before. These are the ones labelled, "Use only on a mountain cliff when a big wind threatens to hurl you over the edge to your death."

I shot a look of panic at Cathy, figuring that if nothing else, her ceaseless patter would shift to a discourse on how to trouble-shoot bad weather conditions.

Wrong. Cathy continued to chitchat about life back home as if nothing were out of the ordinary, as if being on the edge of the Pyrenees with a horrific wind bouncing us around like rag dolls were normal. She did not let anything interrupt her conversation. It was remarkable, really.

I, however, began to silently freak out. Snow had begun fall-ing—*snow!*—and I had no intention of getting stuck on a moun-tain during a snowstorm.

I pulled away from Cathy and her chirpy conversation. This only made her talk louder. As I picked my way down a perilously steep track littered with fallen rocks, the wind screaming in my ears—I'm certain it wasn't Charlemagne—my hair whipping my face, Cathy's gabfest continued:

"And then I told the guy that he was making a big mistake about that brand of socks, because, you know, the sweat doesn't get wicked away as quickly as it does when you have socks with a higher denier count, but he kept telling me, 'You know, I've heard these really are the best brand...'"

In the distance I could make out a huge old building with a spire. Roncesvalles! Hooray! Civilization! I sped up. I was hysterically giddy. I could almost taste the wine and smell the crackling fireplace that surely lay ahead. I surged ahead of Cathy.

A cold rain came pelting down just as I reached Roncesvalles's ancient road that led to the pilgrim office. When I arrived at the appointed place, a sign posted on a heavy, worn door said that the office would not open until 4 PM.

I glanced at my watch: 3:10.

Disappointed that a bed would not be within my reach for a while, I unhooked my pack, leaned it next to the door, and sat down. My legs began to tingle. My calves were throbbing, and my thigh muscles jerked spasmodically, as if they had been tapped by a doctor's reflex hammer. I rubbed them vigorously to calm them down.

Around me sat bedraggled, dirty, defeated-looking people, their heads tilted against the stone wall and their eyes fixed with a catatonic stare. It was a motley bunch of nationalities and ages: fathers with sons on bonding adventures, elderly couples, students, single women, clusters of middle-aged men. All looked utterly beaten and forlorn.

Gradually, the rest of my group began to trickle in. We embraced and congratulated and consoled one another as tales spilled out about who saw whom, who was hurting, who needed medical attention.

With a loud rattle, the door to the pilgrim office swung open, and the formerly moribund pilgrims sprang into action, jostling to get in the door, without a modicum of civility. Europeans, it seems, have nothing on Americans when it comes to being pushy. I stuck my elbows out to prevent anyone from getting ahead of me.

Inside the pilgrim office, huddled on narrow benches trying to grasp stubby pencils in our shaking, frigid fingers and decipher questions in French and Spanish, we filled out forms with our name, nationality, and religion and the purpose of our pilgrimage. The last one was a trick multiple-choice question with a list of options: religious, spiritual, cultural, or athletic. A further subset followed the "religious" options. This is where the dogmatic wheat is separated from the agnostic chaff.

"Don't check off 'none' under religion," I whispered to Joanna. "I heard they put you last on the list for a bed if you don't indicate you're doing this for religious or spiritual reasons."

Our lodging for the night—our first pilgrim *refugio*—was in a cavernous stone barracks, probably eight hundred years old, that had been nicely updated for the modern pilgrim. Huge iron light fixtures hung from the ceiling. There were three long rows of bunk beds, easily a hundred of them.

I snagged a lower bunk and headed off with my toiletry bag and towel to find a shower.

The lower level housed laundry and Internet facilities as well as washrooms. For a place that sleeps two hundred—and before the evening was out floor mats would be laid in the hallways to handle the overflow crowd—there were only three toilet stalls and two shower stalls. What's with that?

After a ten-minute wait, it was my turn for a shower. Only then did I realize that I had left fresh clothing upstairs. I reluctantly gave up my place in line to the next person, returned to my bunk, gathered up the missing items, and returned to the shower queue.

Later that night, I located Georgina in another *refugio*. She was folding clothes and slowly shuffling around her bunk.

"Hey," I said, embracing her. "You did it. I'm so proud of you!"

She looked shell-shocked.

"You want to come for dinner with us?" I asked, trying to cheer her up.

"No, I think I'm just going to stay here and get some sleep. I'm sore."

"There'll be wine," I cajoled.

She smiled wanly and shook her head. She didn't want anything. I asked if she wanted to come to the church service later on, but again the vicar declined. This was not like Georgina, but then none of us were in our normal frame of mind. Try crossing the Pyrenees in a day and "normal," by Camino definitions, includes traces of madness.

I was too tired to attend Mass myself, but I went anyway. A small group of us walked through the doors of the thirteenth-century Collegiate Church and into one of the most beautiful Romanesque churches I have ever seen. The interior was dark, save for sporadic lighting focused on the altar and the numerous bouquets of fresh-cut flowers adorning it.

The place was packed, and we took our seats near the front. I could not understand what the priest was saying, but the gist was that he was thanking God for getting us over the Pyrenees (Amen to that!) and asking for our continued safety and good health on the rest of our journey. (Amen. Amen.)

Tears of gratitude welled up. Yes, it had been an exhausting and at times painful day, but I was lucky to have had the legs to manage it. We humans are quick to bitch about our various aches and pains, but they pale in comparison to what others suffer around the world. I gave thanks for small mercies: family, friends, good traveling companions, a full belly, and a warm bed for the night. At the Communion rail I was, for the first time in a really long while, appreciative of the ritual.

We returned to the *refugio* and the prospect of well-deserved sleep. While packing for the Camino, I had puzzled over what to bring for sleepwear and finally settled on a sage-green camisole and matching patterned cotton pajama bottoms. It looked completely ridiculous in the *refugio*. I might just as well have been attired in a peignoir set. Everyone else was in T-shirts and underwear, if that.

I slid into my sleeping bag. Everything was so alien, not least of which was the fact that I was sleeping in a roomful of strangers. Men were stripping off all around me, and from the vantage point of a lower bunk, I could only see them from the waist down—a smorgasbord of boxers, Y-fronts, and penises.

I turned over in my sleeping bag and there, facing me in the next bunk, was Cathy.

"Hey, Jane! How are you feeling? Where did you go for dinner? What did you eat? Have you seen the others? I saw you at the church service. Wasn't it amazing? It really touched my soul. Did you feel the same way?"

And then, "Isn't this a show?" She giggled, nodding toward the throng of male bodies struggling out of their clothes.

I rolled onto my back and stared at the bottom of the upper bunk's mattress. Jesus. Of all the people I could be sleeping beside, I end up with Cathy. Does she talk in her sleep, too?

A grin crept across my face. Good ol' Cathy. She, too, was away from her family and no doubt feeling out of her element. Being perky, chatty, and upbeat was probably her way of pushing the fear and loneliness to the back of her mind. Terminally cheerful folk like her perform a valuable public service to terminally moody types like me.

I turned my head toward her.

"'Night," I smiled. "Thanks for staying so positive all day. It really helped the rest of us."

"You know what? I talk too much," she admitted almost sadly. "It drives my husband crazy. Sorry if I bugged you."

"You didn't."

I closed my eyes and drifted off to a land without mountains to climb.

5

PITY the poor pilgrim who chooses to walk the Camino in August. Apart from the obvious foolishness of backpacking in the peak summer months, when Spain's sun is at its hottest, the sheer number of pilgrims on the trail exacerbates the ordeal of the journey.

According to the Archdiocese of Compostela, 2004 was the busiest year on record. Nearly 180,000 pilgrims, most of whom traveled the Camino Francés, received their *credencial* in Santiago. About 45,000 of those did so in August, compared with about 17,000 who walked the Camino in May. Bear in mind that those numbers represent the pilgrims who received the *credencial*; it doesn't include those who started out and didn't finish or who didn't bother to collect a *credencial*.

Despite the lighter pilgrim traffic in May, the *refugios* were strained to the rafters, and securing a bed for the night quickly turned into a blood sport.

The Camino crowd spikes during a Holy Year, which occurs when the Feast Day of St. James—July 25, the anniversary of his martyrdom—falls on a Sunday, and 2004 was a Holy Year. In 1999, the previous Holy Year, 154,613 people traveled on the Camino, and in 1993, the Holy Year before that, 99,436 made the pilgrimage.

Statistics point to a renaissance for this medieval trek. In 1988, 3,501 pilgrims registered on the Camino; ten years later, the numbers climbed to more than 30,000; and in 2002 nearly 70,000 hit the trail (none of those years were Holy Years).

The Archdiocese of Compostela hasn't seen numbers like this in almost a thousand years. You see, around the fourteenth century the pilgrimage took a nosedive. Wars, religious schisms, and the rapid spread of the Black Death contributed to a decline in pilgrim activity. But the big factor for the decline was that the Church stopped promoting the Camino because it no longer needed pilgrims. Pilgrims were the Church's foot soldiers at a time when it was trying to gain a toehold in what is now modern-day Spain and weaken eight centuries of Islamic presence in the region. Once the Church got what it wanted, who needed the Camino?

Throughout the centuries a few dedicated men and women kept the Camino alive. It wasn't until the mid-1980s that the Camino got its groove back. That's when the yellow-arrow system was developed and when the Council of Europe formally declared the Camino a European Cultural Route. In 1993 UNESCO added its stamp of approval to the Camino Francés and declared it a World Heritage Site, resulting in a slew of publicity.

Ironically, Western wealth and excess have contributed more to the rehabilitation of the Camino in modern times than has the Church. The Camino de Santiago landed in the crosshairs of a generation that was feeling weighed down by materialism, relentless technology upgrades, and a search for meaning in a complex world. What could be a better, trendier antidote than the simplicity of a pilgrimage? It fit the Zeitgeist like a glove, marrying physical fitness and spiritual nourishment. Furthermore, it fed the

Baby Boom generation's desire for adventure tourism. The same generation that, thirty years earlier, turned backpacking across Europe into a rite of passage, could now, in middle age, return to its youthful roots. If nothing else, the pilgrimage gave them a chance to test their knee replacements.

Not surprisingly, Spaniards are the largest group of pilgrims (about 137,000 in 2004). But North Americans are a growing market, edging out Brits, Australians, New Zealanders, and South Africans. Pilgrims come from as far away as Iceland, Haiti, Sri Lanka, Benin, Paraguay, and Japan and from as close as Portugal and France.

The largest cohort by age is twenty-one to thirty, but lest you think the Camino is a young person's game, let it be noted that the second largest group is between the ages of forty-one and fifty. More than 1,600 pilgrims in 2004 were over the age of seventy, and of those, fifty-nine were eighty years and older. Interestingly, statistics show that almost 10,000 pilgrims were children between a few months of age and fifteen. Now there's a novel form of punishment: "If you're not off MSN in five minutes, I'm making you walk the Camino!"

Getting a true measure of the Camino isn't easy. After a while the Camino's distance contracts and expands like the fish tales of the weekend angler. Some put the Camino francés at 760 kilometers, some say 774 kilometers, others round it off to 800 kilometers, some measure it as 804, and still others insist it's 850 kilometers. In the end, who cares? It is simply a hell of a long way.

If you average twenty-five kilometers a day, the Camino can be accomplished in about a month. But let's face it: unless you're retired, independently wealthy, or between jobs, or you're a student on summer break, it's not easy finding a month to go anywhere. Little wonder many Brits and Europeans section-hike the Camino over a period of a year or five. Cheap flights on an ever-expanding fleet of discount airlines make the prospect extremely affordable.

Walking is the most popular mode of transport on the Camino, but pilgrims also go by bicycle, horseback, donkey, and even camel. In 2004, sixty people rolled the Camino in their wheelchairs, and I can't begin to imagine the difficulties they encountered.

Foot travel is not without its hazards. Yes, the inevitable blisters, shin splints, sprained ankles, and damaged toenails occur, but things can and do get much worse.

Consider the story of Mary Catherine Kimpton from Canada. One June day in 2002, she and her husband, Harry, both retired, were resting with a Spanish pilgrim by the side of the road just outside Estella when a car rounded the corner and struck them. Mary Catherine was killed instantly. Her husband was not injured, but the Spanish pilgrim spent more than a month in hospital. A few years after the accident, Harry returned to the site and erected a cairn to his wife's memory.

Each year about twenty people who start out on the Camino die while walking it, the causes ranging from traffic accidents to falls to heart attacks. We heard of two who died of heart attacks during the month when we walked.

A happier discovery is that murder has not marred the Camino—well, at least not in recent memory. Centuries ago, all manner of catastrophe befell a pilgrim. Today things are more sedate. There have been minor incidents of men pestering women—and a few years ago a man reportedly exposed himself to female pilgrims—but by and large the Camino is a safe trail. That's nice to know; there are so few places left in this world where people can walk for long stretches without fear.

I lay in my bed that first morning in Roncesvalles wondering about the day ahead. It was dark in the *refugio*, but there was a considerable amount of human activity buzzing around me.

It began with the tinny sound of a watch alarm, followed by whispered voices, quiet yawns, creaking bedsprings, a flashlight being flicked on, and the crumpling of paper as people deftly groped for their belongings. The activity built to a symphonic crescendo of zippers, buckles, snaps, and toggles all being played *sotto voce* but at a furious pace until, without a word or glance back, the musicians scampered like mice toward the exit.

Moments later, the overhead lights came on with the dull, slow, echoing thud of a series of institutional light switches being thrown, the sound you might hear in a movie scene about a maximum-security facility. This was the pilgrims' wake-up call.

My eyes squinted in the sudden light, but when they adjusted I noticed that more than half the *refugio* had already cleared out. It was only 6 AM.

I dropped my head back on my pillow and counted back six hours, wondering whether my kids missed me.

I kicked off the sleeping bag, got up, and looked for familiar faces. Some of our merry little band was up; others were still in bed staring into the bunk above their heads, no doubt coming to terms with being on a mammoth hike in a foreign country with a mad, middle-aged woman they barely knew.

"Hey," I said, waving jovially to Joanna, who was getting dressed a few bunks away. "How 'bout we throw in the towel now and just spend the rest of the month at a nice spa?"

She shot me a tight smile and resumed packing.

"Hag flag alert," I muttered to myself, double-checking to make sure I had not misplaced my own laminated warning sign. I wasn't sure about Joanna. We had met a few times when she, Beth, and I did some pre-Camino hiking. At the time, she had seemed friendly and open; now she seemed edgy and grumpy.

Cathy was already up, half packed, and studying her maps. We made eye contact, and she took it as her cue to start chattering.

"OK, so we have twenty-seven kilometers to do today," she began. "That's more than we did yesterday, but at least we don't have that climb. Assuming that we cover five kilometers an hour, that means we'll reach our destination, Larrasoaña—is that how you pronounce it? [she sounded it out slowly a few times]—in five or six hours. So [she looked at her watch and counted ahead five or six hours], um, one o'clock. Just in time for lunch! Hey, what do we do for breakfast? Do you think they'll have. . ."

I grabbed my towel and shuffled off to the washroom. I must really learn to be more patient and charitable, I scolded myself.

It was 6:20 AM when we set off from Roncesvalles. There was a light frost on the ground, and I congratulated myself for packing a pair of dollar-store gloves.

Daylight had broken by the time we stumbled into the tiny town of Burguete, three kilometers later.

The previous day's ordeal began to fade from the conversation. Hardly anyone mentioned the Pyrenees.

The first café we came upon was jammed with pilgrims shouting their orders. The owners—a husband and wife—were wild-eyed with panic, juggling clattering cups and saucers and trying to fill the orders of a clientele that spoke half a dozen languages simultaneously, all of them in an advanced state of caffeine deprivation.

You might assume pilgrims to be a genteel lot. You would be wrong. This scene was an eye-opener; pilgrims can be demanding and, at times, cantankerous, especially in the morning. Older pilgrims were the worst offenders. They thought nothing of shoving one another at the café counters to get their morning *café con leche* and croissant as if they were vying for a senior citizen discount.

Like good little Canadians, our pack waited its turn patiently, but when the Germans began elbowing us, it all became too much for Kate.

"Fuck this," she said through gritted teeth and bulldozed her way to the front of the queue, barking out, "*Seis café con leche, por favor!*"

I liked Kate. She was a nurse, like Beth, but their similarities ended there. Whereas Beth was small, gentle, and quiet, Kate was bigger, tougher, and not afraid to speak up. It was interesting to watch Beth and Kate; they were so opposite one another in personality, and yet they fit together as friends perfectly.

There are two signs pilgrims on the Camino de Santiago learn instantly: one is a bold yellow arrow; the other is a blue ceramic tile inset with a yellow stylized shell. These are the Camino blazes, and they are pervasive. If you don't see either the shell or the arrow periodically, you can rightly assume that you have lost your way.

Shells and yellow arrows have immense significance on the Camino. They are a pilgrim's compass, but they are also a silent cheering squad rooting you on, popping up just when you feel discouraged or lost.

The shell as an emblem of the Camino is said to have been started by St. James himself, who reputedly wore one around his neck as a sign that he was a fisher of men. Later, as the Santiago pilgrimage gained momentum, pilgrims would scour the beaches of Galicia for cockleshells to bring home as proof that they had completed the Camino. Even the Church saw virtue in the shell. *Veneranda dies,* the fire-and-brimstone sermon penned in the twelfth century by Pope Calixtus and trotted out each December 30—the day James's remains were miraculously transported from Jerusalem to Spain—exhorted the faithful to regard the fan-shaped shell's resemblance to the fingers of a hand as a reminder of their duty to serve and help others.

We had been walking for a few kilometers along a highway— the C-135—when, to our relief, the path veered into the sanctuary of the woods.

The major roads were scary. It wasn't so much the traffic— there was very little of it, actually—but when a car or truck did appear, it whipped past at such speed that the resulting gusts of wind almost knocked us off our feet. Not only were we contending with the world from a nonmotorized point of view, we were dealing with a culture that drove like maniacs.

Our worldview changed when we began experiencing the world with our feet pressing the ground instead of an accelerator pedal. We became part of the landscape, and our senses pricked to attention to register the details that one misses when traveling by car.

We entered a dense forest that was struggling to dry out after a long, wet winter. In single file, we walked and talked until the effort to do both became a chore.

Somehow I became separated from my group in the crushing throng of pilgrims as we negotiated a treacherously muddy section of the trail, where thick, slippery globs of the stuff tested our ability to stay upright.

This is when walking sticks come in handy. It is foolish to think you can do a hike like this without one. About half of our group had brought sticks with them or had hastily purchased one in Saint-Jean-Pied-de-Port. Georgina had a beautiful stick. Her husband had whittled it, and it was as smooth and as hard as marble. At the top of the stick, where Georgina's hand would grasp it, her husband had carved a small hole and stuffed it with a lock of his hair and one from each of their two children, as well as strands of hair from the family pets. He presented it to Georgina before she left for Spain with a note attached: *We are all walking with you.*

Not everyone on the Camino used a walking stick. People argued the merits of walking sticks as passionately as if they were debating the death penalty. It was an issue that created two classes of pilgrims: those with and those without walking sticks. If you were a walking-stick person and you had a question, you were more apt to pose it to a person who also carried a walking stick than to one who did not. Or if you were in a group, you would gravitate to those people who held walking sticks and then discuss shape, sturdiness, brand, or the merits of aluminum versus wood. Walking sticks were ice-breakers, walking aids, and buddies. An academic study on this weighty issue is surely pending at some leading university.

My walking stick had been carved from a thick, knotty piece of Pelee Island grapevine. The moment I laid eyes on it in a craft shop, I recognized it as my walking companion. It looked wise and strong. It was certainly proving its worth! The previous day, it had done yeoman's work as a leaning post during my frequent gasping breaks up the Pyrenees; this day it was an anchor preventing me from sliding downhill while doing the splits.

My trusty stick and I were, however, losing the Battle of the Muddy Forest. I planted my right leg firmly into a relatively dry spot and tried to bring my left leg up to meet it, but without a dry patch to plant itself in, my leg slipped farther downhill. I hung on to my walking stick with one hand and flailed about with my free hand for something to latch onto that might steady me or hoist me to drier terrain. I grabbed hold of what looked like a small branch. Only when my hand was firmly clamped around it did I realize it was barbed wire.

I let out a feeble yelp as the barbs sunk into my palm. When I pulled my hand away reflexively, a barb caught under one of my fingernails and tore it off.

There was no time to react. A crowd of zombielike pilgrims was at my heels forcing me onward. I searched the crowd for a familiar face to at least offer a nod of sympathy. No one. I fished a sheet of Kleenex from my pocket and wrapped it tightly around the gush of blood coming from my nail bed.

Christ, what was I doing here? What sort of stupid gift to myself was this pilgrimage? Most sane women would have celebrated their birthday doing something that was actually fun. I had chosen an activity in which I would be cold, smelly, dirty, and sore, and now a candidate for a tetanus shot.

Then again, how was this journey any different from the way I had always treated myself throughout my life? I often sweated out some awful chore at home to feed my rigid and relentless Type A (A for asinine) personality, dangling the prospect of relaxation like a carrot until the dreaded chore was completed. I was a scolding, tyrannical parent to my inner child.

Tears squirted from my eyes. I suddenly missed my children—their hugs and their screaming matches—and I missed my home, missed scrubbing toilets, driving the kids to band practice, dragging the trash to the curb every Sunday night for the Monday morning pickup.

I looked down at my shoes and my trousers, which were caked in mud; I was using the sleeve of my fleece jacket to wipe my sniffles—my sleeve! For God's sake, wasn't this the time of my life when I should be lounging elegantly on a *chaise longue*, sipping a tall, cool gin and tonic while my marabou-trimmed mules dangled seductively from pedicured toes? No sane fifty-year-old woman hits a filthy trail. Oh sure, there were people older than me on this trek—I was walking behind a string of them—but they were European; they were accustomed to deprivation.

A robust, straight-backed, dark-haired Spaniard strode past me with a small group of friends, nodded curtly at me, and smiled.

"*Buen camino!*" he said in a proud, deep voice.

I returned as bright a smile as I could muster as the blood continued to seep from my finger. "*Gracias. Buen camino.*"

Buen fucking *camino,* indeed.

I gave my walking stick a quick squeeze for moral support. It was the only friend I had. Everyone around me seemed to be paired up. I felt ashamed of my singleness and tried to figure out why I always find myself alone at those times when I most need people. What I wouldn't have given at that moment for someone to slip a hand into mine or put an arm around my shoulder to tell me everything would be OK.

Not wanting to fall deeper into a mire of self-pity, I tried to banish the hurt feelings—at least for now—and concentrate on happy thoughts. Come on, I told myself, things aren't as bad as they seem.

But as I looked around I saw that, yes, things were as bad as they seemed. I was in a single file of smelly strangers who didn't speak English. I had a fingernail that had just been ripped from its nail bed by a sharp rusty object; the muscle spasms, a telltale symptom of tetanus, would surely erupt at any moment. The psychic's words came rushing back: "*You might find this experience is a bit more rustic than you want."* "Rustic" was an understatement. I was hating this, hating it more than summer camp. What was really gnawing at me, however, was the realization that somewhere along the road of my life I had become a woman who was too proud to ask for help.

Finally, I boldly stepped off the path, threw down my pack, and collapsed on the ground. I grabbed an apple from a small compartment in my pack and munched on it defiantly. Pilgrims streamed past, some throwing me indifferent looks, others looking startled at the sight of a pilgrim with the audacity to take a break.

"Go to hell," I wanted to scream. Their stupid sheeplike pilgrimage was probably a big Vatican-engineered hoax anyway. Dangle the prospect of eternal salvation in front of people, and there's bound to be a mob ready to bite. Everyone was walking—no, scurrying—toward a city that housed the bones of some dead saint. I mean, really. This was 2004, not 1004. Had we not evolved? Who says those bones lying in Santiago cathedral are really those of St. James? Has anyone done DNA testing on them? Wasn't the human race a little too old for religious fairy tales? The Camino suddenly seemed like a massive joke.

I tossed the apple core, hoisted the pack onto my back, tightened the Kleenex around my finger—how a single tissue was capable of absorbing so much blood without disintegrating into a soggy, useless wad was a mystery—and rejoined the human caravan to ponder the question of faith.

Faith—now there's a thorny subject. In a world that invests so heavily in empirical data and instant replays, faith is like trying to clutch a cloud. How has something as intangible and irrational as faith managed to embed itself so firmly in my psyche that it has become tangible and utterly rational? More to the point, what is it about a belief system that made me leave my comfortable home to slog it out for eight hundred kilometers on a muddy trail?

As secular as the Camino is, it was its spiritual aspect that hooked me the moment the airline steward mentioned it. I wasn't looking for a religious indulgence or a miracle from St. James, and I didn't have any egregious sins to repent, but I was nonetheless drawn to the notion of a Christian pilgrimage because of the sense of community it implied and by the sense of rebellion it stirred within me. I had no idea how or even if I was supposed to demonstrate my faith; all I knew was that the Camino offered a safe haven for people like me—people who periodically question and doubt their faith but who stick with it anyway, people who want to express the spiritual side of themselves without being harassed or viewed as some quaint oddity of the modern age, people who pray and believe in God but who occasionally use profanity and listen to heavy metal.

As a Christian, I have spent as much time apologizing for my faith as I have nurturing it, as much time struggling to understand faith as I have bitng back the urge to slap someone for a condescending remark.

Why are Christians made to feel like freaks? Is it because Christianity is seen as a white person's faith? During a workplace discussion about how to improve inclusiveness in our organization, one person piped up that she felt the Remembrance Day service needed to be reworked because, in her words, "it just seems so... Christian." She practically spat out the word. Interestingly, the room was filled with such a pasty bunch of people that it would have made a slice of white bread look positively multicultural, and yet no one—and to my shame I must include myself—had the guts to object to the woman's remark.

As I continued my lonely trek, I considered how liberating it might be to not have to drag around a belief system all day. It was a short-lived thought; to do such a thing would leave a huge void in my life. I remain part of a group that is afraid to speak up when their faith gets pummeled and who pretend to tolerate a steady tide of low-grade persecution.

I bent down to pick up a palm-sized stone.

On the Camino, stones have immense significance and power. It is said that if you hold one in your hand, it will absorb all the sorrow and grief you want to load into it. Stones can take it; that's why they are so hard. When you have finished depositing sorrow into your stone, you place it back on the path, effectively leaving your or someone's else's sorrow on the Camino. It's another reason the Camino is known as the Trail of Pain.

I gripped the stone tightly. The first person who came to mind was my former father-in-law. Less than a month earlier, he had appeared robust and happy at a family party marking his wedding anniversary. A week later, he was admitted to hospital, where he was diagnosed with cancer.

With the stone in my hand I began praying that the disease that had invaded his body would be transferred to the stone.

After a few minutes of focusing my thoughts, I set down the stone on a dirt lodge beside the trail. As the stone tumbled from my hand, a sudden burst of white light flashed around it and with a *whoosh!* disappeared into the stone.

"What the..." I looked around to see if anyone else had seen the apparition, or for someone with whom to share or at least verify the extraordinary event, but the parade of pilgrims shuffled past, their heads bowed, preoccupied with their own thoughts and sorrows.

I looked back at the stone, but eventuallly I, too, moved on.

Rays of sunshine poked through the canopy of spring growth on the trees and cast a dappled pattern on the ground. The path had become drier, but my finger still bled, the same tissue of Kleenex wrapped around it.

The crowd of pilgrims had suddenly thinned, and there were only about three of them now in my range of vision. I spotted a fellow up ahead, someone I recognized from the *refugio* the night before. German fellow. Tall, handsome young man with his hair tied in a neat ponytail and small round wire-rimmed glasses that gave him a scholarly look.

I sped up, eager to have someone, anyone, to talk to, but just as I did the trail suddenly narrowed into a rocky passage and the footing became difficult.

I kept craning my neck to keep the pilgrim in sight. When I finally caught up to him, he was consulting his map.

"Hi," I said brightly, a little out of breath. "Are you lost?"

He gave me a startled look.

"No," he replied flatly, and returned to his map with Teutonic resolve.

Germans. Would it kill them to smile?

I made another attempt to break the ice, but he clearly did not appreciate my intrusion. I moved on.

The trail left the woods and emptied onto a road. Naturally, the yellow arrow pointed up the hill. I let out a groan and shook my head. Another goddamn climb.

Such fantasies sustain you on the Camino.

Half an hour later, I dragged my sore bones into the tiny village of Larrasoaña, utterly spent. My face was streaked with mud, my finger was wildly throbbing, my hair was damp with sweat, and every exposed inch of skin was caked in grime.

The first person I saw was Colleen, gaily hanging her laundry and, I believe, humming.

"When did you get here?" I asked incredulously, panting out the words.

"Oh, three of us got a taxi," she said in the singsong voice of the domestically contented. "That mud was horrible, and our knees were hurting. I wasn't going to go through that."

She told me that Serena's feet were in bad condition and that Trish and Susie had taken a cab ahead to Pamplona because both were having hip problems. My little tribe was breaking down, and this was only Day 2!

I walked around to the forecourt of the *refugio* to look for someone who would stamp my pilgrim passport and give me a room. The mayor, a short, stout, and brusque fellow, was the keeper of both the stamp and the *refugio*. He wielded this morsel of power for all it was worth in his little Munchkinland.

I presented my passport, and his chubby hands grabbed it. He told me to come back after 5 PM.

I pressed my case for a room.

"*Uno?*"

"*Sí,*" I replied.

"*No uno,*" he responded wagging his finger at me and walking away. With my passport.

"*Que?*"

A torrent of Spanish was the response, which I vaguely interpreted as "You cannot have a room because you are one person; you need to have people to share the room with."

"*Hay quince de nos,*" I said. There are fifteen of us.

"*Quince?*" He pondered this for a moment, putting his forefinger against the side of his nose, as if this would facilitate his thinking.

"*Tres!*" he bellowed abruptly, holding up three fingers.

I followed him, asking for the stamp to my passport, but he waved me away, refusing to stamp it or return it to me.

Outside the *refugio*, I found Joanna and Serena, who had just limped into the courtyard. Serena was in an advanced state of pain. I briefed them on the situation.

"C'mon," I said. "There's a room with three mattresses in it— let's get that one."

We found the mayor, and through a mix of sign language and dodgy Spanish, I presented proof that I had companions with whom to share the room.

His Roly-Polyness led us up a flight of stairs and down a narrow hall. He stopped in front of a room, unlocked the door, and with a dramatic flourish opened it as if he were showing us the royal suite. Three mattresses were stacked in the corner of a room that measured about ten feet square. It was perfect. We thanked him profusely and then shut the door.

Serena collapsed, and we helped her out of her hiking boots and socks. To cheer her up, I began to recount the tale of my torn fingernail. Neither she nor Joanna paid the slightest attention, and I immediately regretted thinking it would be a jolly diversion as soon as I saw Serena's feet: red, blistered, a few of her toenails dangling from their nail beds by strands of skin.

I took off to find Kate and caught her on her way to the café for something to eat. As a nurse, she surely would know what to do. She arrived at our room with a pail of warm water and ordered Serena to soak her feet in it. There are times you are grateful for the bossy practicality of a nurse.

After showering, and feeling marginally human again (my finger had stopped bleeding, but it was whimpering beneath a fresh bandage), I returned to the forecourt of the *refugio* to await the arrival of our remaining members, steeling myself for their tales of mud-drenched misery.

To my utter surprise, they were at the other end of the emotional spectrum, doubled over in hysterics, laughing and babbling about what a great day they had had.

Theresa, who was part of that group, saw me and grabbed my arm.

"This is the best, the absolute best trip I've ever been on," she said through tears of laughter. "Thank you for putting this together."

Stories began to spill out about the various people—pilgrims and nonpilgrims—they had encountered that day and the sights they had seen. They whipped out their digital cameras to show me the evidence, prompting another round of laughter as they relived the shared memory.

Were we on the same trail? I couldn't recall a single happy encounter that day. In fact, I would have pegged it as one of the more miserable in my experience.

I laughed along with their stories, but inwardly I wondered what the hell was wrong with me. How come I missed the fun?

A quick psychological self-assessment followed. Such exercises always clarify for me what a social misfit I am.

For starters, I walk too fast. I have long legs and a stride to match. Everyone—my children, friends, and lovers—complains about how fast I walk.

Second, I become so relentlessly focused on a goal that I often lose my flexibility. It must be a symptom of obsessive-compulsive disorder. For example, I'll embark on a project in my garden and keep working to the point of exhaustion, even when common sense is telling me to take a break before I collapse from heat stroke. The goal gets accomplished but at a personal cost.

Third, this goal-oriented attitude was eroding my humanity. I like to think of myself as a generally helpful sort, the type who will stop to help if your groceries tumble out of your shopping bag or who can be counted on to hold the door open for others, but an episode on the trail earlier in the day made me question whether I had been deluding myself all these years.

Shortly after the fingernail debacle, I found myself in the company of a Dutch man. During our conversation, he told me he was recovering from heart surgery. I asked whether a strenuous eight-hundred-kilometer hike through largely uninhabited terrain was the sort of thing anyone should attempt so soon after major surgery.

"Well, if I die, so what? I die," he replied with an air of *c'est la vie.*

We continued to chat until we hit a muddy patch on the trail. Someone had thoughtfully placed wooden planks over the muddiest portions, but under the weight of so much pilgrim traffic the planks had become partially submerged in the mud, making the passage tricky.

When the Dutch pilgrim and I reached this makeshift boardwalk, we fell into single file. I reached the other side of the boardwalk first and continued walking, figuring that he was just behind me. But when I looked back, I saw him struggling. He had lost his footing, and one foot was on the boardwalk while the other was ankle-deep in muck, his boot almost totally submerged. The more he tried to pull his foot free, the deeper the boot seemed to sink. He managed to wriggle his foot from the boot, but his next hurdle was to retrieve the boot from the mud while keeping his stockinged foot aloft.

Impatient pilgrims came to a standstill behind me when I called out to the Dutchman and asked if he needed a hand. He clearly did, but he replied, "No." I kept on going and never saw him again.

During our conversation, the Dutchman and I had remarked that pilgrims on the Camino were not nearly as forgiving or caring as we had expected them to be. Everyone was out for him- or herself and motored on with little regard for anyone else. If either of us had needed support for this observation, I had just provided it.

Later that night I reflected on the episode and was utterly ashamed of myself. Sometimes when a person says "No" it really means "Yes, please." It would have taken little time to go back and spend five minutes helping this fellow—a recovering heart-surgery patient, for God's sake—but it was easier and less complicated for me to take his "No" response at face value than to treat it as the cry for help that it was. The incident of the Pilgrim in the Mud haunts me to this day.

"ARE YOU WAITING for your pilgrim's stamp?" I asked three young men who were waiting on a long wooden bench in the mayor's spacious office-cum–reception room.

"Our passports are somewhere in that pile," one of them replied wearily, nodding toward an eight-inch stack of pilgrim passports on the mayor's large oak desk.

"He's holding court," the young man's friend smirked, leaning back and crossing his arms across his chest as if settling in for a long wait. And it would be. The mayor, decked out in his chain of office, was working the room.

"But when do we get our passports back?" I asked anxiously.

"Whenever he's ready to give them to us," one of them replied with a shrug. "I guess we just have to wait."

But I don't like to wait, I pouted to myself. I'm tired and sore, and I need a pillow to cry into.

"Where are you from?" one of the boys asked.

"Canada," I replied. "You?"

"The States. Philly," he said.

I gave him a vacant smile. There was plenty of anti-American sentiment on the Camino. The war in Iraq and the ramifications of American aggression angered many people, especially the Europeans, who were closer to the battlefront. Barely two months earlier, bombs had torn through a Madrid train station filled with commuters on their way to work. One hundred and ninety-one people had died; 1,500 were injured. Not surprisingly, the chatter along the Camino often drifted toward politics, and the conversation became more heated and the hand gestures more demonstrative whenever *Americanos* were mentioned.

I decided not to raise the topic of politics. They seemed like nice kids—probably in their early twenties—and anyway, I was too focused on my own inner battles to give a damn about world affairs.

I gazed at the clutter of bric-a-brac, photos, and trophies decorating the mayor's bookshelves. There were lots of photos of him with famous pilgrims, among them the actors Anthony Quinn and Shirley MacLaine. How much sucking up had they had to do to get their passports stamped?

Just then, Theresa appeared in the doorway looking trim and scrubbed, her spiky cap of gray hair fashionably gelled. Behind her wire-framed glasses, she wore a mischievous where's-the-party look and began scanning the room for prey.

I wandered over and apprised her of the situation. Her lips sprung into a sly smile. Without a word she snaked her way toward the mayor, and less than a minute later she was laughing and flirting in Spanish with him; he lapped it up. She acted inordinately impressed with what he was saying, putting a hand to her chest and gasping in awe as he regaled her with anecdotes about each of the awards prominently displayed around the room and boasted of his accomplishments. She displayed wholehearted interest in everything he said, staring intently at him the entire time. She did not take her eyes off him for a second, nor did she let the conversation falter.

Suddenly, the mayor began fingering the thick pile of pilgrim passports. He found the one belonging to Theresa, worked his stamp purposefully on the ink pad, and then pounded it on her passport with an official thud. He picked up his thick pen and dated and signed the stamp with an elaborate flourish of curlicues beneath his signature.

Aha, so that was how it worked. I quickly moved in, but Theresa was way ahead of the game. She had deftly rifled through all the passports and had pulled out those that belonged to our group, cooing constantly in the mayor's ear as she did so. He stamped every one of them.

"Jane!" she shouted as I approached his massive desk. "Come here and have your picture taken with the mayor of Larrasoaña! Isn't he just a cutie?" She drew out the word "cutie" and giggled, wrapping an arm around him. The rest of our group instantly swarmed like groupies to a rock star.

Theresa ordered a grumpy pilgrim in the crowd to snap a group photo, but just before the camera flashed Theresa called a dramatic halt to the proceedings. She straightened the mayor's tie and affixed a small Canadian flag to his lapel. She cooed some more. He blushed some more. She had rendered him utterly speechless. It was a masterful performance.

I looked over at the Three American Boys, sitting in slack-jawed awe at how a bunch of middle-aged Canadian cougars had quietly and quickly seduced their way to the front of the queue. The other pilgrims in the room were similarly agog but in an angry sort of way; Europeans can't stand queue jumpers unless they're the ones doing it.

The camera's flash detonated. Theresa smiled and giggled and hugged the now-bewildered mayor. Then she turned to us, her expression flattening, and murmured, "OK, let's get the fuck out of here. I need a drink."

We squeezed through the crowded room toward the exit as the United Nations of Pilgrims muttered epitaphs against us "Americans."

"Canadians," I corrected them cheerfully as I passed.
Another proud Heritage Minute in the making.

WE REGROUPED in the restaurant's courtyard, where the camaraderie among the pilgrims who had trodden the path between
Roncesvalles and Larrasoaña was in full swing. It was becoming
apparent that the days were for walking, for contemplation, and
for pain; the evenings were for drinking and socializing.

The women in my group were all master minglers, some of
them moving from table to table and sharing jokes with virtual
strangers. Lucy was sitting with two Spanish men and laughing
hard. Auburn-haired Trish, schoolteacher Joanna, and Greta, an
aesthetician—women I hadn't spent any real time with and who
didn't look like they were dying to walk with me, either—were at
another table with a handful of pilgrims they had met that afternoon. How do these people meet others so quickly? Every one
of them was engaged in animated conversation with people they
had met no more than a few hours earlier. I stood self-consciously
at the entrance of the courtyard wondering what group to wade
into or whether I should go back to the *refugio* and console Serena and her nail-less toes.

"Hey, Jane!"

Chatty Cathy waved me over. I walked toward her and smiled
awkwardly at her tablemates.

"This is the *awesome* person who brought us all together for
this pilgrimage!" Cathy squealed to her audience, grabbing me
and putting an arm through mine.

Cathy was a petite woman with long blonde hair and big
boobs, which explained the presence of so many men, most of
them half her age, at her table. None of them cared a whit that
I had organized anything. They were under Cathy's spell. Even
the women were mesmerized. She regaled them with her stories;
trying to get a word in was like merging into gridlocked traffic.

"Come *here*, you!" she said, urging me closer. "How was your
walk today? Wasn't it gorgeous? Weren't those woods *amazing?*

Want some wine? Grab a chair! This is soooo *awesome!* The *day* was awesome."

She gave my arm a little squeeze and giggled some more: "Thank you *soooo much* for letting me join your group! Oh, let me introduce you to everyone. This is Franz and Hans—Franz and Hans, isn't that *cute?*—and Daniel and Mikael." (Mikael was the ponytailed German I had tried to talk to in the woods. I gave him a Teutonic nod.) "Oh, you have to meet Genevieve and her husband, Roland. They're from Switzerland. Isn't that *awesome?* Wasn't the walk today *incredible?* Everything was so *beautiful!* Didn't you think so?"

OK, so she was on crack. I smiled and took a snort myself. "Yeah, it was great! We're lucky to have this terrific weather! That mud was a little challenging, but hey. . ."

I covered my bandaged finger self-consciously, and tried not to wince at the memory.

"Oh, have you got a boo-boo?" Cathy asked, as her smile dissolved into an expression of concern.

"Just a little cut," I lied.

I wasn't going to tell her that my fingernail had been ripped off and that gangrene was likely seeping through my system at that very moment, or that I had had enough and was going to quit the Camino at the first opportunity. No, I sat there with a glass of wine in my hand and a dumb smile plastered on my face.

Lucy was seated close by with a couple of men who looked like construction workers but who were actually doctors.

I hadn't seen Lucy since our lunch on the Pyrenees.

"How's your hip?" I asked.

"God, those Pyrenees," she said as we shifted our chairs closer to one another. "That had to be one of the worst days of my life. It was definitely the hardest. My hip was killing me, so I walked with Sally because I figured she was slower, which she isn't. Man, she can motor on those crutches, eh? Anyway, I figured I was being selfish complaining about my hip when she has to struggle the rest of her life with only one damn leg. I remember when she finally got to the edge of the mountain and that gale started whipping up. Did you go through that, or were you farther ahead?"

I assured her I was in the gale—with Cathy. I smiled at Cathy, who had joined our conversation.

"Well," Lucy continued. "Just as we began our descent, which was real hell on my hips, it started *snowing!* Snowing! Did you guys see snow?"

We nodded and leaned in closer.

"Little white flakes in this hurricane wind! The force of that wind ripped the poncho right off my backpack. I was just about to start bitching about the weather when Sally stopped and pointed out a beautiful hawk riding an air current. She stood there watching it—*in the fucking storm!* At that moment I realized I had a lot to learn about noticing beauty in life instead of focusing on all my woes. I sure hope I can stay as positive as her for the whole Camino."

"And then Roncesvalles," Lucy continued. "What a friggin' hole. As soon as I got some privacy I wrote in my journal: 'Only thirty-one more days left of this goddamn trip.'"

The sun began to dip, glasses were drained, and conversations dried up. People walked or limped back to the *refugio* and to the comfort of their sleeping bags. Come morning, we were all at it again.

6

WALKING releases two things: endorphins and conversation. It is exercise and therapy rolled into one. Words, thoughts, and ideas bubble up from the depth of your soul. There's something about walking and talking side by side that makes conversations more candid than they would be face-to-face. What you have to say isn't influenced by your walking partner's facial reaction.

Beth and Kate were the women with whom I walked the most, mainly because we walked at the same pace. Beth and Kate knew each other from work; both taught nursing at the same university. By coincidence, I was working for a health care organization at that time, so the health care profession was the topic of our conversations that morning.

"So, what is it that you actually do?" Kate asked me.

It was a good question. I had been in my job for two years, and I still couldn't articulate what it involved or describe the *raison d'être* of the organization for which I worked. Whenever someone asked me that question, I would stammer in confusion. This is not a good sign when your title is manager of communications.

Although health care is a vitally important profession the field is crammed with bureaucracy, rules, policies, and procedures. I felt choked. Furthermore, I had the sense I was in the job to fill a position but not to actually do anything.

"Yup, sounds like a government job," Kate nodded.

"I always thought government jobs were godsends because you don't have to work hard," I said. "Good pay, good benefits, good vacation. But there isn't a drop of creativity in that job. Besides, something feels wrong. In nearly thirty years of working, it is the worst job I've ever had."

"Why do you hate it, aside from its not being creatively stimulating?" Kate asked.

"Yes, what is it about the job that really bothers you?" prodded Beth. "It sounds like your problem goes beyond the job itself."

Geez, could we not switch the conversation to something more innocuous, like the thread counts of duvets?

"Is it your boss?" asked Beth gently.

"You got a boss from Hell?" asked Kate.

"Referring to her as the boss from Hell is an insult to people who inhabit Hell," I replied. "But it goes further than a mere person. The place is completely void of compassion. The organization is supposed to care for the frail elderly, and yet I overheard one of the executives refer to them as 'greedy and whiny.' It sent a shudder right through me. That's when I knew I was in the wrong place. The whole health care system smacks of geriatric cleansing, not universal care. I tell you, I'd rather take cyanide than end up in a long-term care facility."

I stopped to catch my breath; hiking and ranting are incompatible activities.

It was the first time I had been able to let loose about my job, to vent with abandon. It was obvious why I had trouble explaining my job to other people; it went against every grain of my being. I moved "new job" to the top of my mental to-do list.

"Maybe I should quit my job and open a café on the Camino," I mused aloud.

The mention of coffee turned our attention to finding some. In just three days, we had become hopelessly addicted to *cafés con leche*, and some of us weren't even coffee drinkers. It had been a good two hours since our last fix.

Our route that day loosely followed the Río Arga through forests, along the highway, and into town. As we approached Villava, the pastoral trail gave way to the Calle Mayor—the Spanish version of Main Street. We ducked into the Paradiso Café, and Beth, who had been complaining of a sharp pain in her lower back, headed straight for the washroom. When she returned, she reluctantly announced that she would have to take a cab to the next *refugio*, which was just outside Pamplona.

It was a distressing moment for Beth. She was a purist when it came to hiking, and for her there had been no question in her mind that she would walk every step of the Camino. The prospect of having to take a cab had never crossed her mind in the planning stages, and now it felt like a betrayal of her personal code. But you can't hike when your body has other plans. Kate and I reminded her as we tucked her into the taxi that there was still a lot of distance to cover on the Camino.

We waved good-bye to Beth, and then Kate and I picked up the trail as it wended its way through a suburban residential district. It felt odd to rely on yellow arrows rather than street signs as guides, especially in suburbia, but such is the off-the-grid world of the pilgrim. We seemed to be off the grid in terms of our treatment by society, too. The nuns and priests we frequently passed shot us dismissive looks and never acknowledged our smiles or our greetings of "*Buenos días.*"

"You'd think they'd smile at us," Kate remarked. "After all, the Camino is a Catholic construct."

Our talk shifted to families and relationships.

I had observed Kate and her husband at the airport smiling into each other's faces as we prepared to board the flight to Spain. Occasionally, one would stroke the other's face or arm, or they would weave their fingers together.

This was a relationship involving a number of adjustments, as Kate began to tell me.

"Many years earlier, I worked as a nurse in Saudi Arabia," she said. I got involved with a Saudi and got pregnant. The man would have been ostracized by his family had it been discovered he had fathered a child with a white Western woman, so he gingerly stepped away from the relationship, thank God."

The situation was just as dicey, perhaps more so, for Kate. For her to remain in Saudi Arabia as a white woman preparing to have a baby out of wedlock would have relegated her to the dangerous fringes of Saudi society. She devised a plan. "Whenever I talked with co-workers, I began to casually tell them that my dad was ill, and I felt terrible about being so far away from my family. I kept this up for a while and told them that my dad's health was worsening and that I really wanted to return to Canada. Tapping the phone lines of foreigners was common practice, so whenever I called home I had to maintain the ruse with my parents. They didn't know what was going on, but they caught on that something was wrong and so they played along."

"It must have been a very tense time," I said.

"It was awful," she admitted. "Had I been caught that would have been it for me."

Kate made it back to Canada safely, and the baby was born several months later. The father never tried to contact her.

A few years later, Kate met the man who would become her husband, and he adopted Kate's daughter.

"A happy ending then," I said.

"Yes," she beamed.

"You and your husband look so devoted to one another," I said. "I noticed you both at the airport."

"We've had our share of problems; don't think it's been easy," she said. "There were times when it seemed as if the relationship would unravel, but one thing I can say is that we are both committed to keeping it going. There's never been any question about that aspect of it."

We spoke about marriage—its complexity, its many forms, the altered state you enter when you form a pact with someone, and the struggle to stay true to yourself in a partnership that melds identity and individualism.

"So, what happened to you?" Kate asked bluntly.

My nose tingled; it does that when a nerve gets hit. It's difficult to bravely and blithely explain two marriages and two divorces without sounding like a misguided idiot or a repeat offender, or like I had it coming.

I took a deep breath.

"After my second marriage fell apart, I thought I would never recover, that the scar of abandonment would never heal. I drank, I smoked, and I took antidepressants. Then one day I woke up and realized the joy that my children brought to my life. They were the only reason I didn't resort to suicide. Single parenting is hard, but I found I could handle it. Quite well, in fact.

"I was thoroughly content, and then one day Love came along and messed up my tidy, happy life. I didn't want to get involved, but the guy was persistent. His flattery swept me away. A month later he proposed and I accepted, and then he dodged the subject saying that 'the timing isn't right' and gradually becoming emotionally abusive. Things didn't feel right but I couldn't let go: you get to a certain age when you are so certain that relationships will work because you're more mature, you've learned from the past, all that stuff, so you keep hanging on. When it splits apart it hurts like hell. It hurts more the older I get."

"Yeah, Beth told me you were having a rough time getting over it," said Kate. "How come it ended?"

"He got a job in another part of the country and told me that his future didn't include me," I replied, biting my lip at the memory of it. "I guess I shouldn't have been surprised. There were so many warnings signs: He cheated on me; he called my accomplishments 'bogus'; he didn't think I was outdoorsy enough. One day I fell while we were rollerblading, and he just stood there looking down at me with a smirk on his face. Didn't offer to help me up. What kind of a guy does that? He was such a cad."

Kate stopped walking.

"He called you 'bogus'?"

"Yes," I answered sheepishly.

"And you didn't smack him?"

"No." I pretend to be a tough broad, but like many women I have been known to sacrifice my self-esteem on the altar of a relationship.

"Look at you!" said Kate, barely containing her anger. "You organized this whole thing. You took a chance on a bunch of strangers. We've walked seventy kilometers already, up a bloody mountain, through acres of mud. Is that outdoorsy enough for him? You know what? Fuck him! Fuck the Cad! You don't need an idiot like that."

She turned on her heel and stormed off fuming, "Fuck the Cad!" as if it were a mantra.

If I had calmed her down, that would have been the end of the verbal lashing the Cad was receiving from Kate, but frankly it was giving me too much satisfaction. Not exactly befitting of a pilgrim, but there you go.

"Maybe the relationship was meant to end," I said stoically, when I finally caught up to her. "If it hadn't, I might not have taken the risk to do the Camino. And here's another bright side: I was so upset after he dumped me that I lost fifteen pounds in two weeks! You gotta love a weight-loss program like that!"

Any attempt at humor would not appease her, so I did the only thing that had a chance of changing the subject: I pulled out a map.

The intensity of our conversation had taken us off course. We had forgotten about yellow arrows. We now stood on an island in the middle of a busy boulevard looking stunned, our maps flapping wildly as the cars whizzed past.

Whenever the Camino's trail brought us into an urban center, it always took us by surprise. We would stare dumbfounded at the

sudden velocity of life as if we were seeing it for the first time—
the ferocious speed of cars, the soaring monuments, the vast
boulevards that stretched like football fields between the lanes of
traffic. Sounds, sights—everything was amplified and magnified.
And yet hadn't we been living in a similar milieu less than a week
before?

The world looks different when you approach it on foot.
There is no set pace; you are controlled by your body's ability, not
by artificial forms of locomotion or by someone else's demands.
When you are on foot, an intuitive calm reassures you that everything is reachable if you simply take the time to walk to it.

We looked up and down the street, then back at our map. I
checked the guidebook.

"It says, 'When you get to a Renault dealer, turn right, cross
the road and make your way to the Magdalena district.'"

We surveyed the landscape for clues. A Mercedes dealer was
farther up the road.

"Maybe the Renault dealership was bought out by Mercedes,"
Kate suggested.

Kate barreled up to a woman, who shook her head, compre-
hending neither English nor apparently a map of the city. Kate
tried another person. No luck.

"What the hell's wrong with these people?" she yelled. "Don't
they know where they are?"

Fortunately, you can get away with saying things like that
within earshot of people you know do not speak your language.

An elderly man eventually helped us by gesturing directions,
shouting at us in Spanish to aid our comprehension, and repeating with emphasis, *"Portal de Francia."*

We found the yellow arrows and the Portal de Francia—the
old geezer had been right—and when we passed under it, we
found ourselves in another world.

This was Pamplona, a medieval metropolis whose sizable
Old Quarter was a hive of activity. All the towns we had walked
through thus far were gorgeous, tidy, ancient, and completely

empty of people. In Pamplona things were different. People were rushing off to meetings, children were skipping rope, grandmothers were pushing toddlers in strollers along ancient streets—the place was buzzing. Above our heads, on elaborately forged wrought-iron balconies, flowers had exploded from the confines of their pots into a profusion of color. We had never seen such a beautiful city.

"This is where they have the Running of the Bulls," Kate whispered, as if speaking a decibel louder might unleash a herd. "Right through these streets."

You may be familiar with the Running of the Bulls. It is a centuries-old festival in which six bulls are let loose in the streets every July 7. Each year newspapers acknowledge the event by publishing a photo showing some poor goof getting speared in the backside by a charging *toro*. It's a dumb idea, but the city is haplessly wedded to the tradition because it draws two million people each year and scads of euros. Yet Pamplona need only throw together half a dozen photos, market itself as a destination for romantics, and the world would beat a path to its doorstep for reasons other than bulls.

Pamplona's roots predate the sixth century, when it was established as an Episcopal see. Its attempts to assert itself were constantly thwarted during the early Middle Ages by various invaders, all of whom seemed bent on destroying the place.

It was not until the eleventh century, under Sancho III, that Pamplona was able to get down to the business of turning itself into a city. A keen promoter of the Santiago pilgrimage, Sancho was canny enough to see that a city through which a steady stream of pilgrims had to pass each year had gold mine potential.

In a move to increase the population of Pamplona, he created three districts—one for the existing population and one each for the foreign artists and merchants who were being lured to this economic boomtown. The plan upset the native population of Pamplona, and eventually all three districts built heavily fortified walls around themselves and spent their time fighting one another in a protracted and bloody civil war.

In the sixteenth century, the trio of districts finally agreed to peace, and they built another wall encircling all three districts. There was never a shortage of work in those days if you were a mason.

Kate and I gravitated to the shop windows to stare down handbags and shoes of buttery leather that were doing their best to tempt us.

"I wonder if I could get a pashmina into my backpack," mused Kate. "Do you think that's a good price—forty-five euros?"

We looked each other up and down. We were sweaty and smelly. We were bag ladies. It was unlikely a store clerk would even permit us on the premises.

We retired to a bench in the expansive Plaza del Castillo with our lunch—an ice cream cone. It was around noon, and the square was swarming with office workers on their lunch breaks and people heading home for *siesta*. Stone fountains, ornate office and government buildings, cafés, *pensiones*, and boutiques swirled around us. It was thoroughly romantic; it certainly seduced Kate and me. For the next minute or so we floated the idea of taking rooms at a *pensione* and spending the rest of the month living like locals in Pamplona.

The people around us were dressed exquisitely; all of them had clearly bathed that day. A woman in an elegantly tailored suit passed by us, her perfume wafting under our dirt-smeared noses. I suppressed the urge to yell, "I have stuff like that at home, too!" because no one would have believed me.

We became aware of an older woman watching us. I smiled at her in the hope that I might erase the impression that we were hookers or murderers. She edged her way closer to us.

"Do you speak English?" she asked tentatively.

"Yes!" we exclaimed, ecstatic that someone would deign to talk to us.

She was from Denmark and was in Pamplona on a bus tour, she explained.

"You're walking the Camino? You are pilgrims?" she asked.

We nodded.

"How wonderful! I walked the Camino last year, and when I arrived here I thought I'd love to come and spend more time here. It's so pretty!"

It constantly astounds me how similar we humans are. We told her we had been talking about the same thing moments earlier and had considered renting a room.

"Oh no, you must keep going," she said seriously. "You will understand why when you reach the end."

"At this point," said Kate, "we're not sure we can make it as far as the next *refugio*, let alone Santiago."

The woman smiled with great understanding. "It is hard. But you will make it. I know you will. Please give St. James a hug for me."

She waved and disappeared into the crowd with her tour-bus companions.

"The post office," I said suddenly to Kate. "I need to find a post office so I can get rid of some of my stuff."

The post office, known in Spain by the antiquated term Correos y Telégrafos, is a place you would assume at least one person might understand, say, five words of English. We were met with shaking heads.

I approached a stone-faced clerk on the other side of a cold marble counter and pulled out my Spanish-English dictionary. Under such circumstances I'm always reminded of the *Monty Python* sketch of the hapless Hungarian using an off-market English-Hungarian phrase book in which his request for a room translates into "May I fondle your breasts?" The poor man can't understand why the people he asks aren't more helpful.

I double-checked what I was about to say.

"Quiero mandar esto paquete?"

"*Que?*" the clerk barked back.

This gal wasn't going to cut me any slack on my pronunciation. I showed her the phrase book.

She sputtered off something in Spanish that amused her colleagues and shoved a form at me from across the counter. I began to fill it out, but she yelled and gestured, again to the amusement of her colleagues, and pointed sternly to a far-off counter. I suspect she was saying, "You are smelly and dirty; get out of my sight and fill out the form way over there."

We shuffled "over there" and pried our tails from between our legs.

I had not purchased any paper for wrapping my parcel—there was no place to buy any—but on a nearby counter rested a lone piece of kraft paper. We looked around warily to see if it had been planted there for our further humiliation. It was unclaimed, and we gave thanks.

From my backpack, I pulled out a bunch of clothing—a tank top, a skirt, the matching pajama top and bottom—and toiletries, stuffed them in a bag and wrapped the kraft paper around it.

I returned to the Stone-Faced Postal Worker and asked for a strip of tape, which she threw at us. I addressed the package to myself and handed it back to her. She weighed it, then demanded 35 euros, about $50. For surface mail. It was outrageous, but I was in no mood for further chastising. I handed over the money. She stamped the parcel, threw it into a bin, and turned her back on us. And that's the last I saw of my parcel.

Later that day a fellow pilgrim said I could have shipped the parcel for an eighth of the cost to General Delivery at the Santiago de Compostela post office. In hindsight, it would not only have been a cheaper option, it might have been a better one. As I write this, three years after posting the parcel in Pamplona, it has yet to find its way to my Canadian home.

The errand completed, Kate and I resumed our journey to the *refugio* in Cizur Menor, which, according to the map, lay just across a highway and the Rio Sadar from Pamplona.

We stumbled through the narrow streets getting more and more lost, consulting unhelpful maps, and trying to get by with about six words of Spanish between us. We knew how to order *cerveza* or *café con leche*, but beyond that we were helpless.

"On the bright side," Kate said, "we'll never lack for beer or lattes."

We spied a tall, clean-cut young man with a knapsack staring up at a building. Was he a tourist? A European who perhaps had a better grasp of Spanish than we did?

We quickened our pace.

"Do you speak English," I asked boldly.

"Yes!" he replied, a little startled.

"Are you a pilgrim?" quizzed Kate.

"I am!"

"Are you by chance heading to Cizur Menor?"

"Why yes! How did you know?" he asked.

We introduced ourselves as fellow pilgrims.

"Do you speak any Spanish? We're kind of lost," admitted Kate.

"I speak some Spanish."

Good enough.

His name was Thomas, he was from Switzerland, and he had just arrived in Pamplona by train. Many pilgrims use Pamplona as a starting point for the Camino. He was fresh-faced and possessed the enthusiastic naïveté of a newly minted pilgrim.

We smiled indulgently.

"What brings you to the Camino?" Kate asked as we started off together.

He let out a plaintive sigh.

"I've lost the passion for my work," he said sadly. "I'm a filmmaker, and I am tired of making the same Hollywood-style movies. They're boring. I want to do something different, but no one wants anything but the same old formula. So I've come to the Camino to think about what I should do next."

"Have you been working in films a long time?" I asked.

"About ten years," he answered. "I've become—how do you say it?—a stereotype."

"Do you mean 'typecast,' as in doing the sort of work people expect from you?" I asked.

"Yes, yes! That's it. Typecast. I feel time slipping away from me, that I've given my best years and now it's too late."

"You can't be that old," I said.

"I am already twenty-six!" he answered in the desperately dramatic way of the young.

Kate and I shot each other a glance that said, "Whoa, he's in for a big surprise when he hits forty."

We trudged on, getting Thomas acquainted with the yellow-arrow system and prodding him to ask strangers for directions when our orienteering skills failed us. We tried to stay upbeat and cheerful, but after a while we could no longer maintain our enthusiasm. Even the novelty of Thomas's conversation did not inject any pep into our steps.

We crossed the Avenida de Sancho el Fuerte and made the long trek across the Pamplona campus of the Universidad de Navarra, crossed the Rio Sadar, and climbed the hill to Cizur Menor.

"You'll get used to it," I assured Thomas when I noticed him struggling and sweating and panting. "We've only been walking two days, and twenty kilometers a day already seems like nothing."

I said this as convincingly as I could, even though sweat was dripping off my face and my mouth was so parched that I could barely speak.

Cizur Menor was a small, suburban enclave of Pamplona. The *refugio*, a white stucco bungalow, lay behind an iron gate. Its pretty courtyard had well-tended gardens and a large fountain in which some pilgrims were already soaking their feet. An amiable woman welcomed us with a big smile and urged us to sit down and relax.

Kate and I fell onto a bench beside Lucy and Georgina, who had just arrived. We were dying for a shower.

I recognized a few of the other pilgrims standing around— Mikael, the ponytailed German, one of the Three American Boys, and a guy we only knew as the Dane Who Wore Black. They were all tall, strapping, good-looking guys. I am, however, one of the few middle-age women on the planet who have absolutely no sexual interest in younger men. I have sons that age, and my undecorated but stalwart tour of duty with that generation is mercifully over.

I led Thomas to the young men and introduced him, figuring he could use a buddy.

I returned to the women, and we went off to claim our bunk beds.

The *refugio* was far more spacious and modern than the cramped quarters of the previous night, and the rooms were large with gleaming tiled floors and freshly painted walls. I threw my pack onto a lower bunk and headed for the showers.

Once again, the beds-to-bathroom ratio was out of whack: two shower stalls and two toilets for every twenty-four beds. When everyone used the facilities at the same time, the water pressure was compromised, as was the availability of hot water.

Still, we were beginning to get used to this sort of life. The languorous bathroom routines we enjoyed back home were now considerably scaled back. We could shower, wash our hair, dry off, brush our teeth, and dress in six minutes. We never wore makeup, not even lipstick. Most of the women had cropped their hair short for this trip. I had kept mine long, thinking it could be tamed into a ponytail, but it was refusing to do so. The humid air and the absence of Velcro rollers, a hair dryer, two brushes, and half a dozen hair products had caused my hair to explode into a cascade of plump, loose curls that made it look as if it were on holiday itself. Naturally, I am unable to reproduce this style at home; my hair only takes on a luxurious, devil-may-care look when I'm backpacking along muddy trails with total strangers in northern Spain.

We gathered that evening in a local bar to recount the day's war stories. Those who had taken cabs from Larrasoaña to

Pamplona's hospital to have their injuries looked at arrived, displaying bandaged feet and toes. Serena announced she had had a couple of toenails removed. Buckets of wine were ordered. Georgina and I threw back a glass each and refilled them.

We were all in high spirits—a little too high. A warm shower followed by copious amounts of red wine has a dangerous effect on body and spirit.

Chatty Cathy took a seat next to me. She seemed quieter this day.

"I talk a lot when I get nervous or upset," she suddenly confided.

"What?" I replied. "I hadn't noticed."

She began to tell me about her childhood, about growing up on the East Coast of Canada, about a brother who had died—suicide, I think—and her mother, who had died while Cathy was quite young.

My heart dropped. I wish I could lose that habit of judging people too quickly, before I knew anything about them.

I put my hand on her arm.

"Oh, I'm OK now," she said, trying to be upbeat, but I knew—we all know—that no one ever fully recovers from traumas of that magnitude.

As the wine flowed, so did the tears. Across the table the Dane Who Wore Black, whose name, we discovered, was Pieter, was locked in conversation with Theresa. Pieter was weeping, and Theresa was pleading with him, on the verge of tears herself, "You can't! You can't! You have to keep going!" she said to him.

"What's going on?" I asked, but Theresa waved me away and returned her attention to Pieter.

I looked at Georgina.

"Is it my imagination, or have people gotten really touchy?"

"Yeah, seems that way," she replied. "You can see little cliques forming. People who didn't know each other a week ago are now best friends. It's an odd phenomenon, eh? You travel from your small little town halfway across the world and encounter strangers who stir your empathy. Before you know it, you become inseparable from them."

She paused. "I'm tired. I want to go to bed."

We walked back to the *refugio*, where a few of the women were already preparing for bed.

"Did you see them?" Susie whispered conspiratorially when we walked into the room.

I had pegged Susie as a shit-disturber and a wildcard from the beginning, and so far my assessment had been bang-on. During our first dinner as a group in Saint-Jean-Pied-de-Port, she had given an introduction so confusing that when she finished no one was entirely certain just what she did for a living, though she mentioned that she sometimes took in kids as a day-care provider. You couldn't tell whether she was independently wealthy or financially strapped. She was divorced and had a few kids of her own—that much we deduced—but it wasn't clear how many she had or how old they were.

She was one of the latecomers to our group. I had tried to talk her out of coming on the Camino because she had never hiked, but she would not listen. She was, she told me, at a crossroads in her life. I tried to picture that intersection, and all I could come up with was Wacky Street and Freak Out Avenue.

Now she was weaving a web of intrigue about one of the women in our group.

"Did I see who?" I asked her.

"They were kissing."

"What?"

"Lucy and that so-called doctor she met."

"Kissing?"

"Someone needs to talk to her," Colleen the social worker said primly as she shook out a shirt and folded it in a precise, deliberate fashion.

"No one needs to talk to her," I said, slipping out of my clothes. "She's middle-aged and knows what she's doing. Maybe it wasn't even her you saw."

"Oh, it was her, all right," Colleen snorted.

"The beds are a little creaky, eh?" said Georgina, trying to change the subject as she tiptoed across the room to kill the lights.

They weren't a little creaky; they were a lot creaky. As everyone adjusted to a comfortable sleeping position, the room sounded like a train screeching to a halt.

The door opened, and in the darkness I saw the outline of a woman I had seen earlier on the trail. Tall, slender, with a model-like figure, she carried a small daypack no bigger than a purse diagonally across her chest. Her signature was a Fendi scarf that encircled her neck in that thrown-together elegance only European women can pull off. She moved quietly toward her bunk, removed some clothing, and hoisted herself into a top bunk, setting off another round of creaks.

I rolled onto my stomach—more creaks—and pulled my maps from under my pillow. I had begun sleeping with what I considered my most important possessions: passport, money pouch, pilgrim passport, maps, diary, and a pen with a built-in light. I pulled out one of the maps, flicked on the pen, and examined the next day's route: only nineteen kilometers, but terrain that indicated a steep climb. I was sick of climbing.

I stashed everything back under my pillow, rolled onto my back, and said a quick prayer along the lines of "God, what the hell have I got myself into?"

The room was quiet. People were lost in their thoughts about families back home, conversations shared during the day's walk, the reasons that prompted them to embark on a tough pilgrimage, the possibility that one of our members was smooching.

The church bell in Cizur Menor tolled 9 PM.

Eyes shut on cue.

7

"**Y**OU'D think they'd be grateful for the business, wouldn't you?" grumbled Joanna as we huddled in the early morning's gray light, alternately rubbing the sleep from our eyes and massaging sore body parts.

Everyone had a complaint: lost toenails, multiple blisters, shoulder strain, sore hips, shin splints. We were like seniors comparing aches and pains after church.

The bitching went beyond physical problems. Thomas the Swiss Filmmaker had only been on the Camino a day and was already annoyed with Spain's lack of twenty-four-hour hospitality. It was a complaint voiced by many Europeans on the Camino. Spain was on its own clock.

"Zee Spaniards, zay are lazy sheet bags," Thomas grumbled.

Lazy? In truth, it was refreshing to find a culture that did not feel obligated to be at the beck and call of everyone else. In North America you get the sense that the entire social order will collapse if someone cannot find coffee at all hours of the day and night. Hey, make it yourself for a change! Better still, go without. There's a concept.

I had been unsuccessful in eliciting any sympathy for my lost fingernail—it had continued to pulse with hot pain—so I tossed out a comment about the soreness in my left shoulder caused by the strain of my backpack. Suddenly, everyone was all over me.

"Really?"

"Your shoulder is sore? Where?"

"Show me."

Two nurses and a physiotherapist prodded my shoulder and then conferred with each other about whether the strain had been caused by the way I wore my backpack.

Cathy, the physiotherapist, announced to everyone within earshot that at the next *refugio* she was going to lead a clinic on how to put on a backpack correctly and how to adjust it to avoid back injury.

"In the meantime," counseled Kate, "you should get that guy to give you a massage."

"What guy?" I asked.

She pointed to a small group of pilgrims milling around the door of the café. Among them was a light-haired, well-built man in his mid- to late fifties wearing wire-rimmed glasses. He looked a bit like actor Richard Gere. I had recognized him among the cohort of pilgrims with whom we were keeping pace.

Kate's shoulders were also sore, and as she massaged one of them, the man she had pointed out was suddenly by her side warming up his magic hands. She slipped off her pack, and Dr. Dan the Massage Man pressed his hands into her neck and shoulders.

I was gob-smacked—not at Dr. Dan's technique or at Kate's shoulder but at how these women managed to meet all these people. As one of the few single women in the group, I was a little perturbed that the married ones were snagging all the guys.

Joanna interrupted Kate's massage session and pointed to me. "Jane's got a really bad shoulder, Daniel. Could you do her?"

Dr. Dan immediately moved from Kate to me.

"Please remove your knapsack," he instructed in a heavily accented voice. No introductions were made; I usually like to shake hands with a person before letting him or her near any part of my anatomy.

His hands touched my shoulders, and I immediately let out a gasp.

"Do I hurt you?" he asked tenderly.

"No, it's just sore," I lied. It had been more than a year since a man had touched my skin, and the shock of male fingers caressing my shoulders had awakened dormant sensations. I hoped he didn't notice the goose bumps that were detonating like land mines on my skin. As his fingers worked their way into my neck, I was tempted to ask him whether he could move his face just a little closer and nibble my ear.

"*Ooooo, c'est catastrophe,*" cooed Dr. Dan.

"I'm sorry?" I asked.

"Very tight moosles," he replied. "Not good. No, not good at all." His face was full of worry.

"You should not be carrying your pack. You send it ahead by taxi?"

This statement was delivered more as a command than a question. I shook my head. I did not want to use taxis—for myself or for my pack. The burden one carried along the Camino was a metaphor for one's emotional baggage, and part of the experience was to learn how to bear it. There was another, less spiritual reason: I didn't trust the system. If someone took my backpack or if it got lost along the way, I was sunk.

"If you walk today, you see me tonight for another session," ordered Dr. Dan. "*Tu comprends?*"

"*Oui, je comprends,*" I nodded obediently. "*Merci.*"

Merde. Were my shoulders that bad? I absolutely did not want to join the rest of the group on the "disabled" list.

Just then, the owner of the café came storming around the corner looking like he had just gotten out of bed. No eye contact, no *"Buenos días."* He roughly unlocked the café doors and went in without bothering to hold it open for his growing crowd of patrons.

"What an attitude," scowled Joanna as we shuffled into the café. "I mean look at this. There's got to be about twenty-five of us. If we all order a coffee and a croissant, that's about two or three euros a person—let's say three—which equals seventy-five euros. That's about one hundred and twenty-five dollars. Pretty good for fifteen minutes of business."

We left Cizur Menor for the Sierra del Perdón, which we had to access via a modern housing development of unspeakable blandness. The beige stucco and brown-trimmed buildings did not possess a shred of architectural elegance, in total contrast to the stylish Old World architecture of the small towns and villages along the Camino. Welcome to suburban Spain.

To the right of us, a building was in the throes of construction. A shopping mall? Apartments? Rock music blared from a radio as a crew hauled lumber and equipment through the job site.

We hollered *"Hola!"* and waved to the workers, who had stopped in mid-hammer swing to watch us, regarding us as a curiosity. They did not wave back. They did not jump up and rub themselves or yell, "Hey, chickie! *Oo la la!"*

The three of us reminisced about the sultry summers of our youth when we could not pass a construction site without enduring a barrage of wolf whistles. At the time we had hated it, but now we confided to one another that it would be nice to get a catcall once in a blue moon.

We stepped off the newly poured concrete sidewalk and onto a dirt path studded with rocks that meandered through a scrubby field rising gently into the foothills.

Two hours and a hard climb later, we were on the Alto de Santa Maria de Erreniega. At nearly eight hundred meters above sea level, it is one of the highest points of the Sierra del Perdón. One of the most riveting sights of the climb was the miles upon endless miles of sleek white windmills strung along the mountain range.

Wind power is serious business in Europe but particularly so in Spain, which is the world's fastest-growing producer of wind power and the second-biggest wind-power-producing country after Germany. About 7 percent of Spain's electricity is generated by windmills, and the goal is to raise that to 15 percent by 2010. Wind power has been growing at an average rate of 28 percent since 1999, and nearly three-quarters of all worldwide capacity is located in Europe.

At the summit other stunning sights awaited us. A larger-than-life-sized ironwork sculpture depicting pilgrims—walking, leading burros, or on horseback—had been erected to honor the Camino de Santiago and its legions of pilgrims.

Then there was the view; it was exhilarating. Behind us spread the Pamplona basin against the backdrop of the Pyrenees, which looked as distant as our memory of climbing them. Ahead were the sequential villages of Uterga, Muruzábal, and Obanos, leading to Puente la Reina, our destination for the day.

Lucy came puffing behind us with the Spanish Doctor at her heels. As we embraced, a look of resigned disappointment passed between us.

I had heard about Lucy through a mutual friend who had planned to walk the Camino with us but had to bail out at the last minute to tend to her disintegrating marriage.

"You'll love her," my friend had said, and she was right. From the moment I met Lucy I knew she was going to be loads of fun. She was married with two teenage children and worked in the male-dominated oil industry in Alberta, where she was underemployed as a secretary. She didn't put up with any guff from her co-workers, and I'd wager she could drink a few of those oilmen under the table. Easy.

In the brief time we had spent together, Lucy and I realized we were cut from the same cloth; we were kindred gypsies. The difference was that Lucy wasn't an approval whore like me. She had an inkling of what lay ahead with a group of middle-aged high achievers, and she had no intention of getting caught in the simmering politics.

Of all the women in our group, Lucy was the one with whom I had hoped to spend much of the time walking.

We now faced each other knowing that although we were on the same trail and taking the same route, we were on different journeys.

"I'm sorry, Janie," she whispered. "I just can't do the Camino with the group. I don't have a good vibe about them."

"Don't worry about it," I reassured her. "Save yourself. There's always another time, another walk—one with fewer women, eh? How's your hip, by the way?"

"Fine, thanks to him," she said, nodding toward the Spanish Doctor. "He's an osteopath—can you believe it?—and he's been able to get me painkillers along the way."

The Spanish Doctor shuffled to her side, and Lucy introduced us. He was a stocky, swarthy man with very sad, dark eyes. He spoke no English, and Lucy spoke no Spanish.

"His son was away at university in Belgium," she explained as we stared into the sweeping panorama before us, "and he died after falling from the window of a campus residence. It was definitely not suicide."

The Spanish Doctor had set himself on the Camino, where his world of grief had collided with Lucy's need for someone who understood hip problems. It was working perfectly for them, even with a language barrier.

A sharp gust of wind was the signal that it was time to move on. Lucy and I said good-bye.

As we began our descent, a dark mood fluttered above me like a silk scarf, drifting over my shoulders and then closing in for the kill as it wrapped itself tightly around my psyche. By the time I reached the bottom of the hill, I was as shocked by my sudden reversal of mood as I was by the ominous feeling that had settled over me.

The path leveled out to a plain of yellow canola and bright red poppies—poppies as far as the eye could see. We paused to take photos, knowing full well that no photo could do the scene justice.

At our lunch stop, Joanna reached into her backpack and withdrew one of the numerous letters written to her by her four children. The dates she was to open them were written on the front of the envelopes, and all held the promise of a homily of encouragement and love.

"Isn't that sweet?" she gushed, after reading the newest installment aloud. "These letters are great. It's just wonderful that they did this."

Kate and Beth had similar totems from their families, which they were also sharing. I sat empty-handed with not a shred of evidence that anyone cared a rat's ass about me. No note was surreptitiously tucked into any of the numerous little compartments in my knapsack. I had checked them all. As the women giggled and waxed on about their loved ones, a big fat tear squeezed out of my right eye and plopped into my *café con leche*.

I got up and made some lame excuse about needing to hit the trail and then stormed off in a rage of shame and anger I can barely describe.

The others scrambled together their gear and followed quickly behind. I walked faster to get farther ahead so that they wouldn't hear my sobs, but I could sense them closing in. I allowed my anger to fuel a warp-speed surge in my stride to put more distance between me and them.

I hated them. I hated their perfect lives, their notes from home.

As for my children, I bled myself for them, constantly trying to compensate for the absent parent in our household, and still they couldn't pull themselves away from MSN long enough to write me a goddamn letter telling me they missed me.

I worked full-time at a good job and even took on freelance jobs to boost my income. Every dime I made was put into making the house comfortable for them, or for paying for school supplies, or for trips, or for the never-ending list of designer-labeled clothing they desired. I said "yes" more often than I said "no" because I didn't want them to feel second-class. Among their friends' families theirs was the only one where the parents had divorced. I seldom said the words "We can't afford it."

And this was my thanks: not one damn note. Didn't I teach them manners and compassion? Did they not learn from my example? I frequently tucked notes of love and encouragement into their lunch boxes or into suitcases and duffel bags whenever they went off to camp or on a trip with their father. They would tell me how those notes meant so much to them, yet they were incapable of reciprocating the gesture. Maybe I expected too much from them—they were teenagers, after all. No, I decided I wasn't going to let them off the hook. I had spoiled them, and they were treating me like the cash cow I had inadvertently created. Wait till I get home, I steamed. Things are going to be different.

The wind slapped my face. Even God was cross with me.

I stormed through Obanos, where a group of pilgrims, including a few from my group, were milling around the fountain of the town square, chatting and laughing.

Some women can cry elegantly. Not me. When I cry, you know it; my face gets flushed, my eyes look like I've been on an eight-week bender, and my nose turns a bright red.

"Hey," someone called out to me. "Your nose is red!"

"Bad cold," I smiled. "Allergies from the canola fields, I think."

I strode past at Mach speed, and when I was a safe distance away from them another string of sobs was unleashed. Hot, leaden tears seared my cheeks. I felt as if I could cry for ages.

The sight of everyone around the fountain having a swell time upset me even more. I wanted to be the type of person who hangs out at stone fountains with my fellow pilgrims, and yet I felt estranged from the human race, even estranged from myself. What's more, I could not understand why I was walking so quickly on the Camino. Something seemed to be pushing me forward, as if urgent business needed my attention.

With Puente la Reina within sight, I dabbed my eyes and fanned the cool air toward them so that the redness would dissipate. I focused on the yellow arrows.

There were two *refugios* in Puente la Reina; the first was full, so I pressed on along the tree-lined Calle Mayor in search of the second. At least I thought it was the Calle Mayor. I discovered the error when I reached a sleek, steel bridge that did not exactly match the guidebook's description of the Romanesque stone bridge I was supposed to be crossing.

I stopped and looked around to get my bearings. On a bridge running parallel to the one I was on—a distinctly Romanesque one—I made out two figures who were wildly waving their arms. It was Trish and Georgina. I scrambled across the bridge and ran to meet them as fast as someone carrying a twenty-pound backpack can.

The *refugio* we arrived at a few minutes later had opened fairly recently. It was modern and spacious and had a bar and a dining room, which meant we did not have to trek back into town for our meal.

Better still, it had lots of showers—about a dozen of them— and they were the most luxurious we had experienced on the Camino. When I stepped inside one of them, I let the water drizzle over me, willing it to purify me and flush out the anger and self-pity through my pores.

I was feeling a bit better postshower. In the hall on the way to the dorm, I encountered Dr. Dan the Massage Man.

"Ah, Jeanne!" he said brightly. "How is your shoulder?"

My hand moved to the afflicted area. Yes, it was still sore.

"Perhaps we should have another session?" he suggested.

Perhaps indeed.

"Where shall we go?" I asked.

"Your room?"

I led him inside. Every bunk was occupied by members of my tribe. Good, I thought. At least it would be a safe environment in case Dr. Dan got out of hand.

Colleen looked up from her book and shot me a disapproving look. Then she nodded smugly to herself as an indication that she had successfully pre-assigned me to the same category as Lucy.

I made an executive decision not to care what anyone thought and lay facedown on my bunk, resting my hands under my chin.

Dr. Dan began administering hand-to-shoulder therapy. God, it felt good. A man's bare hands on my skin can cause innumerable sensations, not all of them befitting a spiritual pilgrimage. Dr. Dan kneaded me.

"Are you a massage therapist?" I asked him.

"*Pardon?*" he replied.

"*Vous êtes un docteur?*" I asked.

"Ah," he said with sudden understanding. He leaned closer to my ear, and lowering his voice said, "Would you like me to be a doctor?"

Jesus. Who was this guy?

"What do you do? *Ton occupation?*" I asked, and immediately regretted the use of the more familiar second person.

"Ummm, how you say," he said slowly as he chose his words. "*Je travaille sur le clavier. Un computer?*"

"You are a writer? *Écrivateur?*"

"*Non, non, je travaille sur les computers. Je suis un consultant.*"

"Ahhhhh," I said as the lightbulb flicked on in my brain. Massaging women was a long way from computer consulting and far more, how you say—enjoyable? Everyone had a purpose on the pilgrimage, and Dr. Dan's was to massage his way into a sexual encounter.

"That feels much better," I said. I turned over on my back and abruptly ended the session. "Thank you very much. *Merci.*"

I might be a naïve fifty-year-old, but I didn't just get off the ark, buddy.

"But your moosles, they are veeeery tight," he said softly. Each of his arms was positioned on either side of my body, trapping me. We regarded one another silently; his bright blue eyes twinkled as he peered down at me over his rimless specs. It did not appear that he was going to blink. Finally, I made a move to roll forward, which forced him off the edge of the bed.

"Yes, that's much better," I said loudly for the benefit of the others in the room. "Thank you so much."

I walked to the door and opened it.

"À bientôt."

Dr. Dan took his leave. I could feel my tribe members staring at me, and when I looked up, they averted their eyes and returned to their books and diaries.

"I'm going for a drink," I said. "Anyone coming?"

IN THE refugio's bar, I logged on to the Internet and was overjoyed to find an e-mail from one of my sons. His news, however, was not good; my former father-in-law had died.

I remembered the incident in the woods when the whoosh of white light had flared into the stone into which I had willed this sick man's sorrow and pain. I wondered whether his spirit had passed from him at that very moment, and I wondered whether this was the death of which the psychic had spoken.

8

A FULL moon ascended just as an emotional shift began to work its way through our group.

Alpha-chick syndrome had invaded our tribe; cliques were forming out of design and necessity. We were lab rats in an experiment probing the social interactions and behavior of middle-aged women randomly thrown together for a month with nothing to do but walk eight hundred kilometers.

Theresa, who had once taken a course in conversational Spanish, had pretty much banned the rest of us from trying our hand at it. She didn't issue an edict or anything—she simply hip-checked whoever was trying to ask directions or a question and completed the transaction on their behalf. I suppose she was just trying to be helpful.

"What are you asking for?" she would inquire of anyone holding an English-Spanish phrase book.

"Well, I'm going to order a glass of wine..."

"*Uno vino tinto, por favor!*" she would command the bartender.

"Actually, I wanted a glass of white wine..."

"No! No No! No vino tinto; vino blanco, por favor!" she would correct the confused bartender.

"There you go!" she would say with a satisfied smile, and then she would take her leave of the linguistically challenged to find another problem to solve.

There seemed no gentle way to break it to Theresa that she was killing the only chance I had to learn Spanish. I had to wait until I was drunk, when my courage was stronger.

If tempers were fraying, so were bodies, but it seemed the complaints about blisters, shin splints, sore hips, and tired feet were merely window dressing for the bigger issues.

Some of the women felt the slower walkers were holding back the rest of the group. Others insisted that we take a bus for a few days and give our legs a rest. There were some who voiced resentment about the women who had found other walking partners because it didn't show commitment to the group. There were even complaints about those women (such as me) who always got the bottom bunks.

You might assume that you'd be safe from this sort of stuff on a spiritual pilgrimage but you would be wrong. Some of the most overbearing, bitchy, and bullying women are found in faith-based milieus where everyone tries to out-God one another. Power trumps piety.

I had often wondered why bonding was so important to women, and lo and behold the pilgrimage was giving me the answer: Women distrust other women, and bonding is often more about keeping enemies close and dependent than it is about shared interests. Men may vie for a job, a contract, or a woman, but women vie for acceptance and acknowledgment. It is not diamonds that are a girl's best friend—it is inclusion. What scares women most is the thought of being shunned.

We had been on the Camino almost a week, and I hadn't bonded with anyone, not in the sense of sharing secrets or having a steady walking companion or snagging bunk beds next to each other. The others had. Slow-walking Georgina had teamed up with one-legged Sally; the two nurses—Kate and Beth—were constant walking companions; Theresa had hit it off with Cathy and Joanna; Greta and June, who knew each other before the Camino, always walked together or shared bunk beds; critical Colleen, shit-disturbing Susie, red-haired Trish, and Serena, the gal with memory loss, traveled as a pack; and Lucy had taken off with the Spanish Doctor and his friend. I wanted desperately to feel part of the group, but at the same time I didn't want to feel pinned down. I intuitively felt something awaited me on the Camino, something that lay beyond the group.

I was thinking these thoughts while hiking across one of Mother Nature's less-than-stellar achievements—a vast wasteland of stunted, parched vegetation coated in dirt, the sort of place where plants come to die—when I stumbled across an astonishing sight. My internal conversation switched from relationships back to faith.

Lining the Camino's path in the midst of this moonscape of scruffy, lumpy clods of dirt and rock were hundreds of miniature inukshuk-like monuments. Out of pebbles, stones, and small rocks scavenged from the desperate-looking vicinity, each was a poetic reminder of a life in progress—a lost dream, a silent scream of anguish, abject loneliness, unimaginable grief, even a celebration of victory over grief—the gamut of human torture. In the place least likely to inspire hope, where nothing could possibly grow, faith and life had nonetheless taken root. I had never seen anything so profound.

And yet it made me sad; it made me want to go home. Badly. The sadness of other people, the struggle of the human spirit—it all made me pine for the comfort and the familiarity of my ordinary but happy life. I always seemed to be looking toward greener pastures for answers to questions I couldn't even articulate when, in fact, my own pasture was perfectly fine, perfectly beautiful. Perfect. I suddenly felt the weight of the Camino bearing down on me, the promise I had made to the others to complete it, the promise I had made to myself to mark the pilgrimage as a midlife accomplishment. But more than that, my ego was at stake.

A few months before I left for Spain, an organization booked me to be their after-dinner speaker, anxious to hear about the adventure upon my return. Naturally I accepted, because at the time there was no question that I would complete the Camino. But from the moment my fingernail had been ripped from its nail bed my first thought—aside from "How soon does one die from tetanus?"—was, "How am I going to bow out of the speaking engagement?" And if I don't bow out, how will I explain why I quit a pilgrimage to two hundred high-powered women who are paying good money to hear a tale about inspiration?

For many kilometers on the Camino, I rationalized my decision to quit within the context of giving the after-dinner speech. I decided my speech would focus on how women spend too much time running after things that are pointless. We worry about our failures when no one really cares whether we win or lose. I would tell them how silly we humans are about taking off from the comfort of our pampered corner of God's kingdom to search for adventure. Most of us were, after all, women who liked a gentle life and drinks with little umbrellas in them; we weren't hardwired to parachute and run marathons and climb mountains and corporate ladders. As women, we constantly set the bar higher and higher for ourselves, and then we wonder why we're so exhausted, cranky, and defeated. It was time to celebrate our blessed yet ordinary lives, to boldly embrace mediocrity as a virtue. I even thought up a title for my speech—Failure: It's the New Success.

AROUND MIDDAY we reached Estella. As luck would have it, the *refugio* opened earlier than others we had encountered—noon as opposed to late afternoon—which meant that I could have a shower before the pilgrim horde arrived.

I threw my gear onto an unclaimed bunk, grabbed my toiletry bag, and made a beeline for the shower, colliding with a man who had the same idea. There were two shower stalls, so I took one and he took the other. I was far too exhausted to care about modesty. I stripped off, turned on the shower, and used up as much hot water as my sweat-soaked greedy body could handle.

The day being still relatively young gave me a nice list of options. I decided to find a restaurant and eat a meal—a real meal—before the Kingdom of Spain shut down for *siesta* and then to stroll leisurely through Estella to take in the ambiance.

Before starting out on the Camino, I was baffled about how pilgrims, after walking twenty-odd kilometers each day, had energy left to sightsee. Never underestimate the power of a shower and clean clothes.

On my way out the door I passed a phone in the lobby, and counting back six hours, I decided to call home. My family would be just waking up, and the kids would be getting ready for school.

The telephone connection was clear, and the sound of my little family's voices elated me. My father-in-law's funeral had taken place—it was, said my mother, "a beautiful send-off"—and the children were coping bravely with their various levels of grief. My mother also reported that a bathroom sink, which had been on back-order for months, was arriving in the next few days and would be installed by the time I returned home.

Content that all was well in the real world, I returned to my pilgrim life.

I was beginning to enjoy the pleasant predictability of Camino life: same clothes, same gear, different town. There was no voice mail or e-mail or errands or chores and no bills to pay, no dental or medical appointments to book, no calendar to check twenty-five times each day to see if a task or obligation had been overlooked. I was a woman without a single responsibility, and I loved it.

Nor did I crave anything beyond food, shelter, and a good night's sleep. Near-orgasmic pleasure could be attained from the smallest thing: a smile from a stranger, a clean *refugio*, space on the clothesline for your laundry, hot *and* cold water in the shower, a hot meal.

I crossed the Roman-built Puente de los Peregrinos, ambled along the Calle Mayor, and ended up in the Plaza de Santiago.

There is no finer, more quintessential hallmark of European life than the town square—*café con leche* notwithstanding. If Europeans didn't exactly invent the concept, they recognized its genius and adopted it with characteristic gusto.

For two millennia the town square has defined European society. It is where justice was meted out, where political debates raged, where victory celebrations were held, where people ran to get the latest news, where Romeo slew Tybalt, where farmers brought their produce to market, where schoolchildren were taught, where a million romances were ignited, where meetings were conducted and hands were shaken to cement a deal, where soldiers gathered in preparation for war, where babies were paraded by adoring parents.

The town square, by its very design, embraces everyone. And here's the poetic and profound thing about that: it is not the square itself that wraps itself around you but democracy itself. The wonderful mix of buildings—religious, official, residential, commercial—represents the panoply of city life and culture and in doing so invites everyone to come together in the town square.

All roads within a medieval town lead to the plaza or square. The maze of narrow cobblestone lanes framed by an oppressive and uninterrupted wall of buildings heightens the anticipation. You scurry along skinny sidewalks, peer down dark, narrow laneways, and hustle forth toward your destination. You round a corner and there, suddenly, it is: the plaza. It immediately overwhelms you with its openness, its sense of freedom, and the exuberance of life you find there. I suppose the shopping mall was intended to be the North American equivalent to the European square, but I'm sorry, there's no comparison. One is an organic fusion of art, tradition, and necessity; the other is a temperature-controlled, artificially lit fish tank.

In Estella's Plaza de Santiago, café tables were filling up with the lunch crowd. The place was teeming with the drama of everyday life. I found a bench and sat down to soak it in.

The thought began to percolate: I could really live here. I didn't have a lick of Spanish to my vocabulary apart from *cerveza, vino tinto, café con leche, sí,* and *gracias,* but what more does a person need?

Estella was a Roman settlement long before it was officially founded in 1090 by King Sancho Ramírez. An enterprising chap, Ramírez managed to divert the Camino's route, which was three miles away, through Estella. He did this ostensibly so that pilgrims could have decent food and drink (three cheers for Ramírez!), but I think we can safely assume he was after pilgrim pesos. No one seemed to object, and Estella quickly earned a reputation for hospitality.

Over the centuries Estella continued to prosper without losing its sense of history. The weekly farmer's market has been going strong since the fifteenth century, and the city has an active cultural life ranging from the Gustavo de Maeztu Museum to the Ancient Music Week festival held each September.

In the Middle Ages, the city was an occasional royal residence, and today Estella's greatest architectural treasure is the Palace of the Kings of Navarre, built at the end of the twelfth century. The Romanesque cloister of San Pedro de la Rúa and the elegant porticos and reliefs of San Miguel Arcangel are other monumental must-sees, but all these would have to wait for a future visit, because right now there were shoe stores to check out.

I adore shoes. What woman doesn't? Shoes are exquisite pieces of fashion, marvels of workmanship, design, eccentricity, and style, but above all they are paragons of forgiveness. Shoe size does not fluctuate with weight: I can gain ten pounds or lose ten pounds, and my shoe size will still be 7½.

On the Calle Mayor my eyes were drawn to a brightly lit window display of sleek pumps in rainbow-hued silk with a pointed toe box and kitten heels. I ventured into the store, where a stiff-looking sales clerk eyed me suspiciously as I turned over the object of my desire to look at the price and get a sense of the shoe's weight. Could they fit in my backpack? How much weight would they add? Would they be crushed and ruined before I got home? Would I be ridiculed if I showed up at the *refugio* laden with shoe boxes?

I put the shoe down, nodded politely to the sales clerk, and left the shop. Maybe later.

As I strolled along the Calle Mayor, my thoughts about shoes got distracted by the architecture, specifically by doors. Doors thrill me almost as much as shoes. Almost.

I passed a door that was studded with metal rivets. It was ajar. Hmmmm, I thought, perhaps I'll just push this open. Behind the door a dark, cobblestone corridor beckoned, and I dutifully followed it to the end where a grand wrought-iron and stone staircase curved to the second level. I tiptoed up the stairs—they had deep treads and lower-than-normal risers, which create the effect of a person floating as she ascends or descends. At the top of the staircase a heavily carved door presumably led to the main quarters of the house. Above the stairwell was a domed ceiling painted with a skyscape—a mini–Sistine Chapel that looked to have been done about six hundred years ago—inset with windows, which let natural light into the interior of the house. The wall space in the stairwell was large, perfect for hanging a massive tapestry or two. What a great place to live, I thought.

I imagined a wrought-iron candelabra on a pedestal in the corner of the landing, the rustle and swish of silk and taffeta gowns, and the flutter of elaborate fans as beautiful women descended the stairs to a waiting coach. I practiced my best *doña de Estella* walk.

At the bottom of the stairs, around the corner, a worn ramp led to what I assumed was a stable or carriage garage. It was dark down there, and I resisted the temptation to investigate further.

The horse and carriage would have been brought up to the main level to await the *don* or *doña* of the manor and whisk them to their daily appointments. I could almost hear the clip-clop, clip-clop of horse hooves on the cobblestones.

My love for Estella was confirmed when, farther along the street, I came upon the town's public library on the Calle Ruiz de Alda. You can get a pretty good idea of a town's appreciation of culture and arts by checking out its library. This one was the best I had ever visited.

The library was housed in a Renaissance palace owned by one of Estella's most distinguished and decorated upper-class families. Miguel de Eguía y Jaso followed the tradition of his family as a high-ranking military man serving the Navarre monarchy. He established the town's first printing press in 1546 and was considered one of the best typographers of his time.

By the time the library got its hands on it five hundred years later, the building was dilapidated; only the façade and the escutcheon of the los Eguía family remained intact. New glass doors were discreetly installed beneath the arched entrance. Inside, a stunning renovation had been undertaken around the building's bones.

The ground floor, the former reception hall of los Eguía, was now the reading lounge, delineated by four ancient pillars. Light wood coffee tables, area rugs, black leather and steel chairs were modern concessions to comfort. Pole lamps topped with dainty cream-colored lampshades were stationed around the perimeter, augmenting the natural light from two sources—from a huge plateglass window overlooking the Rio Ega and the Roman-built Puente de los Peregrinos and from the skylight two stories above. The open skywell afforded a glimpse of the other floors, which contained a study room, children's space, and an audiovisual room. The study tables on the uppermost level hugged the rim of a colonnaded balcony. It was as if someone had taken the home of the Capulets and turned it into a library.

It was an inspired integration of old and new. Like the town itself, the library was buzzing with activity as the after-school crowd charged through its turnstiles and raced to meet classmates at prearranged tables to huddle and confer over homework.

I sat down in the reading lounge and leafed through books about Spain, pretending that I was a native, that I could understand the language, that this was just another ordinary day in my extraordinary life in Estella. Yes, I thought, I could really live in this town—it had a great library, Old World architecture, and shoe stores.

I decided to check my e-mail, so I moved across the room to a bank of computer terminals, sat down, and logged on.

For the first time since the start of the trek I felt relaxed and totally happy. This really was the best adventure, I told myself. What a stroke of luck to have learned about it from the Steward. Sure, it was a hard, dirty trail, but look at how much I was seeing and learning. I loved the Camino now. I loved the freedom of walking every day. I loved the easygoing, polite Spaniards and their unhurried pace of life. I even loved our group. There were a few personalities that rubbed me the wrong way, but I bet I rubbed them the wrong way, too. Maybe I needed to be a little more relaxed and upbeat with the others.

"Everyone wants a meeting. Now."

The voice jolted me from my blissful state. I spun around to find Susie the Shit-Disturber peering at me with her beady eyes.

"Hi!" I beamed. "Isn't this the best place . . ."

"Everyone wants a meeting."

"A meeting? About what?"

"The group wants to know where we're going, and they want to map out the next few days," she said.

Map out the trip? We all had maps. There was no need for mapping. A meeting? Hadn't I taken this trip so that I didn't have to have a meeting? My government job back home was full of meetings; my eyes glazed over at the very mention of the word "meeting." The last thing I wanted on the Camino was structure. However, as a show of cooperation I nodded agreement, and reluctantly I left the library with Susie.

A few minutes later, our group was arranged around a dark wood table in a dark bar that shut out all indications of the warm, sunny weather outside. We bought a jug of *vino tinto* and passed it around the table.

Cathy took charge. As soon as she started talking, I began daydreaming about the silk shoes in the shop window down the street. Should I buy them or hold off in the hope I'd see the same pair farther along the Camino? If I bought them, what did I have at home to wear with them?

I checked out of my daydream and back into the meeting.

Cathy was prattling on about the "incredible bond" that was being forged with the group. Her voice was caught with emotion.

How nice, I thought. Everyone is getting along so well. When you throw a bunch of strangers together you just never know whether they will gel. Still, you can "bond" without holding meetings, and this one felt suspiciously like it was going to erupt into a weepy hug-a-thon. The combination of wine and women can prompt that to happen. My active imagination conjured up a new mathematical equation:

$$women + wine = Oprah\ orgy$$

Back to the discussion. Around the table there was talk about whether the group should be allowed to break up so that others could strike out on the Camino at their own pace or whether the group should travel en masse as a single unified force.

It was an odd idea to bring up, because we had already unintentionally adopted the former system and it was working well. We all got up each day at the same time and set off at roughly the same time, knowing that if we didn't stick together all day we would meet up eventually by late afternoon at a previously agreed-upon destination. It was a sensible strategy, and no one had voiced any objection to it.

Now a degree of control was carefully being exerted. The alpha chicks were fluffing their feathers.

"Let's go around the table and hear from everyone about what they want from this adventure," Cathy began.

Oh Christ, why do we need to do this? I fixed an indulgent smile on my face so that I wouldn't come across as a spoiler; I remembered what befell the dissenters in *Lord of the Flies*. An uneasy feeling came over me.

All the women droned on about how great the group was, how "awesome" and "powerfully moving" they found the Camino. They were concerned, however, about the foot problems some of the women in the group had; about how we needed to consider the slower walkers among us; about how we needed to hold back for a day or two to allow the injured to heal. Doing so, we were told, would ensure the continuation and maturation of our bonding process.

As for Santiago, everyone agreed there was no way the group would make it there by our goal of May 30. Besides, the women decided, the important thing was the group, not reaching Santiago.

I could not believe my ears. More than a year of planning had gone into this trek (far more planning than I had put into anything else). Everyone had had an opportunity to train for the mental and physical rigors of the Camino. If someone was injured or didn't feel like walking, she could keep up with the group by taxi until she was able to walk. To expect the entire group to wait around for someone's blisters or sore knees to heal was unreasonable.

Things had changed behind my back. For most of the women, the Camino was no longer a pilgrimage; it was a movable consciousness-training exercise.

New Age crap about "needing the group," "bonding with our sisters," "connecting with each other's souls," and the "incredible magic of the Camino" began to piss me off. If I heard the word "awesome" one more time, I was going to scream. I had a sneaking suspicion someone was going to suggest we all break into "buddies."

Was this what Lori the psychic had meant when she warned about the group floating off on a cloud of profundity? *"They'll be going on and on about how magical everything is, reading stuff into everything they see, and you'll be saying, 'Hey, I just like pizza.'"*

The ritual rhapsodizing of these women reminded me of a cult. I looked around to make sure no one was standing by with a jug of Kool-Aid and the promise of eternal salvation. I poured another glass of wine.

One by one, the women spoke. Most were in favor of only moving forward if all fifteen of us were healthy and able to do so.

Beth, ever the diplomat, felt that bonding—though important—should not be done at the expense of the journey itself. Using herself as an example, she said the pain in her lower back had left her with no alternative but to take a cab for a while, but in no way did she expect or even want anyone to wait for her or change their plans to accommodate her.

Joanna in her teacherlike fashion insisted we all stick together. She waxed on about what a magical experience this was for her. Susie, Colleen, Trish, and Greta, all of whom were content to let everyone else make the decision, purred agreement.

Theresa and Kate weren't as stridently passionate about the all-for-one-and-one-for-all idea, but they didn't argue the point.

June, who rarely spoke to anyone except Greta, kept enigmatically quiet. I had walked with her earlier that day, and after four or five hours together, I was no better acquainted with her. Facing her across a table was like playing poker; what she said and the hand she played were two different things.

Georgina and Sally were slower walkers and hadn't yet arrived in Estella.

Serena and her nail-less toes were resting at the *refugio*.

Lucy had wisely bolted from the group before anyone could say "group dynamics."

"We haven't heard from Jane," said Cathy, turning to me and nodding as a signal that I could now speak. It was like being at a meeting of the Imperial Order of Daughters of the Empire and being asked to deliver the report on the previous weekend's afternoon tea and bake sale.

It was hard to know where to begin, because I was fuming inside. As I struggled to get my words out, Cathy mistook my stammering for shyness and gently prodded me: "Come on. It's OK. What is your goal on the Camino, Jane?"

"M-m-my goal is to finish the Camino," I blurted out. It was a heretical statement under the circumstances. "I've been preparing for this for a year and a half. And you're wrong. We can still make it to Santiago by May 30, but we're not going to get there if we sit around having meetings to decide whether we need to stick together as a group. This is a pilgrimage, not a trip to the bloody Outlet Mall."

You'd think I had told them I was resurrecting the Third Reich.

They stiffened a bit and looked at Cathy, who pursed her lips, put her hands together, and said, "I think we need to give Jane permission to walk her Camino."

That was it. I was ready to slug someone.

"With all due respect," I smiled through gritted teeth, "I don't need anyone's permission to walk the Camino or to do anything for that matter."

That was the bucket of cold water that doused the warm glow cast by the wine, the camaraderie, and all the talk about bonding.

We paid the bill and left.

I staggered from the dark bar into the glare of the afternoon sun. Blinded and disoriented, I looked around for a buddy, but everyone had dispersed quickly in different directions.

I sauntered off. Alone. Toward the shoe shop. When the chips are down, there's always retail therapy, even on a pilgrimage.

What had happened to my group? Before the Camino, everyone had come across as bold and independent—well, at least they had in their cyber correspondence. What was all this psycho-babble crap about "We need to give Jane permission"? Who gave *them* permission to give *me* permission? *"Women and their sanctimonious tones,"* I muttered to myself angrily.

There were people in the group who were really needy—needy in the sense that they needed to mother—no, smother—the living daylights out of anyone who came within ten feet of them. They set up a sort of domestic construct of mother and child. There were some in our group who wanted to be babied and led by the hand, and there were others more than willing to step in and administer hot tea, bed tucks, and punishment. The punishment was usually delivered in the form of the silent treatment.

As I stared into a store window, pondering what to do next, Susie's face popped up in front of me.

"There's talk of a mutiny," she said conspiratorially.

"W-W-W-What?" I asked, shaking myself back to reality.

"Some of the others weren't happy with the meeting," she said.

"Oh, that's too bad," I cooed.

What I was really thinking was, "Try to imagine how little I care."

9

"**I** COULD lie here all afternoon," said Kate dreamily.

"Me, too," sighed Beth.

We were stretched out on our backs in tall grass, the sun washing over us as we watched wisps of cloud coalesce into shapes that were left to our imaginations to decipher. Did that large white puff resemble the shape of Spain? A child's face in profile? A stingray? A shell? No sooner had you identified the shape when the cloud would break apart and spin itself into a new shape.

It was lunchtime, and Kate, Beth, Theresa, and I had settled on a hillside beside the ruins of a crofter's cottage, its timbered roof hopelessly collapsed and weathered by a good century or two of neglect. We unpacked a picnic of cheese, chocolate, and a bottle of beer, which passed for a balanced meal on the Camino.

The roundtable discussion that had taken place in Estella the day before was never discussed again, at least not in my company. Change was in the air. Spring had sprung, and so had the canola, poppies, and wild thyme. The landscape was in a rapid state of color change; browns and grays were transforming into vibrant greens, bright pinks, cheerful yellows, and hot reds. When the wind blew, the pastures became a massive green sea of languorous waves. Bales of hay were piled high in the fields to dry, and some were arranged—rather considerately, I thought—in a way that provided shade and shelter for the flood of pilgrims that passed by daily.

En route to our picnic spot, we had passed a group of pilgrims lolling around one such makeshift pit stop munching their lunch. Among them was Cathy, who had taken up with Pieter the Dane Who Wore Black. The day before, in Estella, she had waxed on about how our "magical group," needed to "bond." Now it seemed she had cast her bonding chips with someone else.

We did not care. The political machinations of the group had worn many of us down. It was only a matter of time before someone had the courage to pipe up about wanting a few creature comforts.

Beth, the least likely to complain about anything, was the first to utter what we were all thinking: we wanted a hot bath, big fluffy white towels, clean clothes, some privacy, and no bunk beds. Once the idea was launched, we were like slobbering dogs straining to get our maws around a ham bone dangling in front of us.

As we gazed at the clouds, Kate, Beth, Theresa, and I listed the little things we missed from our off-Camino lives: a fat fresh bar of soap, a pot of strong hot tea, a big towel to wrap around your washed and conditioned hair while you sat on a sofa with a nail file and a new bottle of nail polish, a bubble bath, more than three minutes in which to do your business in the bathroom, a blow dryer.

The single item of luxury I had brought with me on the Camino was a small bottle of Vitabath gel. This little potion—I am referring to the Spring Green scent—could catapult me into a stratosphere of cleanliness in which I barely recognized myself. Each day after a long hike, I would smuggle my Vitabath into the shower. As soon as I removed the cap, the aroma would instantly transform me. It was magic dust and a soothing blankie rolled into one. When I discovered I had left it behind in the shower stall in Estella, I was so upset that I seriously considered hiking the nineteen kilometers back to retrieve it.

Yes, a one-night break from the *refugio* routine, we reasoned, might be just the ticket to raise our flagging spirits.

We pulled ourselves away from cloud spotting, stuffed our lunch garbage into our backpacks, and prepared to resume our march. As I stood adjusting my backpack, one of my legs suddenly buckled.

"You OK?" asked Theresa.

"My knee is a bit wobbly," I said. "I think it'll be fine once I get walking again."

"Maybe you need a knee massage," she said lasciviously as she hooked her arm through mine. "And I know just who can give it to you."

"Shut up," I chuckled. "He's not a doctor, you know."

The others paused and waited to be enlightened about Dr. Dan.

"He's a computer programmer," I said. I told them about his would-you-like-me-to-be-a-doctor comment.

"Are you shittin' me?" gasped Theresa. Nothing escaped her scrutiny, and she was a bit miffed that she hadn't seen through Dr. Dan's ruse.

"Ha! The guy just loves rubbing women," laughed Kate.

"Well, who can tell on the Camino?" said Theresa. "I mean, we all dress the same, we're all dirty and smelly."

"It's very democratic, isn't it?" smiled Beth, who liked democracy.

For single people the Camino can be an exciting prospect; newspaper articles have referred to it as "the new singles bar."

Based on anecdotal evidence, I would say there were slightly more men than women during our May trek, though the 2004 statistics for the Camino contradict that, reporting more female pilgrims (56 percent) than male pilgrims (44 percent). Certainly there were more singles than couples.

Pilgrims may curb their passions on the trail, but that doesn't mean that promiscuity is uncommon. An old saying provides a blunt reminder of human frailty in this department: "Start out as a pilgrim, return as a whore." Not surprisingly, extracurricular activities of a sexual nature are kept under the radar, away from the watchful eyes of *refugio* owners. A pilgrim can be kicked off the Camino for unpilgrimlike behavior.

None of this was of any concern to me—romance was the furthest thing from my mind—but that didn't stop a few of the women in our group from trying to change my single status. There's nothing more exasperating than well-intentioned people playing matchmaker, which is, when you get right down to it, just a polite term for pimp.

Some of the women had noticed that Dr. Dan the Massage Man was paying a lot of attention to me. I assumed he was simply being friendly, but then I'm not the brightest person when it comes to deciphering romantic overtures.

As Kate, Beth, Theresa, and I reached the *refugio* in Los Arcos and stood in line waiting to register, Dr. Dan came running toward me with arms open wide.

"Ah, Jeanne!" he exclaimed hugging me. "You are staying here, yes? You must stay! It is very nice."

I nodded and smiled.

"We must organize to go out for dinner!" he said.

"Yes, of course," I replied politely, accepting yet another hug as he took his leave.

Did he mean dinner as in the two of us, or did he mean with his two friends and me and my group?

As the line inched closer to the registration desk, I became increasingly undecided about whether to check in. I still had energy to walk, and it was only mid-afternoon. A five-kilometer walk would put me in Torres del Rio, the next town with a *refugio*, in about an hour. Whether there was a spare bed in Torres del Rio was a crapshoot, however.

It would also mean missing a possible dinner date with Dr. Dan. By moving ahead a few kilometers, I might not see him again on the Camino. *Mais, c'est la vie*; how many times in my life had I altered my course in order to please a man rather than follow my intuition?

I stepped out of the line and explained my idea to Theresa. She said she was game. "I'm getting sick of the group, anyway," she confided. We were all getting sick of the group.

As Theresa and I stood outside the *refugio* discussing the road to Torres del Rio, my right knee spasmed again. I limped to a bench and sat down. We were immediately joined by Willem, whom we referred to as the Guy Who Creeped Us Out.

"Are you walking ahead, because I am walking ahead, too," he said noticing the maps we held in our hands.

His eyes looked at us hungrily. Willem and his friend—whose name escapes me—were walking the Camino to score babes. Although, like I said, most pilgrims kept their passion under the radar, these two Dutch chaps were exceptions. Their intentions were so patently obvious you could practically see the drool dripping from their mouths.

A strange thing had happened with Willem and his pal a few days earlier. Seeing that there were fifteen of us and only two of them, they figured that scoring with at least one of us was within the realm of possibility. Sadly for them we were smarter than we looked. (Or so I thought. After the Camino was over, I learned that one woman in our group had succumbed to Willem's dubious charm. The very thought of that encounter gives me shivers to this day.) Anyhow, while a bunch of us sat at a table enduring Willem and his pal's swaggering chatter over a *café con leche* one day, Serena suddenly asked Willem about his two children. The question startled him as much as it did us; he had never even mentioned a wife, let alone children. He stammered a few lines about them, but it was clear that a discussion of his family was off script.

Later we asked Serena how she knew about Willem's children. "I see auras around people," she confided. It was one of the "gifts" she had received as a result of her Amazon-acquired coma. "With this guy and his friend, I can clearly see ovals above their heads, and inside those ovals are their families. They're both married with kids. These guys are so on the prowl."

In Los Arcos, Theresa and I now faced a dilemma: should we strike out on our own to get away from the herd and contend with Willem, or should we stay put?

I stared into the maps to buy some time, pretending to calculate the true distance we had to travel to Torres del Rio.

"We're staying," I said abruptly. Theresa held her surprise in check.

"But why?" argued Willem. "It is not very nice here. The *refugio* in Torres del Rio is supposed to be much nicer." He sprayed bits of saliva as he spoke.

"My knee is really sore," I said. "It's better that I stop here and let it rest."

I turned to Theresa. "We're staying here."

Willem continued to argue the point, his face getting redder and redder. I got up and limped back into the lineup and left it to Theresa to tell him to piss off.

"Wow, fast thinking coming up with that knee injury," Theresa chuckled when she eventually joined me at the registration desk.

"It wasn't a lie," I said. "My knee really is painful. If I walk even a few more kilometers, we'll be adding another name to the injury list."

ALONG WITH THOSE we had come to recognize on the Camino— the Woman with the Fendi Scarf, the Dane Who Wore Black, the Stocky Spaniard Who Always Said *Buenos Días* with a Smirk on his Face, the Austrian Nurse, the Three American Boys—Dr. Dan the Massage Man was a familiar face. All of us were part of a nomadic tribe, surging together twenty-five kilometers at a time toward Santiago. There was comfort in belonging to a group that stumbled over the same worn path together and that suffered through the same mud or the heat or a particularly arduous climb. Misery does indeed love company, and there was an abundance of both on the Camino.

People in the tribe began asking after each other. The welfare of each other's aches and pains became cause for both idle chatter and serious discussion. Those who had been total strangers a week before became the people who mattered most in our lives. This is what happens when your world shrinks to the size of fifty people: deals are made, relationships are forged, quid pro quo established. It's the tribal way.

I showered and changed and was delighted to find some quiet and privacy in the Los Arcos *refugio's* walled courtyard among the few items of laundry hanging on the clotheslines. I pulled out my journal and was ready to jot down some thoughts when the silence was broken.

"Ahhh, Jeanne!" Dr. Dan was practically skipping toward me. "We go for a drink, yes?" he said making drinking motions with his hand.

Why not? ·

Dr. Dan guided me through dusty, deserted, depressing Los Arcos as we hunted for a bar.

"I have been making nice dreams about you, yes?" he giggled.

I hadn't heard lines like that in a while, but I decided against asking him to elaborate.

When we arrived at the bar, it was already packed with pilgrims. Cigarette smoke as thick as a funnel cloud hovered above tables littered with wine bottles and ashtrays overflowing with cigarette butts. A cacophony of chatter, clinking of glasses, and riotous, drunken laughter filled the air. A few people were having trouble staying upright in their chairs. It was only 3 PM. Wine had edged out prayer as the currency for spiritual nourishment. The Camino was a booze can.

As Dr. Dan and I made our way through the crowd in search of an empty table, several women from my group grabbed my arm.

"Oooooo! Are you guys on a date?"

"He's so handsome, isn't he?"

"You know, I've heard of people meeting on the Camino and then getting married!"

Another round of drunken cackles.

"It's just a drink, maybe dinner," I said through a tight smile.

"They think I am falling in love with you, no?" whispered Dr. Dan merrily as he steered me toward a small table at the back of the bar.

No sooner had we settled in our seats when Theresa rushed over and plunked down a bottle of *vino tinto* on the table.

"This is from all of us for you guys on your first date," she gushed before scurrying back to her tablemates.

I turned around. Half the room was staring back at us, drunken smiles on their faces, giving me the thumbs-up.

Cathy was the next visitor to our table.

"It's totally awesome that you guys met," she said with a little squeal. Pulling me closer in an embrace she whispered: "I have a really good feeling about this. I think this is the man, the soul mate, you are meant to be with."

Jesus! This was like high school. I felt like the class geek who had been matched up for a mercy date. Did these women think I was some hopeless case who never dated? OK, so what if I was?

"Maybe I give you another neck massage, and..." Dr. Dan was leering.

We drank our wine, and I sat like a good girl listening to him talk about himself. Between his fractured English and the deafening noise in the bar, I barely made out a word he said, so I just nodded while his mouth moved.

Dr. Dan appeared to be in his mid- to late fifties. He was about five foot eight, with a solid build that suggested lots of exercise and a healthy pride in his body. Good teeth. Trimmed gray hair. Small rimless glasses. Bright blue eyes. His hands were strong, with short, squarish fingers. They're exactly like my father's hands, I thought. Dr. Dan's blue eyes twinkled—just like my dad's. I smiled. Dr. Dan probably thought that whatever he was saying was making me happy, but the truth was I was sitting there remembering my dad. Was Dr. Dan a reincarnated version? Was I meant to meet this guy? Was this a sign? Was I going insane?

Dr. Dan was still yammering the following day as we resumed the trail out of Los Arcos. The night before, Kate, Beth, and I had made a quiet pact to get a hotel room together in Logroño, our next stop. I attempted to convey this bit of news to Dr. Dan, but something got horribly twisted in the translation and he assumed I was trying to tell him that I wanted to get a hotel room *with him.* My attempts to set the record straight proved futile; he put his arm around me and continued talking so that I could not get a word in edgewise.

Despite his assumption that we would share a room that night, Dr. Dan did not offer much in the way of verbal foreplay. During the entire twenty-nine kilometers to Logroño, he delivered a comprehensive history and geography lesson about his home of Freiburg, Switzerland, as well as an exhaustive and somewhat interesting account of his time in the army. Not once did he ask me a question about myself. Did I have a husband? A boyfriend? Children? What did I do for a living? Where did I live? Did I have any pets? Hobbies? Communicable diseases? When he mentioned his sixteen-year-old daughter I tossed off a comment that I, too, had a daughter, but he did not take the bait and did not so much as ask her age.

Now I do not expect a three-page questionnaire from someone who has designs on me, but there is a tacit understanding in dating circles that if you are a man who hopes to get a woman you have just met into bed that night, it's to your benefit to ask the woman about herself and sound halfway interested in her answers.

While Dr. Dan blabbed on and on, I turned my attention to the rolling landscape. The path led through olive groves and vineyards, past ancient cemeteries and a hermitage, and over the Ebro River's Puente de Piedra (Bridge of Stone, though I confess to not gleaning the significance of the name, since all the bridges were made of stone). We also walked though mud, but we had become so accustomed to mud as a fact of daily life that if we failed to encounter any during the day the omission would be raised at dinner that evening. "Did you walk through mud today?" "Where was the mud?" "Have we seen the last of the mud?"

Was mud perhaps a metaphor? Everything was a metaphor on the Camino. Shells and arrows were, too, and everything seemed to take on their shapes. The yellow arrows painted along the route began to resemble crosses. Ripples in the creeks and rivers fanned out in a shell-like formation; the whorls on tree trunks possessed shell-like patterns. Even the soles of my boots appeared to leave a shell-like imprint. If I stared hard enough, I might have seen clouds move into the shape of arrows, shells, or the Virgin Mary.

It's easy to become shell-shocked on the Camino; the shell is everywhere. Had a pair of them been handed to me as eating implements in restaurants along the Camino, I would not have been surprised. During the long day's walk I found myself coming up with marketing and tourism schemes based on the shell. And once the Camino was over, I continued to look for these symbols for guidance, my heart fluttering whenever the Shell Oil logo came into view. Escape the shell and you effectively remove yourself from the Camino.

ON THE OUTSKIRTS of Logroño, I unbuckled my backpack and let it drop with a thud on a wooden bench that had been thoughtfully placed on this barren stretch of path.

"I need to rest and wait for my friends," I told Dr. Dan with a forced smile. God, I hate it when I have to pretend to be nice. "You can go on ahead if you like."

"Oh no, Jeanne, I wait. We will get a hotel tonight, no?"

"Yes, I'm definitely getting a hotel tonight," I replied wearily as I slumped onto the bench.

We sat in silence, him smiling and thinking about a night in a hotel with me, me fuming about his arrogance in not asking me one question about myself. Not that it mattered. As well-intentioned as he seemed, as jolly, talkative, handsome, and genial as he was, I just wasn't into him.

Kate and Beth came striding down the trail. They looked embarrassed, as if they had caught a friend in a compromising situation, which in this case consisted of me seated next to a man on a bench on a public road. They gave me a quick smile and walked right past.

"Hey! Wait up!" I yelled, grabbing my gear and running after them while Dr. Dan, alarmed at my sudden departure, struggled to pull on his backpack and catch up.

"Are you guys still keen to get a hotel room tonight?" I asked urgently. They nodded.

"I am, too, but this guy thinks I want to share it with *him*. I don't. You have to save me!"

Their eyes immediately registered understanding.

"And I want us, just us, to share a room," I added to drive home my point. "We're not sharing the room with him."

Both vigorously nodded agreement.

Dr. Dan scurried to join us.

"Have you lost Raymond and Giselle?" Beth asked in her sing-song voice, referring to Dr. Dan's traveling companions. "I think we saw them back there."

"Ah, yes, but I am with Jeanne now, and we are getting a hotel room," he said proudly.

Sweet Jesus.

We located the *refugio* in Logroño and decided to check in with the others in our group and let them know our plans.

"We saved you some beds," said shit-disturber Susie upon seeing us.

"We're not staying," I said. "We're going to a hotel. We need to do laundry. We want a bath and a real bed."

"But this place is *nice*," she insisted. "It's got everything! You can do laundry here. And it's only three euros."

She was absolutely right. The three-story *refugio* was situated on one side of a large, sun-drenched walled courtyard. Pilgrims were dangling their legs in a pool, reading, writing in their journals, chatting, or hanging up their laundry. The stucco building itself was modern and scrubbed clean. It was an idyllic, peaceful sight, completely at odds with the normal pilgrim *refugio*. It looked like Club Med.

Still, the thought of bunk beds could not compete with visions of thick, fluffy white towels and en suite bathrooms. With Dr. Dan in tow, we set off down the Calle Marqués de San Nicolás to the Calle Mercaderes and then to the Plaza del Mercado, where we paused to watch storks the size of pterodactyls circling the Catedral de Santa Maria de la Redonda, their monstrous nests wedged between the cathedral spires. We crossed the Calle de Portales to the gorgeous Paseo Principe de Vergara, with its lush decorative topiaries. We dodged rush-hour traffic while jaywalking across Rey Juan Carlos. We trolled the streets of Logroño hunting for anything that resembled a hotel, or had the words *hotel* or *pensione* in its signage. We passed the modern and majestic Carlton Rioja, which positively screamed, "Big, fluffy bathrobes," but Kate and Beth did not want to spend the money. For a fleeting moment I considered casting my lot with Dr. Dan in exchange for the chance to bury my face in a thick pile of looped pima cotton.

The search for a hotel became a Camino in itself.

Two hours later, exhausted and disoriented, we ended up at the Hotel Issa, a small, bland, unappetizing place with no laundry facilities, threadbare towels, and the clone of Basil Fawlty manning the reception desk. We casually but quickly told the clerk that we wanted a room for three. Dr. Dan was given his own room.

There are times when you know exactly what your body and your spirit need but you are forced to settle for less. You try to bite back the disappointment of not getting your way because it seems childish, yet the craving persists and magnifies. A rarely expressed but delicious benefit of being a single mother is that you almost always get your way because no one is around to oppose your decisions. I did not get my way this time.

Our hotel experience fell far short of all our expectations. The lesson of course is that if you want something badly enough, don't compromise.

As for Dr. Dan the Massage Man? He called me the moment he got to his hotel room, but by then I was already soaking in the tub. I did not return his call. The following morning when we checked out of the Hotel Issa he was gone, and I never saw him again.

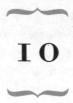

10

IN A CAFÉ on the road out of Logroño, we ran into one-legged Sally and Georgina the vicar. They were now traveling with a middle-aged German who was convinced his purpose on the Camino was to protect and assist Sally.

"Is the German guy bugging you?" we asked them, as Kate prepared to roll up her sleeves and deck him.

"No, he's the kindest man you could imagine," said Georgina, who would not tell a lie, at least not a big one. "It's weird. He doesn't speak any English, and I'm using what high school German I can dredge from my feeble brain. But the language barrier isn't an issue. We're all comfortable with one another."

Over a *café con leche*, Sally showed me her palms, which were badly blistered from the constant pounding they were getting from her crutches—in a way her hands were her feet. Undaunted, this one-legged wonder was forging ahead with an indomitable will and determination lacking in most two-legged wonders. Georgina, a slow walker, admitted that she had to hustle to keep up with Sally.

Kate, Beth, and I left them, and we trudged on to our destination that day—Nájera. There, chaos awaited. The *refugio* was full, and the owner grumpily refused to help anyone find alternative accommodation. A handful of the women in our group had arrived earlier—by cab—and managed to snag beds in the *refugio*; the rest of us were left to our own devices.

A whiff of revolution was in the air. People were angry, panicky, and near tears from the combination of physical exhaustion and emotional stress. Stress on a pilgrimage! Who would have thought it possible? The Camino had morphed into a highly competitive sport, and things were getting ugly.

Agitated pilgrims clogged the lobby of the *refugio* and in half a dozen languages demanded beds, but the *refugio* owner refused to enter discussions with anyone. He sat at a small table with his arms resolutely crossed and his eyes staring off into the middle distance.

Meanwhile, Kate and Beth discovered to their considerable dismay that their backpacks, which they had sent by cab earlier that day from the Logroño *refugio* to the Nájera *refugio*, had been turned away by the Nájera *refugio* owner because he did not want their bags cluttering up his place. As I said, he was a most unhelpful man. Their faces flushed with anger and worry, the nurses pushed their way outside, hopped into a cab, and headed back to Logroño to find their packs.

Not wanting to be stuck in the midst of a full-blown riot, I squeezed through the shouting crowd toward the door. In the square, pilgrims milled about trying to make other arrangements. It was the first time we had been turned away from a *refugio* and forced to consider Plan B. Naturally, none of us had a Plan B.

I spotted Greta, Trish, and Joanna and migrated toward them. "What are we going to do?" soft-spoken Greta implored to me. I was hoping someone else would have the answer.

While we discussed possible options, we were approached by a glamorous mother and daughter from Vancouver who overheard us speaking English. The daughter, I was later told, was a plus-size fashion model of some repute, though she hardly fit the description. North American women who don't possess the body of a premature baby are automatically consigned to the column marked "plus-size."

Like us, the mother and daughter had been turned away at the *refugio*, but instead of fretting about it, they simply got a hotel room. They suggested we do likewise. We demurred.

"Let's get a cab to the next town," suggested Joanna.

It was as shocking a statement as you're likely to hear on the Camino, especially coming from someone like Joanna, who, despite having taken a cab up the Pyrenees, insisted on walking every step of the Camino. None of us wanted to take a cab, but then again none of us wanted to be without a bed for the night. After considerable debate Joanna, Trish, Greta, and I hailed a taxi.

"It will get us ahead of the pack," I said, trying to justify our actions.

I was wrong. As the cab reached Azofra, five kilometers from Nájera, we encountered a couple of pilgrims who were walking away from the village.

"There's no room at this *refugio*, either," one of them shouted to us.

We looked at each other, then at our maps, and finally at our cab driver. We asked him to drive us a further eight kilometers to Santo Domingo de la Calzada.

Enjoying his complicity in our search for *refugio* beds, the driver put the pedal to the metal and took off at warp speed for Santo Domingo.

"*Lento! Lento!*" I gasped as the speedometer edged its way to 170 kilometers per hour. Princess Diana speed, I thought.

The driver laughed off my concern and then took both his hands off the steering wheel to prove that driving 170 klicks per hour with no hands was a thoroughly manly thing to do. I thought I would pass out.

He deposited us at the entrance to the medieval town of Santo Domingo. We hiked up the cobblestone road to the *refugio* only to learn there was no room there either. We were directed further up the road to yet another building. By this time, our anxiety levels were high enough to warrant medication.

We did get beds that night. Well, not beds, per se, but floor mats. Never have there been four more grateful pilgrims. We practically sobbed our thanks when the friar at the second *refugio* accepted our money and let us in.

The floor mats were stacked in a corner, and we each claimed one, dragged it to the end of a long row of other mat dwellers, and set up camp. We unrolled and smoothed out our sleeping bags and arranged our meager possessions around the perimeter to stake out our territory. We drew coveted items from our backpacks and fondled them lovingly. A comb, a pen, a hair scrunchie. These were our luxuries, and we hoarded them protectively.

In my rush to pack for the Camino, I had neglected to pack photos of my children—I'm not sure this was entirely unintentional at the time—and now, craving to be reconnected with them, I turned on my back and stared at the ceiling, trying to re-create their faces. I'm not the type who travels with photos of my loved ones—I don't quite know why. Perhaps it's because a celluloid image does not do justice to them or anyone. I prefer the memory of action and voice—the laughter, the cries, even the sarcasm-laced sound bites of adolescence. But lying there on a cold floor—without letters from home, without wallet-sized photos—I suddenly wished to be like normal people who are heavily armed with such totems whether they are heading across the planet or around the corner to the grocery store. As I thought of my children's faces and voices, I wondered what they would have thought of their mother sleeping on a mat on a cold floor. Would they have recognized me with my long, straggly hair, gaunt, makeup-free face, and sweat-stained clothing? This was only our eighth day on the road, but in a strange way I felt that I had always lived this way.

In the *refugio* we recognized a few familiar faces from our tribe—the Three American Boys and an older couple, to whom we nodded a greeting. Still, the separation from our own group worried us.

"I think we should wait here a day for the others to catch up," said Greta in her soft German-accented voice as she rubbed cream into her cuticles. "Look at these nails," she tutted, shaking her head. She was an aesthetician, so it was natural for her to have packed a small arsenal of expensive European potions, which I eyed covetously. She wore no makeup, and her hair, skin, and nails were always immaculate.

"I think we should keep moving," said Trish.

Joanna agreed, as did I.

"These *refugios* seem unprepared for the number of pilgrims along the way," observed Joanna. "What are they going to do in July? This isn't even peak season."

"I heard that there were tents being erected up ahead to handle the numbers," said Trish, running a comb through her shiny, chin-length auburn hair. Her hair was perfectly straight—you could shake it, and it would still fall neatly into place. "I mean, they have to do something. Look at this place—it's already packed, and this is the overflow *refugio*."

"Then we need to keep moving, group or no group," Joanna affirmed.

By morning she had reversed her decision. In a manner befitting her teaching profession, she told us that we should wait a while for the others to show up.

It was Mother's Day, so after repacking our gear we headed across the square to attend Mass in an ancient and unadorned little church. Afterward, we walked back across the street to visit its polar opposite, the Catedral de Santo Domingo de la Calzada, and, to be honest, to kill some time until the rest of the group arrived.

The cathedral did not look like much from the outside—at least not from the south façade, where we entered—but you know what they say about judging a book by its cover.

Inside, the cathedral was everything the Roman Catholic Church is criticized for—its noxious display of wealth, its architecture that induces equal parts fear and reverence, its Disney-like legends and characters that are so outlandish you have no choice but to believe. We were drawn in. Open-mouthed and wide-eyed, we groped our way to a pew and fell to our knees.

The Catedral de Santo Domingo de la Calzada was a mesmerizing cornucopia of architectural styles—Roman, Gothic, Renaissance, Baroque—and every artistic fusion in between. Stone columns shot up to the heavens like Douglas-firs, their bases bearing the handprints of generations of saints and sinners.

Saint Dominic, the cathedral's namesake, was born in 1019, in a neighboring village. He attended the Abadía de Valvanera and the monastery of San Millán but the monks considered him too slow and uncouth for their liking. In spite of his commitment to the Church, he was shunned by the Benedictines. (The tourist pamphlet in the cathedral euphemistically refers to Dominic's attempt to enter the monastery as "unsuccessful.")

Dominic was nevertheless sanguine about it all and quietly became a hermit, devoting his life to helping pilgrims along the Camino. He was surely history's most industrious hermit. His major achievements consisted of the construction of a bridge over the Rio Oja, a pilgrim's hostel, a hospital (now a four-star Parador hotel), a church, and a thirty-kilometer road between Nájera and Redecilla del Camino—hence the addition of *calzada*, the Spanish word for highway, to his name. Not bad work for a lifetime. The buildings he erected constituted the beginnings of the city that now bears his name.

But what really put Santo Domingo de la Calzada on the map was the legend of the resurrected roast chickens. It goes something like this:

A couple and their teenage son, Hugonell, were traveling the Camino in the fourteenth century. They stopped for the night in Santo Domingo at an inn where the innkeeper's daughter took an immediate shine to Hugonell. Being a virtuous chap, he rebuffed her advances. She did not take it well. To avenge the slight, the girl hid a silver goblet in Hugonell's backpack. When the family was leaving the next morning, the missing goblet was discovered in Hugonell's backpack, and he was denounced a thief. Hugonell was taken out and hanged.

With their only son dead, Hugonell's poor, distressed parents decided to carry on to Santiago. As they passed the tree from which their son's body hung, they heard him call out that he was still alive. Depending on the version of the story you hear, either St. James or St. Dominic had saved the boy by holding him up on his shoulders beneath the gallows tree.

Hugonell's parents ran to the home of the district judge and told him what they had witnessed. The judge, who had just sat down to a sumptuous meal of roast chicken, scoffed at their report. Their boy, the judge told them imperiously, was no more alive than the chickens on his plate. With that, the chickens stood up, grew feathers, and crowed, thus demonstrating the boy's innocence.

In honor of the miracle, a niche was carved in the cathedral's west wall, and a pair of live white chickens—a cock and a hen—were installed to scratch and strut behind an ornate iron grill.

It was a goofy, cheesy display that left you wondering whether the humane society had been notified. Then again, in a country that puts bulls in rings or lets them loose in city streets, you shouldn't be surprised to find cocks in cathedrals.

We explored every nook and cranny of the cathedral, paced up and down its three naves, inspected the crypt containing St. Dominic's remains, and visited the ten chapels that frame the nave and the apse.

The centerpiece of the cathedral is a magnificent high altar, one of Spain's Renaissance jewels. Dioramas of the usual Biblical stories were embellished with gilt and, upon closer inspection, delicate polychrome work and filigreed details. Dazzling artistry notwithstanding, piety and profanity existed side by side, and some of the friezes looked positively pornographic. Others were just plain weird; the carved depiction of the Last Supper showed someone's head on a plate. I couldn't quite figure out what that was all about.

As with most architectural gems along the Camino, you could stand for hours studying the artistic flourishes and skilled workmanship of every frieze and sculpture. But if you did, it would take you a few years to finish the pilgrimage.

Suitably humbled by our cathedral tour, our quartet repaired to El Corridore Hotel for coffee. As we tucked into a *café con leche*, it dawned on us that we could have easily taken a room there instead of begging for a floor mat in a barracks the night before. Then again, we were thinking like pilgrims, not like ladies with credit cards.

Gradually, the rest of our group began to trickle into Santo Domingo bearing tales from their evening. One cluster, having arrived from Azofra, recounted a night spent with the host from hell in a private *refugio*.

"The man was so weird," Serena said. "He welcomed us graciously and offered us wine and food. His place was gorgeous and the rooms were lovely, but as soon as I showered and put on lip gloss he called me a whore and started screaming at me. I thought he would throw us out!"

I wouldn't have traded my floor mat for that accommodation, thank you very much.

As our group assembled and expanded, the dynamics shifted. Decisions made by a small group on the barracks floor the night before were back on the table for a large-group discussion. Why do women analyze everything for hours, come to a conclusion, and then revisit the issue and subject it to another round of microscopic analysis? Because, apparently, we can. And just what occurs in women's washrooms that makes women flip-flop on their decisions?

An example: as I mentioned, the night before Joanna had suggested we move on without the rest of the group. In the morning she had changed her mind, which was fine, though it appeared that her definition of "waiting for the rest of the group" referred only to those women she liked. Then, after asserting once again that she would wait for the others, she suddenly announced in the hotel's café that she wanted to take a cab to the next town. She got up from the table, went to the washroom, and emerged from the loo with an entirely different decision—she would walk. A few minutes later she changed her mind yet again and said she would stay put in order to pass a message on to the others who had yet to arrive. The to-ing and fro-ing drove me mad.

Fed up, Trish and I put on our backpacks and announced we were heading out.

"The others will catch up, or they will troubleshoot this on their own," I said.

"But we need to be here when they arrive!" argued Joanna.

"Maybe they took a cab to the next town," I countered. "How can you be sure when or even if they will arrive? Besides, no one has to babysit anyone here."

Oh, but yes they do. There were plenty of anxious babysitters on this Camino.

"I hate the group dynamics," an exasperated Trish muttered as the two of us marched out of Santo Domingo de la Calzada.

I was looking forward to having Trish as a walking buddy and getting to know her, but just when we reached the edge of town she stopped.

"It's Mother's Day," she said. "I need to call my mother."

"Shall I wait for you?" I asked, trying to decide whether to do likewise.

"No, you go on." And she disappeared to find a phone booth.

I considered returning to the hotel to find another walking buddy, but the idea of re-entering the estrogen pit turned my stomach. The Camino was no longer about fulfilling my heart's desire but about placating a pack of women who did not know what they wanted and who based every decision on what others thought.

My temper inched up. I considered digging the hag flag out of my backpack, but since I was alone, would it even matter? (If a woman silently rages, is she still considered a bitch?) Then, just like the women I had walked away from, I began waffling—between the wish to fulfill a dream and the wish to belong to a group.

For as long as I can remember, I have existed uncomfortably on the periphery of belonging. I don't have problems making friends or being a friend; I have a problem feeling like a friend who matters. I never get the sense that I am more than a cast member, when what I really desire is to be someone's Best Supporting Actor.

Over the years I have joined various groups, clubs, organizations, and boards, but none of them made me feel as if I truly belonged. I don't fault the organizations; I think it has something to do with me. In every situation it was as if I were missing a page or two of the meeting minutes, as if an elemental piece of information had not been communicated to me, and had I possessed it I would have been brought to the epicenter of belonging. Instead, I loitered awkwardly on the margins until I eventually lost interest and bowed out.

I tried solitary projects and pursuits to see if they were a better fit, but although individually enjoyable, none of them gave me the satisfaction that comes from human community and sharing a common cause or goal. Despite the disappointing outcomes, I persist in trying to click with something or someone, wandering like a gypsy in search of her true tribe. It was fitting that I had been steered toward the Camino—the rootless, vagabond lifestyle was a metaphor for my own emotional homelessness.

Although the path out of Santo Domingo de la Calzada was broad and invited ambling, I gravitated to the outer edge. The gravel crunched beneath my feet, my walking stick and my right hand began their practiced conjoined propulsion, and in short order my legs picked up the pace, and my body settled in for the hypnotic journey ahead.

At times it felt as if my brain and my body were acting independently of each other—that my body was saying, "OK, I know what to do. You just concentrate on your thoughts, and I'll take it from here." I would marvel at the instinctive automation of my physical self, how I felt more like a passenger than the driver of my own body.

A church bell rang, the dewy morning air infused my senses, and suddenly I was lost in the white noise of internal thoughts.

Four kilometers out of Santo Domingo, in the tiny village of Grañón, I ran into the nurses. They had retrieved their backpacks in Lograño and had taken a cab to Grañón. Beth's lower back pain was worsening. She and Kate had made a pact that if one of them faltered on the trail, the other would remain by her side.

"We're going to walk slow and maybe stay here a few days," Beth explained with a pinched smile.

I didn't know what to do or say or whether it was rude of me not to offer to stay with them. My gut told me to keep walking, so that's what I did.

At the edge of town, the Camino veered right and down a short hill, its wide dirt path cutting a stark, impressive swath through a panoramic green meadow before disappearing into the distance. I sighed for the natural beauty before me and for the conflicting emotions in my heart.

At a crossroads on the path, a yellow arrow—bent, rusted, sharp—on a short metal pole pointed the way. How apropos, I grumbled, gleaning way too much significance from this sign.

How can someone be on a pilgrimage and be so crabby? I had cursed this walk every step of the way, so how come I was still walking it? Why not just go home? It was physically demanding, but it was also taking an emotional toll on me.

"Arrrrghhhh!" I screamed out loud. I wanted to throw my backpack on the ground and kick it and jump all over it. I was so furiously frustrated. Nothing was turning out the way I had planned.

I thought of some of the others in the group and began to hate them. Their contradictions, their neediness, their high-maintenance whines, their secretive and bitchy cliques, their lack of drive. Their ease at developing a friendly intimacy with others.

I was a mass of rage, the burning bush in a peaceful wilderness. I threw off my backpack and fished about for a water bottle. (The plastic water pack I started the Camino with had proved to be a colossal waste of money.) I alternately belted back gulps of water and stood seething, staring at the crooked yellow arrow.

I rooted around in my backpack for my camera and snapped a picture of the sign. As I returned the camera to my backpack, I accidentally knocked over the water bottle. I now had less than three fingers of water to last me until my destination, and I had no clue how far that was.

Farther up the road, I made out the figure of an old man with a cane walking toward me. I brushed away the tears with my dusty, grimy hands and struggled with my pack—God, it was heavy—as I hoisted it onto my back. I wanted to avoid the old guy because I didn't feel like making nice with anyone. Surprisingly, he reached me before I could get away.

"*Buenos días,*" I smiled, my face streaked with tears and dirt.

Señor launched into conversation. Why do foreigners, upon hearing you utter two words of their language that are universally known, assume you can speak their entire language fluently?

"I don't understand. *No español,*" I fumbled.

But he continued, speaking urgently and gesturing emphatically. Something about Redecilla, the town I was headed for.

"*Ah, sí,*" I said figuring he was telling me that Redecilla was four kilometers ahead.

But no. He knew I did not understand, and he was prepared to stand there until I did. He kept waving his stick, signaling something beyond. "Viloria de Rioja," he kept repeating. At the time, all I heard him say was "Rioja," and I assumed he was telling me that I was in the Rioja Province of Spain and that the wine was good.

I nodded, but he would have none of it. He kept waving and carrying on about Rioja.

"*No Redecilla!*" he said with tremendous agitation.

Had the town disappeared? Was the road out? Had guerrillas overtaken the region? What was he going on about?

"*Ah, gracias. Buenos días,*" I said, and took my leave.

The road snaked on ahead, dusty, pebbly, and empty. I hated being alone, but it was dawning on me that that was the only way I'd get to Santiago. If I did not stick to my dream of completing the Camino, it would slip from my grasp, and I would be sucked into a vortex of group politics and hot flashes.

"By the blisters of my shell-shocked soul," I fumed to myself, "I will get to Santiago."

Thunder rumbled; the air felt twitchy. The body, being an intuitive vessel, knows when a shift is about to happen.

I shuffled into the one-horse town of Redecilla del Camino, which surely translates into Shithole of the Camino. It was hard to imagine an uglier, meaner, and more inhospitable town.

The *refugio*, which appeared to do double duty as the village bar, was run by a hard, cigarette-sucking blonde. She wore a look of utter contempt for each arriving pilgrim, stamping pilgrim passports with unnecessary severity and swatting the air as if we were a swarm of mosquitoes. Her homies, the inebriated bar flies conducting sentry duty from their stools, resembled the stone gargoyles and grotesques that embellished the churches along the Camino's route.

As I gulped back a glass of wine at the bar, a dust-up erupted at the front door, prompting the pie-eyed sentries to swivel unsteadily on their bar stools to gape at the spectacle.

A French pilgrim, who had started his Camino in Le Puy and had already logged a thousand kilometers, was crazed with fatigue and began shaking his first and railing against some of the pilgrims who claimed to be injured.

"They take buses and cabs from one *refugio* to the next and manage to get beds," he wailed, "but even though I walk the entire distance by foot there is no place for me to stay!"

It was hard not to sympathize with him. His accusations were aimed at certain pilgrims, some of whom were in my group, who were abusing a system that permitted injured pilgrims to take cabs to *refugios* and receive priority treatment there.

The innkeeper snarled back at the pilgrim from Le Puy and said she had a room for him at her overflow *refugio*. She grabbed a set of keys and her ever-present cigarette and barked at him to follow her. A few of us tagged along to see if the accommodations were any better than the sardine can–like quarters of the main *refugio*. When we arrived, it was hard to decide which was worse—a room crammed to the rafters with bunk beds or a mattress on the floor in a roomier space. The pilgrim from Le Puy threw his pack defiantly onto one of the mattresses and, without any acknowledgment or thanks, began stripping off. It was becoming apparent that the farther we progressed along the Camino, the shorter the tempers.

Back at the bar, I settled in at a table with Theresa, Trish, and a couple of French-Canadian women we had just met. We drained a bottle of sharp red wine in about five minutes and ordered another.

Theresa gabbed cheerfully with the French Canadians but ignored Trish's and my attempts to converse *en français*. If we managed to utter anything, Theresa would laugh dismissively and apologize to her French tablemates: *"Ce qu'elles disent..."* ("What they are trying to say..."), making us look like pathetic Anglophones.

Noticing my thinly disguised irritation, Theresa took me aside and suggested we slip away for a quiet dinner together.

We found a suitably unappetizing restaurant run by a sour-looking couple—likely relatives of the woman back at the Inn of Les Misérables. The owner grudgingly took our order—what was eating these people?—and yelled some words to the cook, words

I took as ". . . and make sure you blow your nose on their French fries and add cat droppings to their vegetables."

Emboldened by the five glasses of wine I had had earlier at the *refugio* bar and another two gulped as we waited for dinner, I told Theresa I thought she was a pushy broad. I said this, however, in my nicest female-speak.

"You're so confident and gregarious," I gushed. "So much so that it intimidates me. For instance, when I try to speak Spanish or French, you're always correcting me or translating. It's nice of you, but I'll never learn on my own if you don't let me try."

Theresa was less diplomatic about what was bugging her.

"I'm bored with the Camino," she confessed.

"How can anyone be bored with the Camino?" I asked, taken aback by the remark.

"I just am. Getting to Santiago isn't a big deal for me anymore," she shrugged.

I FELL ASLEEP that night at about 8 PM, but it wasn't long before I was wide awake. A few bottles of wine will do that to you. My sleeplessness was also due to the snorers, who were going full bore. One person was making honking sounds, while another was whinnying during the honker's silent intervals. From a corner bunk came snorting sounds; from another bed someone cried out in her sleep: "Dad!" It was an insane asylum.

I could hear water running somewhere, but when I got up to investigate I could not find the source. I returned to my bunk and lay awake trying to guess the time without turning on a light and checking my watch.

Just then the church bell—which, it bears noting, was a mere twenty feet from the bedroom window—began to toll. I counted them off. Forty-two. Yes, forty-two. Short of war, I don't know what would prompt a church to ring its bells forty-two times in the middle of the night. Maybe it was an alarm meant entirely for me: four and two are my lucky numbers. Was this some sort of message?

I threw off my sleeping bag, gathered my belongings—I didn't care if I made a noise, there was plenty in the room already—and made my way through the maze of bunk beds toward the bedroom door.

"Jane, where are you going?" someone whispered.

"I can't sleep," I replied. I had no idea who was speaking to me.

I dragged my gear into the washroom, flicked on a light, and looked at my watch: it was just past midnight; I had slept only four hours.

Lack of sleep was becoming a serious issue. Rarely had I had an uninterrupted night's sleep since beginning the Camino.

I washed and dressed, then lugged my gear downstairs to the lobby.

I thought of the old man with the cane I had encountered on the road to Redecilla that day, and now I understood what he had been trying to tell me: he was warning me about Redecilla, urging me to go beyond this crappy town to the other town with Rioja in it. What was it? Viloria de Rioja? Too late now.

I looked at my watch again. Seven minutes had passed since I last looked at it.

I pulled everything out of my knapsack to see if there was anything I could discard. Then I folded it all up again and neatly replaced it in my pack. That killed eight minutes.

I pondered my options: Go back to bed. Start walking. Quit this stupid pilgrimage and go home.

At 1 AM, I consulted my maps, one of which illustrated the topographical elevations along the Camino. The next leg of the journey looked especially grueling. It was hard to decide if it was better to walk in ignorance or knowledge; knowing you had to face a big climb could make you feel defeated before you hit the trail.

At 2 AM, I studied my English-Spanish phrase book. I could not believe I had come to Spain for an entire month so ill-prepared to speak Spanish.

At 3 AM, I stared at the walls, wondering where some of the characters on the Camino were—the Woman with the Fendi

Scarf, Thomas the Swiss Filmmaker, Pieter the Dane Who Wore Black, Mikael the Ponytailed German. Where were Cathy and Lucy? We had not seen them in days.

By 4:30 AM I was beyond bored. I decided to strike out on my own. I considered leaving a note for my group, but there was no place to post it where any of them would see it.

I strapped on my backpack and headed out the door into the dark, deserted (I hoped!) streets of Redecilla. It was really dark. Really, really dark. And rainy.

I trudged up the main road wondering how, in the darkness, I would be able to see the yellow arrows and Camino signs along the way. Out of nowhere an enormous transport truck screamed past me like a monster on a tear.

Terrified, I sprinted across the highway and then stopped; it was so dark I could barely make out the footpath as it disappeared into what looked like an abyss. It would have been foolhardy to walk in such a place, especially alone, so I turned around, retraced my steps, and reluctantly headed back to the *refugio*.

I resumed my post in the solitary chair in the lobby. And waited. And waited. I decided that the first person who came down the stairs would be the person I would walk with that day.

That person finally materialized at 5:30 AM. I did not know his name, but I knew him as someone who was part of our tribe. He was an older, serious-looking man; tall, fit, and gray haired, with a neatly trimmed gray moustache. Theresa had overheard him making an off-color joke one night and, relaying the incident to our group, suggested that we collectively ignore him.

Now here I was facing someone I had pointedly shunned. I considered changing my decision to walking with the second person who came down the stairs, but I was too worn out to manipulate the rules of my own game.

"*Parlez-vous français?*" I asked, for no other reason than it seemed more logical to ask a question in French than in English. I stuffed my Spanish phrase book into my backpack.

"*Oui*," he replied.

"Well, do you speak English?" I asked, for no other reason than to confuse the situation.

"Yes, I do," he replied impatiently.

"May I walk with you today?" I inquired. "It's dark and rainy out there, and I don't think it's wise to walk alone."

He regarded me with an irritated air for a few seconds, then shrugged. "Sure."

We introduced ourselves stiffly. He was from Belgium, and his name was José—the French pronunciation (Jo-zay), he instructed, not the Spanish one. Naturally, for the first few hours I kept inadvertently calling him by the Spanish pronunciation of José (Ho-zay).

He was securing the last buckle on his backpack when June hobbled down the stairs.

June was the enigma in our group. She didn't share an iota of herself with others and wore the same impassive expression whether people were laughing or having a serious discussion. Her guardedness made her hard to befriend, so most of us steered clear of her.

"I think I have shin splints," she said to me. "I don't think I should walk today at all."

"Do you think you might have to go to the hospital?" I asked.

She shook her head. "I think I just need a rest day."

I told her about my sleepless night and about my decision to quell my restlessness by hitting the trail earlier than usual.

"I'm going to walk with this guy," I told her. "Please tell the others I have left and that I'll meet you all at the next stop—San Juan de Ortega—this evening."

She didn't reply; she simply gave me a tight, enigmatic smile.

She never did relay my message. It was the last time I saw anyone from my group.

I I

AN EERIE calm drifts through the 5 AM world. It's not a frightening time so much as an unknown one. The day's script has yet to be written or even considered.

You have different thoughts at 5 AM than you do at, say, 7 AM. Daylight kick-starts your pulse and brainwaves, and before you know it a to-do list starts to assemble. But in the very early hours, before the Earth has awakened, before the veil of night is lifted, before the mind is contaminated by visual and aural distractions, possibility reigns. In blindness there is clarity and courage.

"This is the earliest I've started out," I said to José, trying to make conversation with my new walking companion. "Do you normally start out this early?"

"I get up a little later," he replied flatly.

"I could barely sleep," I continued chirping away. "Did you hear the church bell last night? It tolled forty-two times! I couldn't sleep after that. I've been awake since midnight."

I was beginning to sound as annoying as Cathy.

"No, I did not hear them," he responded. His short answers indicated he was not a morning person, so I shut up.

Darkness lifted, revealing gunmetal gray skies that drizzled rain. Beth's clever mantra sprang to mind: "There's no such thing as bad weather, just bad gear."

My thoughts turned to rain ponchos, a piece of gear I had contrarily refused to pack for a couple of reasons. Rain ponchos cover your pack and your body, which is a good thing; but they can fly up around your head in a strong wind, which is not a good thing.

The other thing I had against ponchos was their color: I could only find orange ponchos. Honestly, even in the dark and the rain, even on a pilgrimage, who in their right mind would don an orange poncho? Oh sure, orange is meant to make you visible, but who wants to be seen wearing an item of clothing that makes you look like a walking garbage bag?

Serena had picked up a few disposable plastic rain ponchos in a clear blue color from a hardware store in Canada and had thoughtfully given me one. With the rain showing no signs of letting up, I had been forced to fish it out of my soggy backpack and put it on. To say it was hideous was stretching the bounds of understatement. Even José looked embarrassed to be seen with me.

As happens with thoughts that are pondered privately for a little too long, opinions emerge until they morph into a Big Complaint that is so obvious you are left wondering why the rest of the world has not cottoned on to it. The Big Complaint was this:

What are the designers of outdoor adventure clothing thinking when they sit in front of a drawing board? Do any of them, perchance, possess a geek filter? A practical, middle-age woman, the type who wears sensible shoes and watches an endless loop of the *Antiques Roadshow* or gardening shows would likely not object to something like an orange poncho. But what about her hipper counterparts, the refuseniks caught in midlife with a few pairs of pointy-toed, spike-heeled boots in their closet?

The garb of the hiking world is dowdy and shapeless, nowhere near as sexy and sleek as what the running crowd wears. Is it so difficult to design hiking pants in, say, a straight-legged, relaxed version with Velcro legs that tear away into capris? Something that can take you from the hiking trail to a casually elegant restaurant? Would it kill designers to use real colors, like moss green, cranberry, Wedgwood blue, black, or soft pink? What's with paramedic orange? And Gestapo gray? Who wants to pull on gray pants in the morning? And those tops? Please. No one looks good in pale green or lavender. No one. It is as if a warehouse filled with bolts of rejected fabric exists somewhere solely for the use of designers of outdoor adventure clothing.

I glanced up at José, who was walking ahead of me and seemed deep in thought. Do guys think of this stuff? Is he regretting his decision to pack two T-shirts instead of three? Is he having a heated discussion with himself on the merits of, say, socks? Is he wondering whether the medium-density padding was worth the extra cost over the pair with a higher polypropylene content?

He was probably thinking about sex. They say men think about sex every fifteen seconds.

"What part of Belgium are you from?" I asked in a worldly manner that suggested I was well acquainted with the parts of Belgium.

"Brussels," he replied. "You know Belgium then?"

"I visited it many years ago," I answered casually without letting on that "many years ago" actually meant thirty-five years ago. "There was a lovely town called Bruges. It had a beautiful square, and there was a gorgeous stone bridge that spanned a small river. It was such a romantic town that I vowed to move there one day."

"My mother-in-law lives in Bruges!" He perked up at the mention of something familiar. "You're right. It is a beautiful place. And I know the bridge you're speaking about."

"Then you must know the art gallery, too," I said. "I set off the alarm system and almost got arrested when I got too close to a painting. It was the triptych by Hieronymus Bosch—*The Garden of Earthly Delights*—do you know it? It mesmerized me as a teenager; to see it in person took my breath away. I leaned in to examine the multitude of tiny characters and the paint strokes

that created them. I couldn't help myself. I thought I could touch
Bosch himself and absorb a smidgen of his soul if I ran my finger over a tiny part of the canvas, and so I did. Suddenly all sorts
of alarms went off and the guards came rushing into the gallery
pointing their machine guns at me!"

"What did you do?" José asked.

"What every Canadian does—I apologized."

He chuckled. I can be such a card early in the morning.

The ice was now broken, and the superficial layers of our lives
began to melt.

José was sixty-five and had retired from a career as a bank
manager. He and his wife had raised a son, and now they were
raising a granddaughter; the son and his wife had divorced and
both were too busy with their careers. José did not begrudge this.

"She is like our daughter," he said with grandfatherly love. "We
cannot imagine her not being in our lives."

José's granddaughter—her name was Fiona, he said—was
about the same age as my daughter, and soon we were trading
and comparing stories about the challenges—to put it politely—
of raising twelve-year-old girls.

"Does your daughter get embarrassed when she walks with you
in public?" he asked. "I used to love the way Fiona held my hand
when we went out for walks, but now she is suddenly repulsed by
it. Yet when I tuck her into bed at night, she doesn't hesitate to
put her arms around my neck and say, 'I love you, Poppa.' I don't
understand it."

It is always a relief to hear other parents voice complaints
about their children; what we perceive to be unique to our own
children is, in fact, universal.

"So, why are you walking the Camino?" I asked. After "What's
your name?" it is the most common question pilgrims ask one
another.

"I am walking the Camino because of my wife," José said with
a plaintive edge to his voice. "She has a very strong faith, and I

do not. It has always been an issue in our marriage. So I am walking the Camino to see if I can find faith."

That was heavy.

"I'm amazed at how she accepts faith without question," said José. "She doesn't intellectualize it nor does she make apologies for it. And yet I wrestle with faith like it's an alligator."

The banking business, José admitted, was not a place where faith had much of a chance to be stoked. He said he had bartered his soul for a comfortable life and a measure of security.

"I was always compromising what I felt was right," he said, shaking his head in shame. "Eventually I no longer recognized myself. It was stressful. Banking is not a very nice business. Too much greed."

I had heard similar stories from other pilgrims—lawyers, educators, managers, health care workers, artists, researchers, entrepreneurs, CEOs, accountants—all of them expressing disillusionment with a working life that had overtaken their personal lives like purple loosestrife. They had come to the Camino with the hope of reclaiming their self-respect and their integrity. The curious contradiction here is that we live in an era of the so-called enlightened workplace, which purports to be all about balance and ethics. Yet, employees feel more duped and conflicted about their work than ever before.

"You can feel it in your body when your work is wrong," said José.

"Yes," I nodded remembering my own experiences. "In your throat and your stomach. It's the feeling of guilt."

For miles we persevered through squishy, rain-soaked fields, along hard asphalt roads cloaked in fog, our heads bent against the wind and rain. Occasionally José and I would launch into an animated conversation lasting several minutes, then our words would peter out as we drifted back into ourselves, bowing our heads in contemplation as the rain sluiced off our headgear.

Outside Tosantos we spied a roadside café. José wanted a

coffee to warm himself up; I was in need of something cold to quench my thirst.

"*Una cerveza, por favor,*" I told the bartender, glancing at the clock behind him that read 10:30 AM. It's never too early for a beer in Spain.

I shook off the rain like a dog. My hair was plastered to my soaked scalp. My flimsy rain poncho clung to my backpacked body. I was chilled to the bone, and my nose was dripping with rain or snot—I am not sure which. Whatever. I slid my sleeve across it and immediately embraced my inner bag lady. I could not begin to imagine how awful I looked; I was just grateful no one was around to see me.

"Hey, it's El Camino Jane!" someone shouted

I spun around and saw the Three American Boys sitting at a table. They began to pound the table with their hands and chant, "El Camino Jane! El Camino Jane!"

I smiled broadly, knowing that at this point my smile was my best feature—hell, it was my only feature. Seriously, had there been an Attractiveness Code in this bar, I would have been grabbed by the ear and thrown out the door. Still, as dirty and unkempt as I was, I felt great. My body was stronger than in my off-Camino life; my normally sensitive, dry skin—on which I had slathered hundreds of dollars' worth of face creams with little visible benefit—was naturally hydrated and clear thanks to daily exercise and the fresh, dewy air of Spain's northern climate. I looked like hell, but I felt heavenly. Slovenly and heavenly.

The Boys rose from their seats to greet me—such wonderful manners—and I introduced them to José.

"You've been rockin' us," one smiled at me, as he sat back down.

"Pardon?" I asked, slightly taken aback. In Canada, the term "rockin'" has a slight sexual connotation. I think they meant "You're smoking us," which means I was either keeping pace or surpassing them. Occasionally there's a language barrier between Canadians and Americans, at times conveniently so.

"Yeah, you're El Camino Jane," grinned the other lad. "You've got a reputation, you know."

Like the Woman with the Fendi Scarf or the Guy Who Creeped Us Out, I too had a moniker. Although the boys had their own pet name for me, I learned that I was referred to on the trail as the Canadian Woman Who Walks Fast. (Later I would become known as the Canadian Woman Who Walks So Fast She Lost Her Group.) This was the lingua franca of the Camino—pithy identifiers that dispensed with the need for elaborate detail. It was easier to reduce everyone to an easy summary than to say, "Do you know John?" and then describe John's hair color, height, nationality, profession, backpack color, etc.

The Three American Boys had become a familiar sight in my corner of the Camino. They were in their early twenties, college kids. Ben and Ian were brothers—they looked like twins, in fact, and I confess I was always calling one by the other's name—and Peter had been their friend since toddlerhood. "He's like an honorary brother," Ben said. Ben and Ian were tall, lanky fellows with short dark brown hair. Trim, youthful beards outlined their angular jaws, and a tuft of hair had been groomed to punctuate the area just below their lower lips. Their mouths seemed perpetually curled into a mischievous smirk. They wore matching deep blue jackets and beige soft-brimmed hats that tied under their chins. Peter was slightly shorter and fairer skinned, with sandy red hair and the same hint of beard bordering his jaw. The trio was never apart.

"We should get going," said José, draining his coffee cup. We bade farewell to the boys and took our leave.

It rained for the rest of the day. The map indicated a hostel, about five kilometers away, in Villafranca Montes de Oca. But one of the first things you learn when you hike is that maps lie. They especially lie when you're desperate and cold and straddling the fine line between madness and murder.

Pilgrims also lie. A couple we encountered on a steep climb out of Villafranca Montes de Oca told us there were no beds in San Juan de Ortega.

"No, no, there is no place to stay in San Juan," they said in halting English, as they scrambled to get ahead of us. "Nothing there. Just a church."

"No room?" I asked. "My guidebook says there's a place to stay."

The pilgrims quickly changed their tack.

"It's full," they replied.

"How can that be?" I countered. "You can't book in advance at these places."

"Maybe they don't want us to go because they don't want us competing with them for beds," José whispered.

We continued to climb, plodding up a muddy, rocky steep hill behind the Foreign Couple.

"There is no room there," they insisted repeatedly to us.

José and I pressed on.

It was hard not to just call it quits; the climb was excruciating.

"Don't take such long strides," José suggested. "It makes you more tired. Take small steps when you climb a hill."

I took his advice, and to my surprise I did not feel nearly as winded; still, the climb was tough.

Half an hour later, when we thought we would die from the strain, the grade eased somewhat but continued upward through pine forests. On a clear day, this would have been rather pretty terrain.

I tried to distract myself from the exhaustion and the pouring rain by concentrating on the surroundings. Were those little white flowers edelweiss? Was that a cuckoo I heard in the woods? But mind games were of no use; I was beyond exhausted. There seemed no end in sight, and yet there was no alternative but to keep walking.

The trail finally leveled out, but it was hard to decide which was better—climbing, or trudging through a wet, muddy, rut-infested logging road. We careened all over the trail, trying the left side of the road to see if the ground was firmer, then sidling back to the extreme right side to test the ground there. To no avail; it was wall-to-wall slop.

The forest bordering the trail was thick with fog and suspicion. A cuckoo's distinctive cry startled the silence.

According to a medieval manuscript known as the *Codex Calixtinus*, this was the site of one of twenty-two miracles attributed to St. James.

The miracle in question took place in 1108 and concerned a man from France who was desperate to have children but, owing to the considerable weight of his sins (unfortunately, his transgressions were not explained), had been rendered sterile. In a last-ditch attempt at forgiveness and fertility, the man took his pleas to St. James. At the Cathedral of Santiago de Compostela he wept and begged "with all his heart" for a son, according to the *Codex's* report. The man returned home, and after a three-day rest period he made love to his wife. From that union a son was born. His delighted parents, not surprisingly, named him James.

When the boy turned fifteen, he and his family made the pilgrimage to Santiago. But along the way, in the area where I was now walking, the boy became ill and—as is dramatically described—"breathed out his soul."

His mother, torn by grief, screamed to the heavens and demanded that St. James restore her son's life or she would kill herself. The next day, during the funeral procession, the boy suddenly stirred to life. He told the stunned mourners that St. James had received his soul but had then been commanded by God to return it to the boy's body. (Apparently, decisions made by middle management get second-guessed in Heaven, too.) St. James took young James by the hand and directed him to continue the Camino with his parents.

It was a hat-trick miracle: forgiveness, restored fertility, and resuscitation all rolled neatly into one little story. But the circumstances surrounding this miracle vexed the Church. Was it possible, the Church asked itself, for a dead person (St. James) to bring back to life another dead person (young James)? There had been stories about people raising the dead, but never had the Church encountered a dead-person-to-dead-person resurrection. After much debate, the issue was settled with lawyerlike hairsplitting. If a dead person cannot bring another dead person back to life, but a living person is able to do so, then one can only conclude that St. James is not dead; he is alive with God. The Church ruled that henceforth saints have the power to bring a dead person back to life with God's help.

This is probably as good a time as any to explain the *Codex Calixtinus*. This illuminated manuscript, which glorifies the cult of St. James, was penned by the monks of Cluny around 1150. Scholars of medieval literature refer to the *Codex* variously as Europe's oldest tourist guide and the first written piece of French propaganda. It is much more than that; it is a rare glimpse into the Camino's earliest days from a musical, ethnological, artistic, historical, political, and literary perspective. Want a slice of medieval life? Read the *Codex*.

No historic era was so wrapped up in faith and mysticism than the medieval one. Liturgy, rites, rituals, miracles, cults, rumor, and mythmaking abounded. Everything had meaning—layers of meaning—with myriad interpretations.

Pope Calixtus II was a well-known booster of the Camino, but it is his secretary, an enterprising monk named Aymeric Picaud, who is widely credited for creating the *Codex*. He is listed as its editor as well as one of the authors. A first folio edition now resides in the archives of the Cathedral of Santiago de Compostela.

Picaud is also the one fingers point to when questions are raised about who tinkered with the timeline of the *Codex*; the foreword and a few of the miracles attributed to and recounted by Calixtus are dated *after* the Pope's death. There is little doubt that Picaud appropriated his master's name to give the book papal authority.

The *Codex* is a five-book anthology. Book I is a collection of sermons and hymns, Book II lists the twenty-two miracles, Book III explains the significance of the shell, and Book IV links Charlemagne to the Camino via the visitation by St. James.

It is Book V, Picaud's little masterpiece, that gets all the attention, however. It's a vivid, zesty, and at times scurrilous and heavily jingoistic bit of travel journalism. It was the Fodor's of its day. Under Picaud's quill, the French are paragons of civility, while the Spanish, particularly the Navarrese, are knuckle-dragging heathens who sodomize their women and their livestock and affix chastity belts to their mules. (No mention is made of the same courtesy being extended to the womenfolk.) In addition, the Navarrese wear black kilts and hairy leather sandals, and they eat with their hands and drink from a communal cup. Picaud writes:

> This is a barbarous nation, distinct from all other nations in habits and way of being, full of all kind of malice, and of black color. Their face is ugly, and they are debauched, perverse, perfidious, disloyal and corrupt, libidinous, drunkard, given to all kind of violence, ferocious and savage, impudent and false, impious of mouth and uncouth, cruel and quarrelsome, incapable of anything virtuous, well-informed of all vices and iniquities.

I was grateful to be traveling in this century and not an earlier one.

JOSÉ AND I continued to pound the mud-drenched trail to San Juan with increasing despondency. We were not happy campers.

A forest bordered the path, and fog was packed like cotton batting into the spaces between the trees; ghostly wisps encircled trunks and limbs. God, I thought, it looks just like my brain: so cluttered and jumbled, so jammed with confusion.

A few hours earlier I had felt clear and clean, but the weight of the Camino was once again bearing down on me. The Camino had a way of inflicting this mood swing on pilgrims; you would be happy one minute, and then inexplicably your mood would darken the next. Conversely, within an hour of being sad, you would find yourself on the brink of shedding tears of joy and contentment.

But now, the darkness had returned and with it an internal inquisition framed around an acute desire to go home.

What am I trying to prove? In the grand scheme of my life, will it matter whether or not I finish the Camino? Why do I need to test myself? Why is any of this important?

I could not come up with convincing answers to my questions, and that pretty much nailed it for me. I didn't need to be tested; I did not need to wade through slop to achieve enlightenment or endure sleepless nights or bitchy women or torn fingernails. What was abundantly clear was that I couldn't stand the Camino any longer. The rain, the cold, the mud—it was relentless, oppressive, and pointless. And so I decided that my Camino was over.

If nothing else, nearly two weeks on the Camino had taught me that my lot in life, all things considered, was far easier than that of other people. Stop complaining, stop searching for something better, stop mourning lost relationships, I told myself. Just concentrate on being a good mom. Really, get over them now, I scolded myself. So what if I'm single? I have the love of my family and friends. I should be grateful for that. What sort of romance had I hoped to find in a relationship where someone was messing with my head and my affections?

When I finally acknowledged that the Camino was too much for me and that I had had enough and had learned my lesson, I felt an incomparable sense of relief. I felt free, liberated from my guilt.

I heard the cuckoo a second time. I glanced over at the foggy pine forest, and to my astonishment the fog had lifted. The cotton batting between the trees, the wispy ghosts—it was all gone and the vista was perfectly clear. I took that as my epiphany, my sign from God that it was OK for me to go home.

Strategizing the end of the hike began immediately. Once I reached San Juan, I would rally my comrades and tell them it was over for me. I was going home! Yes! Home! Where it's warm, where people love me, where I can retreat into my sanctuary with my family, where there is no mud latching itself to shoes and clothing.

The cuckoo cried a third time. I watched a handful of pilgrims ahead struggle with their footing through the mud. Poor wet, cold, dirty suckers, I thought. I am so out of here. As soon as I get to San Juan, I'll check the maps, locate the nearest city, get a cab, find an airport, and go home.

My pace quickened. Ha! Ha! I was practically delirious. Home! Home! I could already smell the crisp sheets on my cozy bed. I started a mental list of the groceries I needed to pick up once I got home; I thought about the summer months ahead. Should I work on my garden? Fix the fence?

I was so busy making plans I hardly noticed when José and I reached our destination. I decided I would wait before telling him about my decision to quit the Camino.

"Shall we get a drink?" he asked as we paused in the downpour.

"No, let's get a bed first, and there'd better be one," I muttered, remembering the cautionary comments made a few hours earlier by the Foreign Couple—now forever known as the Pilgrims Who Lied.

I prepared for the worst when we were greeted—and I use that term loosely—by the *refugio*'s gatekeeper, a sour-looking old crone. She indeed had beds for us, she said, and pointed a crooked finger in the direction we were to go.

We paid our money and signed in.

"G-G-*Gracias*," we shivered through blue lips.

Two flights upstairs and a long haul through two cavernous rooms later, we found our bunks. We flung our wet packs onto the floor and then ourselves onto the bunks. There were plenty of unclaimed beds. Loads, in fact. The lesson here: never trust a pilgrim.

"I need a drink," said José. I nodded.

The lone bar in San Juan—a cozy, low-ceilinged establishment—was jumping when we stepped over the threshold. A huge fire was burning and warmed our wet, cold bodies immediately. The sight and sound of happy people cheered us up. Every inch of the place was crammed with pilgrims. With nowhere to sit and no energy left in us to stand, José and I found a step leading into the kitchen and crouched down there. The waiter served us anyway.

José began chatting with an older Frenchman who was seated at a table next to our stoop. José explained to me that this was the Frenchman's sixth time walking the Camino.

I looked at him with incredulity.

"Six times? *Six?*" I held up six fingers.

The Frenchman smiled back and nodded proudly.

The bar was so noisy that I could barely hear myself asking, "What made you want to do this more than once?"

"Every time I do it I see something different," he said. "It always looks new to me. I learn new things and meet new people. Each time is a new experience."

Right, buddy. There's a big world out there, more lovely and stirring than the Camino de Santiago de Compostela.

A couple of people left, and José and I got seats at a table with a young woman from Australia and a fellow from Austria. We filled our glasses to the brim with red wine, gulped them back voraciously, and poured a second round. The wine warmed my frozen veins and hardened heart.

After ordering dinner, we exchanged information with our tablemates about the route that day. By our calculation, José and I had walked thirty-eight kilometers, the longest distance I had done on the Camino. Actually, it was the longest distance I had walked in one day in my entire life. And I felt every step of it.

"There's a Mass tonight. Are you going?" José asked as we walked back to the *refugio*.

"What time?"

"I think it's at eight," he answered.

Jesus. Is it not enough that I've walked thirty-eight kilometers through rain and rocks and mud and hideous steep climbs, and now I'm supposed to go to church, too? Is this a pilgrimage or boot camp?

"I probably will," I answered sweetly, "though eight o'clock is rather late, don't you think?"

I untied my boot laces and pried my shoes away from my soaking socks. The shoes rolled like two-hundred-pound boulders on the bare floor. There was no way in hell I was going to Mass—I was going to bed. I undid my backpack, reached in for my toiletry bag, a towel, my wallet, some clean clothes, and headed for the bathroom.

As I stripped off and got into the shower a woman a few stalls down from me let out a gasp.

"*Il fait froid! Il n'y a pas d'eau chaud!*"

Sucks to be her, I chuckled to myself. I turned on the tap. It was as if Death himself had entered the room. I groped for the shower taps to shut them off.

With every second I remained on the Camino, I felt myself edging closer to the stereotype of the Ugly American. What sort of goddamn country doesn't have hot water? Is this modern Western civilization, or did I take a detour somewhere and end up in the fourth century? If tetanus wasn't already marching through my system, pneumonia was following close behind.

"You had a cold shower after walking all day through the rain and the cold?" José scolded me the next morning as we set off for Burgos. "Then you walked around with wet hair?"

I didn't care. I was going home.

My plans had altered slightly from the day before. I wanted off the Camino, but I also wanted the piece of parchment attesting that I had completed it. I hadn't flown across an ocean and stomped nearly three hundred kilometers just to return home empty-handed.

I had learned from several pilgrims that to qualify for the *credencial* you only had to complete the last hundred kilometers of the pilgrimage by foot. Well, that was doable. I decided I would walk to Burgos, take the train to Sarria, walk from Sarria to San-tiago—a distance of about 110 kilometers—and then fly home. If I stuck to the map, I would be done in four days. Still, four days is a long time when you want to quit something.

I was fine with my abbreviated Camino—really I was. I would get to Santiago but not the way I had originally planned. I would tell the group—when I saw them—that they would have to make their own decisions about when, how, and where their Camino ended.

Speaking of my group, where the hell were they? I had scoured the *refugio* the night before and again the next morning before José and I left, but they were nowhere to be found. I was certain that I would reconnect with them in Burgos.

The pelting rain had been replaced by a steady drizzle. The thick fog had stayed with us, however, and at times it was impos-sible to see where we were going. I resisted the urge to ask José whether all this was worth his search for faith. Had Satan materi-alized from the fog and asked, "Will you renounce your faith in exchange for a five-star hotel, big fluffy white towels, a body mas-sage, and endless pots of *cafés con leche*?" José and I would have been tripping over one another to be the first to enlist.

That morning José and I had availed ourselves of the "con-tinental breakfast" that was included in the price of our board. Never have I seen so many miserable, sullen people gathered around a table. I've been to funerals that were more upbeat.

In the spacious Spartan kitchen of the *refugio*, we were given the luxury of tearing a chunk from a baguette that had long passed its best-before date and drinking coffee reheated in a bent metal saucepan on a stove that Methuselah had used.

If this was the epitome of a Christian life, then I was ready to join the Scientologists. Oh, I know, the whole idea is to be grate-ful for small mercies, to be thankful that you have a morsel of stale bread to nibble and a cup of hot liquid to warm you. But if you think you can bring humanity to its knees in gratitude with this sort of stuff, you're wrong. Such pathetic offerings make people grumpy and resentful, not grateful.

The Camino was beginning to strike me as a spiritual exercise for those who liked their spirituality with a side order of whips. Worse, this was manufactured penury—I knew it, and every other pilgrim knew it. We were there because we could afford to be there. We were all pampered pilgrims.

Was the tired, wizened old woman shuffling around the kitchen before me any kind of an advertisement for a life devoted to God? How much more uplifting it would be to have vibrant men and women running these places to invigorate the spiritually cynical. I don't intend any disrespect, but a bunch of ratty people shuffling around looking as if they're ten minutes from death do not make me want to fall on my knees except to say, "Get me the hell out of here!" Note to Pope: your pilgrim routes could use a face-lift in the human resources department, and while you're at it, throw some cash at some of the shabbier *refugios*, starting with San Juan de Ortega.

Not that I cared so much; I was going home.

The fog had lifted somewhat when José and I arrived at the top of a large, sloping meadow.

"Barbed wire fencing on the left and a quarry and telephone poles on the right," said José, reading from his guidebook. He surveyed the scene to spot the landmarks and nodded with satisfaction. "We're on the right track."

What the guidebook failed to mention was that the meadow, under certain conditions, was prone to viscous mud and dung. These were the certain conditions. Every step we took coated our boots in thick clops of the stuff, which clung to our trousers. We walked four steps. Stopped. Scraped the mud from our boots. Walked four steps. Stopped. Scraped. Walked four steps. And on and on. The mud, in just a few steps, would be packed four to six inches thick on our boots. It was like walking in platform shoes through quicksand. How on Earth would one-legged Sally manage this? I could not imagine a more difficult descent. Usually a descent could be relied on to offer respite but not this time.

Somehow José was able to get through the mire more quickly than I did. He was so far ahead that I hoped he couldn't hear me scream and sob obscenities to the Creator: "Why must everything be so harsh, God? Is it not enough that it's pissing rain? That I'm fucking freezing?"

Then again maybe José had heard me, because at the end of the fence line he suddenly stopped and waited for me. He was an awfully decent fellow.

By the time we arrived in Burgos, José and I were beside ourselves with exhaustion. The city was large and noisy and bustling with traffic; the yellow arrows faded into a landscape of multi colored directional signs, massive billboards, flashing traffic lights, honking horns, and looming buildings.

"There's a travel agency," José huffed as we reached the main square of Burgos. I followed him in.

He paused at the door and turned to me.

"I am not going to the *refugio*," he confessed. "I need a hotel—a bath and a real bed. I'm exhausted. I need a few days here to just rest."

"I understand," I said. "I'm going to carry on to the *refugio*. My friends are probably there. I'm not sure what I am going to do afterward, whether I'm going to leave the Camino or rest or keep going."

We exchanged e-mail addresses and embraced like old friends.

"I could not have come this far without you," I said. "Thank you for being so kind and generous to me."

And then he was gone.

I stood alone, wondering what to do next.

"Can I help you?" the travel agent said in clear, welcome English.

"I need to know where to find the pilgrim *refugio*," I said. "And the bus station. I need to take a bus or a train."

She took out a tourist map of Burgos and drew a line from where we were standing to the *refugio*.

"It looks like a long way," I said.

"It's about two kilometers," she said. "Not far."

No, not far if you haven't already walked twenty kilometers through shit and mud.

"As for the bus or train, you should come back tomorrow morning. You cannot buy tickets ahead of time. Unless you want to go now. You could get a bus or train to Sarria right now. The station is very close. Here, let me show you."

She drew another line and gave me directions, but I didn't pay attention. I was panicking. I had the power and ability to end the Camino at that very moment, but I hesitated. Should I stay? Should I go? Wasn't there a song by the Clash about that?

A few minutes later, I stood in front of Burgos Cathedral staring vacantly at the fifteen or so steps that led to the front portico. I did not have the energy to climb half of them. I stared at the façade, wondering what to do and where to go. Bus? Train? *Refugio*? Door number one, door number two, or door number three?

I had lost all understanding of buses and trains. They had become unfamiliar territory. The only thing I knew were *refugios*, so I headed toward the Burgos *refugio*. Maybe my group was there or had left word for me.

I quickened my pace, crossed a bridge at the Plaza Castilla, and turned right at the Avenida de Palencia. I saw a yellow arrow and farther along a large sign: *Refugio por Peregrinos*.

I handed the *refugio* keeper my pilgrim passport.

"Ah, another Canadian," he said ruefully and then, narrowing his eyes: "You came by bus, too?"

"I walked," I said indignantly. "From San Juan de Ortega. Are there other Canadians here?"

"There were many last night," he said pointing to the registry.

I turned the registry around to scan the list. Ten members of my group had signed their names. I looked at the date.

"Last night?" I asked.

"*Sí*," the man replied. "People were not happy. They said the Canadians came by bus. They are not real pilgrims."

I flushed with embarrassment and anger. So that was it. They had traveled here by bus. Theresa had said she was bored with the Camino. Now I understood. All of them were now on a bus tour of Spain, and they had not left so much as a note of explanation.

I nursed my hurt feelings over wine and a salad in a nearby bar. Damn women. First they beg to come along with me on this odyssey, and then they band together and abandon me.

For the next hour, I wore myself out trying to decide what to do next and how to do it. I was afraid to make a hasty decision about going home, because I knew that once I got there I would instantly regret the decision.

I stared at the maps, hoping for direction in a choppy sea of options. Should I take the train to Sarria? Should I hop a bus for Villafranca and stay in a hotel for a few days to rest? Should I find an Internet café and contact my travel agent?

My thoughts drifted to my children. For the last several months, I had longed to escape them, craving a respite from parental obligations and teenage angst. (You can't spend enough time away from teenage angst, in my opinion.) Now, barely two weeks away from them, I was desperate to bury my face in their hair and kiss their hands, desperate for the sanctuary of familiar and familial love.

Back at the *refugio*, I ran into the Three American Boys, minus one.

"Have you seen my brother?" Ben asked.

He wasn't frantically worried that his brother was missing— he knew he'd show up eventually—but loss of any kind was felt acutely on the Camino. All you really had to save your sanity was your walking companions.

I told Ben about my group, careful not to let bitterness creep into my voice or allow the gathering gloom of loneliness to set off a flood of tears. I confided that I was tired and that I was going to quit.

"No! You can't! You've come this far! You have to finish," Ben urged. "Maybe you just need a day off or a good sleep."

I retreated to my bunk still wondering what to do. It was only 6:45 PM, but I could think of nothing I wanted more than to burrow deep into my sleeping bag and escape the barrage of options crowding my head and demanding resolution.

Infuriatingly, there was too much activity around to allow me to sleep. By 8:30, the din had risen: crinkling chip bags, slurping drinks, people packing and unpacking their knapsacks, or expelling phlegm from their throats.

I rolled onto my stomach and sighed. Desperate situations require desperate measures.

I reached into my backpack and pulled out a small pouch.

I do not take medication of any kind, not even vitamins, but when my mother had pressed a few tabs of morphine into my hand before I left for Spain "because you never know," I had tucked them in my backpack to humor her. You've got to love a mom who dispenses with equal gravitas advice and morphine.

I split a tab in half and swallowed it. I wanted sleep, a very long, deep sleep. An enormous German had claimed the bunk above me, and I wanted to be comatose before he hoisted his orcalike frame into it. If the bunk caved under his weight, I reckoned I'd at least be asleep before I was killed.

As I waited for the morphine to take effect, somewhere in the hallucinatory haze of noise that permeated the room I heard someone call my name very softly.

I poked my head out of my sleeping bag. Ben was standing in the doorway of the dorm scanning the room. When his eyes landed on me he smiled in recognition and came over.

"Did you find your brother?" I asked.

"Yes," he whispered kneeling at my bedside. "Yes, he arrived a little while ago. How are you feeling?"

My quivering lower lip was his answer.

"You know something? Whenever I feel down or homesick my mom gets me one of these," he said as he gingerly unfolded a napkin and displayed a large coconut macaroon. "It always makes me feel better, and I thought it might make you feel better, too."

My tears could not be restrained a second longer, and they tumbled out drenching the hem of my sleeping bag. Here I was, alone in the middle of Spain, and this young man whom I barely knew—but wanted to adopt immediately—had shown true compassion. His gesture overwhelmed me.

"I'm so sorry," I sobbed.

"No, don't cry," he said patting my arm. "We're all sore and tired. The Camino is really hard. We're going to keep going until León; then we'll get a hotel room and take a day off. Go to sleep. You'll feel better in the morning. But first have a taste of this. I swear you'll feel better."

"Thanks," I sputtered. "Goodnight."

I burrowed back into my sleeping bag, took a nibble of the macaroon, and closed my eyes. But sleep continued to elude me. Perhaps when taken with a coconut macaroon morphine loses its potency.

I heard voices whispering in French, and I opened my eyelids just a crack. A young couple in the next bunk was looking at me, checking to see if I was asleep. Certain that I was, the man got out of his sleeping bag wearing only a skimpy pair of black briefs, flicked off the lights and scooted back to his bunk. I heard the rustle of sleeping bags, and against the faint light coming in from the window opposite me, I caught the silhouette of his girlfriend moving her legs into a bent position. She let out a muffled moan. Trust the French.

Several minutes later pilgrims began entering the room, groping their way in the dark toward their bunks. Another interminable din arose and then subsided.

Just when I thought things had finally settled down for the night there was a loud commotion at the front door of the *refugio*. Someone struggled with the latch, then burst through and ran across the hall toward the bathroom. For the next few minutes we listened to a man vomiting. Loudly and prodigiously.

Each of us, tucked tightly in our bunks, held our breath. Please God, I prayed, don't let him be the fat man above my bunk. Pleeease!

The door to our room creaked open. Every eye darted toward the door—and then we uttered a collective sigh of relief when we saw that it wasn't the Vomiting Pilgrim but a sweet and very sober Australian woman who had returned from a sightseeing tour of Burgos.

12

BY THE time I hit the two-week mark, I couldn't remember whether the Camino was about St. James or Rick James. The pilgrimage was turning me into a superfreak.

I waded into the *meseta*, the legendary crazy land of the Camino that, based on past accounts, packs an experience equivalent to two hits of LSD. The *meseta* is a vast, treeless plain. It is here that pilgrims lose their minds—if they haven't already done so—to a psychosis not unlike Jerusalem syndrome, the psychological disorder that causes normally sane visitors to the Holy Land to trade their clothes for togas, convinced that they are Christ, Mary Magdalene, or disciples of either. They roam the city shouting psalms, Bible verses, hymns, and spirituals. I did all those things save for singing spirituals; I don't know any spirituals, so I substituted heavy metal.

I know what you're thinking: hey, wasn't she going to board a train or a bus for Sarria and pick up the Camino there? Well, yes, I was, and then I changed my mind—at least twelve times.

When I emerged from my morphine haze at the Burgos *refugio*, almost all the pilgrims had cleared out. The French Couple

Who Had Sex had left; the Fat German was cramming the last few belongings into his knapsack while clearing his nasal passages through his throat. His tricornered felt hat sat at the end of my bunk, and I resisted the urge to kick it off.

In the bathroom I bumped into the young Australian girl. She was going into Burgos for breakfast, so I invited myself along. We arrived at a dismal, dirty hole that, in its off hours, must have been a heroin den.

I fell into conversation with some other pilgrims who were mapping out their day: a thirty-something guy from Chicago, an older woman from France, and a lost-looking young woman from Denmark.

Chicago was expounding in his thick Midwestern accent about how Americans were getting the shaft from the rest of the world, given what they had suffered on 9/11.

"How long are you guys going to dine out on 9/11?" I said with irritation. "Why don't you stop invading other countries and start looking in the mirror?"

A fearlessness rose in me. It felt good to speak my mind. In Europe, I didn't have to censor myself like I did back in Canada, where the media were behaving like lapdogs in swallowing and regurgitating the propaganda coming out of Washington about poor, misunderstood America for a public that accepted it without question. Contrary opinions could get you shunned from polite society or, worse, earn you passage to Guantanamo Bay. Europe was more tolerant of free speech.

"Hey, at least we do things," Chicago shot back. "You Canadians just sit on the sidelines and cheer the winning team. I'd rather go in with my guns blazing than sit on my ass when my values and principles are being attacked."

"How far are you going today?" interjected Denmark, hoping to ward off an international incident. She wanted the Canadian Lady Who Walked Fast to set the pace for the day.

I wanted to reply, "Well, I'm heading to Burgos, taking a bus to Sarria, and walking the last hundred kilometers because I'm lazy and I want to go home." But I didn't want to be known as the Canadian Lady Who Bailed in Burgos.

What I did say was, "I'm heading into Burgos for a while. Might stick around for a day. Haven't decided."

That was God's truth. I had no idea what I was going to do. After my stale-bun-and-a-coffee breakfast, I wandered back into the Plaza de Santa Maria, dominated by Burgos's stunning thirteenth-century cathedral square, to wait for the travel agency to open. It was 9 AM, and the travel agency did not open until 10.

I sat down on the cathedral steps, opened my backpack, and pulled out my maps. I looked at them for a flash of divine guidance, but nothing popped up. I thought about having another coffee, then decided against the idea. I thought of getting a hotel for a night, then dismissed that idea too. I could not make up my mind about anything, and I feared I had lost my decision-making capabilities altogether.

I tried not to look like the bag lady I was becoming. I crossed my ankles in a ladylike manner and looked appreciatively at the decorative latticed features on the spires of Burgos cathedral, but even the dogs sniffing for crumbs steered clear of me. A little boy toddled toward me, smiling innocently, but when I smiled back and said, "Hola!" his grandmother sprang into action and pulled him away as if I were a leper.

I thought of the Three American Boys and their kind gesture of giving me the macaroon. That morning Peter had solicited my advice about his feet and said something that had warmed my heart.

"Since you're a real mom," he had said, "can you tell me what to do about these blisters?"

A real mom. Was there a nicer compliment?

I had examined his feet, given him some packets of gauze and a glob of Vaseline, and instructed him to slather it on each morning before setting out. If he stuck with this regimen, his feet would be blister free, I assured him.

Suddenly I jerked to life on those cathedral steps. That's it! The Three American Boys! They need me! I jumped to my feet and checked the time. It was 9:50. I could not wait ten minutes for the travel agency to open; I had to find the Three American Boys.

I stuffed my maps into my backpack, grabbed my walking stick, and retraced my steps to the *refugio*. The sun came out. I walked faster. Past the *refugio*, past the little stone restaurant where I had had dinner the night before, past the college, and finally into an industrial area that was waist-high in grass.

The yellow arrows cheered me on. I walked under an overpass just as a tour bus rumbled across. I wondered whether my group was on it, singing camp songs and having a jolly time.

At the edge of Rabé de las Calzadas, a small, caramel-stuccoed church surrounded by a sparse but brave stand of Cyprus trees stood against a bright blue sky. Beyond it the hypnotic *meseta* stretched into infinity.

IF YOU WERE praying on May 12, 2004, it is unlikely that God heard you; He was too busy with me. Sorry—I sucked up a lot of God time that day. I'm sure He put His hands over His ears when He heard me calling His name. I wasn't indulging in blasphemy, there was no "For the love of God, what was I thinking when I decided to do this?" or "God Almighty, when will this day end?" No, this was more along the lines of "Hello? God? I've messed up big time. I'm not a pilgrim; I'm playacting at it. The psychic was right about this being too rustic for me. But it's more than that—this is completely beyond my ability. I've failed. I cannot be the pilgrim You want me to be."

I looked behind me, then ahead. The planet was deserted.

But I did not slow down. Some force pushed me forward, forcing me to walk faster and faster, refusing to let me rest. I wanted to drop to the ground and weep, but I was incapable of stopping, so I just walked and cried.

I thought of my children. I yearned to tell them how much I loved them, to tell them that if they knew the depth of my love it would break their hearts. I was desperate for their touch, for tangible proof that I was connected to them. But I also craved their approval, craved their forgiveness for the years when I was too worried about the household finances to spend time on the floor racing dinky cars through tunnels of sofa cushions and toilet paper rolls, too busy creating a standard of impossible perfection for myself to play Barbie dolls, too busy making a living to join parent-teacher councils or Little League clubs.

I had let those years slip from my grasp while I rushed through projects, through playtimes, through hobbies, through vacations, through relationships, through life. Now I was rushing through a pilgrimage.

"Forgive me!" I bawled to God. "I'm not the pilgrim You want me to be."

Bible passages, psalms, confessions from the Anglican *Book of Common Prayer* spilled out: "*. . . We are not worthy so much as to gather up the crumbs under thy table, but thou art the same Lord whose property is always to have mercy. . .*"

"To Be a Pilgrim," an old school hymn that I had loved and memorized in grade eight at St. Clement's School but that had sat dormant for four decades suddenly sprang up in my throat, and I began to sing it as loud as I could.

> *He who would valiant be 'gainst all disaster,*
> *Let him in constancy follow the Master*
> *There's no discouragement shall make him once relent*
> *His first avowed intent to be a pilgrim.*

"*To be a pilgrim, indeed,*" the Critic Within mocked. "*You are not a pilgrim. You're as much a pilgrim as you are a Spice Girl.*"

I burst into tears and sang the second verse louder.

The Critic Within snickered, and I screamed at her to leave me alone.

What could I sing that would not make me cry, a song that would distract me from my anguish? I mentally scanned my vast AC/DC repertoire.

Nah. What else? "The Teddy Bear's Picnic?"

Try as I might, I could not get my mind to fix on anything except my wretchedness. Why hadn't I waited for the travel agency to open in Burgos? What was ten minutes? I could have been on a bus to Sarria by now. I wanted to go home, but at the same time the notion of telling people I had not completed the Camino was too frightening and too shameful to contemplate.

I tried on a conversation:

"So, how was the Camino?"

"Oh great. Wonderful experience, but really taxing. Hard on the body and the spirit. I could not do it."

"Really? That's hard to imagine given that you spoke with a few seventy-five-year-old women who completed it."

Damn the seventy-five-year-old women! If they could do it, why couldn't I? What was holding me back?

Loneliness. That was it. I longed for a connection with another human being. And therein lay yet another puzzle. How does one reconcile a love of solitude with a desire for companion-ship? God! Why was life so complicated?

Three figures silhouetted against the sky floated in and out of view as the landscape undulated. The American Boys? I sped up, frantic to talk to someone other than myself, but as I got closer I realized it wasn't the American Boys but a trio without backpacks out for a walk. Here? Were they crazy?

The sky darkened in the north. Pewter-colored clouds coa-lesced into a single mass and moved ominously like the mother-ship of an alien civilization. Please, God, don't let it rain.

Eventually I reached the edge of a plateau where the path dropped sharply into a valley. A village appeared in the distance at the far end of the valley floor: Hornillos del Camino, according to my map. A spectacular panorama of cascading hills and mountains wrapped itself protectively around the valley.

I spied a cluster of ant-sized people surging along the ochre dirt path. Could they be pilgrims? I hurried to catch up to them, careful not to stumble and trip on the rocky descent.

Again, my eyes had played tricks on me, for it was not a group of pilgrims but a group of schoolchildren on a class outing. When I reached them, their teachers alerted them to my approach, and the group parted to let me through. They stared at me, then erupted into cheers of *"Buen camino!"* A little girl stood in awe and called out, *"Peregrina!"*

No, I am not a pilgrim at all, I wanted to correct her. I am a mother. I had lost count of the number of times on the Camino that I had thanked God for bestowing on me the gift of motherhood. Then again, how do you explain to schoolchildren, to anyone for that matter, why a mother leaves her kids for a month to wander in the wilderness?

On the deserted main road that ran through Hornillos, I spied a bar marked Casa Manolo—the thought scooted through my mind that perhaps Manolo Blahnik secretly owned a café—but it appeared to be closed.

A sign indicated a *refugio* nearby, so I followed it around the corner.

There a woman greeted me and invited me inside.

"Una cama?" I asked, requesting a bed.

"Sí, sí!"

But something made me stop short of signing in.

"Dónde está el café?" I asked.

She pointed to Casa Manolo.

I wandered back across the road to the café and tried the door. Manolo Blahnik was not inside, but the Three American Boys were, or, rather, two of them were.

"El Camino Jane!" they called out. "You didn't give up!"

"Where's your brother?" I asked with concern.

"He's on the phone over there," Ian replied, pointing him out just beyond the bar. Brother Ben waved back. "He's speaking to our mom. We thought she'd like to know we're OK. So, what happened?"

"I went to the travel agent this morning," I explained. "But ten minutes before it opened I kind of panicked. I thought of you guys and your encouragement, so I'm continuing on, at least for today. Are you stopping here or are you going farther?"

They were continuing on to Hontanas, about ten kilometers away, they said.

"Do you mind if I walk with you?" I asked. They were delighted.

I celebrated by ordering a huge salad and a beer and set into my meal like a ravenous wolf. The salad had arrived with bread, which I could not eat, so I offered it to the boys, who swooped on it like hawks. The salad proved to be more than I could eat, and the boys dispatched the remains of that quickly, too. They eyed my beer. I drank every last drop.

After lunch we returned to the expansive *meseta*.

The conversation drifted from college to careers to their part-time jobs. In the summers Ben and Ian worked for their uncle, who had invented a portable swimming pool. Peter sometimes worked there, too. They would return to their jobs after the Camino.

We covered world affairs, American politics. I told them of my fondness for Jimmy Carter's gentle style of politics (though he has been castigated for it ever since), and showed my age by telling them I was present on the White House lawn when Carter, Anwar Sadat, and Menachem Begin signed the Camp David Accord.

"Wow," Ben said. "I was born during the Carter administration."

I might as well have told them I had been in the audience when Lincoln was shot.

We discovered we shared a favorite TV series—24—and we dissected its implausible though riveting plotlines and probed the big questions: How come Jack Bauer always manages to get the president on the phone? Why does presidential aide Mike Novak act like such a sinister weasel? Why are all the wives and girlfriends of elected officials portrayed as ditzy sluts and traitors? Why can't the U.S. elect a president like David Palmer in real life? How is it possible that all the characters can get through a twenty-four-hour period without visiting an ATM or eating?

The conversation switched to music. When I mentioned that I had recently attended a Tom Jones concert, my cool quotient shot up.

"Wow, was he playing with the Art of Noise?"

"No, with his usual backup band, who were really good."

"He does that song 'Sex Bomb,' doesn't he?"

"I love that song!"

On a plain in Spain with no rain, three twenty-something American guys and one fifty-year-old Canadian gal shattered the meseta's ominous grip and broke into song.

In the blink of an eye, we were transformed into a hot Broadway chorus line, grooving in unison, kicking up our heels, thrusting our pelvises, hands behind our heads, shoulders jerking to the rhythm of the song. The Boys hoisted me onto their shoulders, and when I turned my head I saw a sea of pilgrims behind us using their walking sticks as dance barres, strutting and hoofing their way across the meseta, all of us grooving to "Sex Bomb."

OK, so it didn't happen exactly like that. My imagination gets a little carried away from time to time. Still, whenever I think back on that moment I dress up the memory in klieg lights and dazzling sequins because it was an epiphany; that's when I began to understand what it truly takes to survive a pilgrimage—of any type, really: companionship and a guiltless sense of fun.

For a moment we forgot the weight of our packs, our weary legs and muscles, our individual heavy thoughts, and our yearning for home.

Across the field, a church spire rose from the ground as if it had pierced through the underside of the Earth.

Hontanas. It's a small village that sits in a shallow valley and unfolds like a sunrise as you approach it across the plain.

We arrived at a small but charming stone *refugio*. The boys spoke Spanish well, and we got our pilgrim passports stamped and were signed in.

The *refugio* keeper then led us out of the *refugio* and back into the glare of the sun.

"We have to leave?" I asked.

"The lady says it's full," said Ben. "She has other buildings connected to this *refugio*, and that's where she's taking us."

She beckoned the boys to follow her into what looked like a stone barn and signaled for me to wait.

The Boys turned and waved to me and entered the building. It was the last time I saw them.

I waited on the dusty road for the *refugio* owner to return, and when she did she led me down the dirt road to a long, modern, one-story building and gestured to me to go inside.

I looked around at the roomful of pilgrims who had already claimed bunks to see if I could recognize any one. One woman, who was Dutch, waved to me with delighted surprise. I remembered her from the beginning of the trek in Roncesvalles, although we had never spoken to one another.

Dinner—served at 6 PM in the main *refugio*—was one of the most enjoyable on the entire Camino. Chicken, salad, macaroni, wine, and yogurt for seven euros. I sat at a table with five other women, from England, the Netherlands, Germany, France, and Spain. I adored the linguistic plurality of the Camino; despite the language barrier, we managed to make ourselves understood.

The surroundings lent themselves to the convivial atmosphere. The small, domed dining room in the lower level of the building was like a cave; a log crackled in the fireplace. The owners—a young couple with small children—had purchased the building, my tablemates explained, and were slowly renovating it into a home. To help pay for the renovations, the couple took in pilgrims and served them dinner. It was the nicest, most hospitable *refugio* I had been in.

Back on my bunk bed that night, I pored over the maps yet again. Where was I meant to go? What should I do?

Before the lights were shut off, I resolved to go directly to Villafranca, stay two nights to relax, take a bus to Sarria, and walk the final hundred kilometers of the Camino in order to get the *credencial*.

By sunrise the next morning, I had had a change of heart.

13

ENTERING Castrojeriz, ten kilometers beyond Hontanas, I could stand it no longer. I decided to quit, *credencial* or no *credencial*. For sure this time.

I had started the day as I started all days on the Camino—with unbridled optimism and steeled determination. It usually worked; by the time I had come to my senses, I was already so far along the path that there was no choice but to keep walking and following the arrows and shells. As soon as I surrendered to the Camino for yet another day, the little aches and pains that plague all pilgrims magnified as if making you suffer for your audacious belief that you could get another day closer to St. James.

But now extreme sleep deprivation was added to my growing list of physical complaints. The night before the *refugio* dorm had once again been serenaded by inveterate snorers, the worst offender being a fat Spaniard in the bunk beneath me. I was beyond livid. As I lay awake pondering what the Spanish prison term for murdering a snoring man in his sleep might be, an Australian fellow, four beds away, summed up what my fellow insomniacs were thinking when he screamed into the darkness, "Shut the fuck up!"

His outburst had no effect whatsoever on the Snoring Fat Man in the Lower Bunk, but it scared the bejesus out of the rest of us.

At first light I got dressed, grabbed my gear, and started walking to escape my exhaustion.

The world had been rinsed of the preceding day's dust; the air was clean, the vegetation lush and glossy. A glint from the rising sun reflected off the morning dew and turned the landscape into a shimmering fairyland. On a hillside path I paused and bowed my head in prayer as the sun peaked above the horizon and exploded across the sky. It was a beautiful peace.

The climate and vegetation had changed dramatically as I progressed across Spain. In Roncesvalles remnants of Winter had been visible—bare-limbed trees, brownish grass, and new growth in its pregestation stage. Now Spring, unable to restrain itself a second longer, had busted out of its buds and was sprinting to hand Nature's baton to Summer. It was the kind of seasonal rejuvenation that inspires resolutions to be a nicer person or to lead a simpler life.

Beneath a Gothic double arch of the fourteenth-century Convento de San Antón, birds were fussing over the finishing touches to their nests. New life was being breathed into old ruins. The breadth of antiquity along the entire Camino was as bracing as the spring air. I felt like an explorer on the cusp of discovery. My trusty guidebook noted that Castrojeriz dated back to the time of the Visigoths. Visigoths, for God's sake!

But not Spring nor antiquity nor Visigoths could keep me on the Camino. In addition to being sleep deprived and lonely, I was sick of being mired in a swampland of introspection. The sound of my own whining internal voice was driving me crazy. If I needed to rationalize my decision to quit, I could throw in several physical complaints that had started to gnaw at me: my back and shoulder muscles were twitching painfully, and I could no longer get relief by adjusting my backpack; a jab of pain in one of my toes had intensified, and my eyesight was inexplicably dimming. My body was breaking down, and it was simply time to stop.

In an old *taverna* I ordered a *café con leche* and a cab. An achingly melancholy Bach aria, at once incongruous and perfect, soared through the place. It was a dramatic soundtrack to my denouement, and yet in that moment I couldn't help but feel a sense of triumph. I had extricated myself from the clutches of the Camino and from the spiritual shackles of being a pilgrim.

An older Dutch couple, whom I recognized from the trail, wandered in and joined me at my table.

"Why not walk with us today?" the husband urged. "We're stopping at Boadilla del Camino; it's only twenty-two kilometers away."

But even the promised beauty of the *refugio* in Boadilla—advertisements for it plastered along the Camino made it look like Shangri-La—could not tempt me. I had been wrestling with this moment for days, and the fight had worn me down. The last punch had been swung; the bell had sounded. It was time to admit defeat.

"How sad for you to give up now," said the wife. "We are almost halfway to Santiago. You've already traveled so far."

I hugged them good-bye, wished them "*buen camino,*" and surrendered my backpack to the cab driver. I climbed into the front seat and slumped self-consciously as the cab drove past clusters of happy pilgrims on the road.

The cab gathered speed, and in the bat of an eye towns that I had come to know from my maps began to whip by faster than I could keep track of them: Itero del Castillo, Itero de la Vega, Bodegas, Boadilla del Camino, Frómista, Carrión de los Condes. Within twenty minutes of leaving the *taverna*, forty-five kilometers had been lopped off my journey, a distance that would have taken me two days to walk.

In Carrión de los Condes the cabbie, who spoke no English, walked me to the Café-Bar España–cum–bus depot. He spoke to the man behind the bar on my behalf, and a ticket was purchased for León.

I paid the driver and thanked him. Plucking dejected pilgrims from the road and delivering them to this very bus depot was probably a regular occurrence for him.

He indicated on his watch that there was a bit of a wait before the bus arrived and proceeded to order two *cafés con leche*. He waved away my attempt to reimburse him. I doubt that North American cabbies ever display this sort of generosity, but then again I've never backpacked across my own country.

I thanked him for the coffee and walked across the street to a stone bench.

There was still an hour to wait until the bus for León arrived, so I had time to review my latest plan. Once I got to León, I would transfer to another bus and travel 125 kilometres west to Villafranca.

I was fixated on Villafranca for one reason: Villafranca had a Parador.

Parador is a government-run program that converts historic country houses, castles, and monasteries into luxury hotels while preserving their architectural integrity. From a travel brochure I had picked up in a café several towns earlier, I learned that four such hotels were located right on the Camino—in Santo Domingo de la Calzada, Villafranca, León, and Santiago. The one in Villafranca was the cheapest.

While I pondered Paradors, pilgrims filed past. Distressingly, a few were on cell phones:

"Hi, honey. Yup I'm in—what's this place?—Carrión de los Condes, yeah, that's it. Oh, it's going OK. What's new? How did Timmy's game go last night? Scored three baskets? Excellent! Hey, did you order the drywall for the back room? Think I'll tackle that when I get home. I'll check in again tomorrow. Yup. Love you, too. Bye-bye."

How can you get in touch with your soul and with God when you're tethered to a cell phone? How can you experience absolute isolation when emotional rescue is only a dial tone away? Even on a pilgrimage many people can't bear to be disconnected from humanity. I felt that fear myself, seesawing as I was between wanting to be alone and searching for people to walk with. Or running to get home to the very routine and people I could hardly wait to flee two weeks earlier.

I looked around and wondered what day it was. Thursday? Friday? Wednesday? What day had I told my family I would call home? I fished around in my pockets for my watch. As I studied the time, my hands inexplicably began to shake. Christ. What was happening to me? I needed to get help.

Where was my group? How was Sally faring? Lucy? They were not among the ten from my group who had registered the other night in Burgos. I hoped José was doing OK, too. What about Georgina? Her family had asked me to carry a birthday card to give her as a surprise from them on her big day. That day was tomorrow, and I was pretty certain I wasn't going to encounter Georgie on the trail again. It was a shame she wouldn't get it: She was homesick—I could read it in her face—and the card would have given her a good boost.

I dropped my head wearily and looked at the charm bracelet encircling my wrist. Two of its charms—a pair of hearts intertwined and a gold cross—glittered to the point of inducing blindness. I accepted it as a sign that God loved me regardless of my failures and my complexities. I had nothing else to believe in.

I sat on that bench, head bent, pondering the humbling yet profoundly simple fact that in an uncertain world you can at the very least always count on God's love.

And then a louse dropped onto my shirt and broke any sense of holiness I might have been feeling.

Christ Almighty! I screamed to myself. Is there no end to the calamities?

The thought of contracting head lice had flashed into my mind the night before as I lay on my bunk and wondered how many heads had touched that pillow.

I squeezed the louse between my fingers until I heard its body crack and flicked it away. At the same time as I was annihilating the louse, I took stock of my finger, the one missing a nail. It was pulsating with a heat that indicated advanced signs of infection.

Could things get any worse?

I walked back across the street to the café to make sure I had not misunderstood the departure time of the bus. As I stood reading the chalk-written bus schedule, a young woman, having spotted my walking stick and backpack, asked me—in German— where I was going. I replied—in English—that I was headed for León.

She switched to English—Europeans are brilliant that way— and said she and her friends were also headed to León.

She extended her hand. "Why don't you travel with us? Perhaps we can share a cab once we get to León."

"Yes, I'd love the company," I said. "I lost my group a few days ago, and I haven't a clue where to find them."

"You've been walking alone since then?" she exclaimed. "That must be so lonely. Is there some way we can help you find your group?"

Her concern was awfully nice, but if I had found my group at this point, I would have throttled them rather than hugged them. I didn't say that to the German Girl. No sense looking like an angry, bitchy, resentful, ungrateful, snarling, vindictive, lice-infected pilgrim.

I stuck like glue to the German Girl and her gang while trying not to appear to be sticking to them like glue. I hoped the head lice wouldn't become an issue.

We boarded an air-conditioned coach, and I sat across the aisle from the German Girl and her three friends. The seat beside me remained blessedly empty until a pretty, stylish teen with an insouciant air (teens wear that so well, don't they?) sat down beside me.

I smiled at her, and she recoiled, glancing nervously toward the back of the bus in search of another empty seat. She was stuck

with me. Her perfectly manicured nails began furiously pound-
ing out a text message on her cell phone. I imagined her SOS:
"Sitting next to gross old woman. Ratty clothes. Smells. Pilgrim?
Smiled at me. Thought I'd puke. Need drugs. For her. Not me."

The bus arrived in León, and I was so excited about being part
of a group that I completely forgot about Villafranca and eagerly
agreed to share a cab into the center of the city with the German
Girl and her friends.

"We're staying at a convent," she said. "Would you like to join
us?"

After all the withering looks I had received from nuns and
priests on the Camino, a convent was the last place I wanted to
stay. We parted company in central León, and when the German Girl and her posse were out of earshot, I asked the cab driver
to suggest a four-star hotel.

He held up four fingers to ensure he had heard correctly.

I nodded my head.

He reluctantly directed me around the corner to La Posada
Regia, and off I went.

La Posada looked thoroughly charming. According to the
plaque on the front of the building, it dated back to 1370. I pushed
open the heavy iron and glass doors with an immense amount
of confidence and approached the front desk, where two female
clerks did their best to ignore me.

"Excuse me," I said eventually, with polite irritation. "I would
like a room."

The two women stared back at me. One said, "We're full."

I looked at them as if I did not comprehend the term "full."

"No rooms," reiterated the other.

A brief digression is in order here. Of the forty-five women
who had originally expressed interest in walking the Camino
with me, a small cohort had asked about doing only half the
Camino because they were unable to get a month off work. One
of them, a university administrator from England named Sharon,

offered to organize the group. During our e-mail correspondence, Sharon mentioned that her group had decided to start their
trek in mid-May in León, with the hope of meeting up with my
group so that both groups could walk together to Santiago. I was
certain she had mentioned that her group would be assembling
at this particular hotel. Had they already arrived?

I mentioned Sharon's name and those of a few of her walking companions to the Two-Headed Hydra behind the reception
desk.

There were no such guests, they assured me, without consulting the register.

"I'm certain they are staying here," I insisted.

One let out a weary sigh and leafed through the book. Sure
enough, I was right, and because I was right and because I knew
real guests who were staying there, the Hydra accorded me a
smidgen of respect.

"But they are not here until Sunday," the Hydra said.

"What day is it today?" I asked.

This is apparently the wrong question to ask in a fancy hotel.
One of the Hydra's hands moved slowly under the desk. I heard
a click behind me: the front door was being unlocked. That was
my cue to leave.

The Hydra forced a smile.

"It's Thursday. May 13."

"Can you recommend a hotel in the area?" I asked. "One that
will do laundry?"

"The Hotel Paris. Up the street and around the corner."

The reception was not much better at the Hotel Paris. The
two gents behind the desk eyed me as if I were Medusa sweeping
into their sterile-looking establishment. What was it with people
here? Hadn't they ever seen someone with head lice? (I was sin-
cerely hoping it was confined to head lice.)

In their oleaginous manner they told me, oh so sympatheti-
cally, that they had no room.

I asked for directions to another hotel.

"A nice two-star around the corner has just opened," they informed me. One of them drew me a map and handed it to me, careful not to make contact with my skin. The other gent was already holding the door open to speed my exit.

I followed their map but got hopelessly lost. People stared at me, and I could sense them cringing when they walked past me, making sure their backs were to the wall.

I looked down at my clothes. OK, they weren't couture, but they weren't hideous. Only the smallest clods of mud still clung stubbornly to the hem of my pants. Was it my walking stick? Did it look too much like a weapon?

I caught a glimpse of myself in a store window and gasped. My face was sunburned, my hair could not be called a rat's nest without offending the rodent species, and my gait had changed— I was loping. I wanted to raise my stick in the air and scream: "I am not an animal! I am a homeowner, a taxpayer, a recycler!"

I ducked into a café and handed my map across the counter. The waiter in his starched white shirt and smooth dark hair tried to help but admitted with polite apology that his English "is no nice."

A puma at the end of the café bar looked up from her book, slowly uncrossed her long legs, and glided toward me.

"You speak English?" she asked in a voice as flawless as her skin.

"Yes," I answered with relief. "I'm completely lost."

I hoped she would detect in my voice the sort of inflection that indicates that the world of mud-splattered polyester and fleece was not my usual habitat. I really hate this sort of snobbism, but I was desperate.

The puma smiled kindly, collected her things, and gave a slight nod to the waiter. Then she put her hand on my elbow and guided me outside. She went further than giving me directions to a hotel; she actually walked me to one. I thanked her but was careful not to overdo it as a signal that although I was grateful for her help I would expect no less from someone of my class and would reciprocate in exactly the same manner.

The nuances of class were new territory for me. I had never worried about such niceties before, but now I was someone without references. I was on the lowest rung of the social ladder, dependent solely on acts of human kindness. I thought of the street people in my hometown, whom I ignore, people who look as if they want to say something to me, maybe ask for help, but who shrink back when my body language says that I am too busy and can't spare the time, let alone a dime. Now I know what it feels like to be shunned, ignored, and really alone. It's a scary place to be. I will never treat anyone like that again. Ever.

At the next hotel the proprietor eyed me with suspicion but said he had a room available. I asked about clothes cleaning, and he began to give directions to a Laundromat. I cut him off.

"*No lavado en el hotel?*" I ask.

"*No, no,*" he said.

I dropped my head and stared at the map in my hand. Exhausted and forlorn, feeling immensely sorry for myself, I reviewed the list of evaporating options. I could smell my own foul odor, and I was ready to cry. My nose tingled, but I bit my lip. To cry right now, right here, will finish you, I told myself.

I was broken but not completely beaten; I had one card left to play.

I turned to the owner. "*Quisiera un taxi, por favor.*"

He ran to the curb and hailed one in a matter of seconds.

The cab driver took my bag and put it in the trunk while I climbed into the back seat. He returned to the driver's seat and turned to me, waiting for his orders.

I looked straight at him.

"*El Parador, por favor.*"

He let out a gasp.

"*El Parador?*"

He looked me up and down.

I kept my gaze fixed on him, and through clenched teeth, I repeated: "Sí. *El Parador.*"

He took off like a shot. We whipped past important buildings and shops, shops, shops. Businesspeople were on their lunch hour. Everyone looked clean and in control, heads held high. Reflexively, I straightened my spine, elongated my neck, and drew in my stomach muscles.

At the traffic circle, the cab made a quick left into a driveway that ran for hundreds of meters in front of a long, ornate building. The driver spoke into a speaker, and the entrance barrier was lifted. We continued driving alongside this magnificent edifice festooned with carvings of historic and religious figures until the cab pulled up to a set of steps leading to glass doors tucked beneath an impressive archway.

I paid the driver, grabbed my knapsack and walking stick, and entered the Parador San Marcos.

I scanned the signs hanging above the various counters until I was intercepted by a bellhop.

"Where's reception, please?" I asked.

"Reception?" he repeated, looking me up and down.

Was there an echo in here?

"Reception," I confirmed haughtily.

He moved swiftly behind the main desk, alerting the front desk clerk in urgent whispers.

The clerk looked up with a bored but wry expression on his face.

"Sí?" he asked me.

"Do you speak English?"

"A little."

"I want a room, please," I said, while rooting around in my wallet until I had found what I was looking for.

"A room," he smiled, as if indulging my insanity.

I held his gaze and slowly withdrew my weapon. MasterCard. I snapped it crisply on the polished mahogany counter in front of him and continued staring at him.

"A room. One night," I said evenly.

The clerk held my gaze. A Canadian and a Spaniard were locked in a Mexican standoff.

"Do you have a passport?" he finally asked tauntingly.

"Pilgrim passport or passport of citizenship?" I shot back without blinking. I slid both toward him.

He opened my passport, then lowered it out of my range of vision. Interpol check. I rolled my eyes in a show of unworried irritation. Whatever. I was so worn down that I would have submitted to a cavity check.

Having passed the security check, I was handed a registration form, which I proceeded to fill out. I was about to ask whether the hotel had laundry service when I changed my tack. I summoned my best imperious tone—making it sound as if I do this with some regularity—and matter-of-factly stated, "I would like all my clothes washed. Please send a maid to my room right away."

"You'd like your clothes washed for tomorrow?" the Clerk asked.

"No. Immediately. Have the maid at my room within five minutes."

I signed my name with a dramatic flourish and allowed the pen to loudly stab a dot over the i.

The bellhop carried the room key but left me lugging my knapsack and walking stick. I had an impromptu internal debate about whether I should tip him just to show that I was above his snooty attitude. No. I was sick of sucking up to people. No tip for him.

As we made our way to Room 332, I played the nonchalant traveler while stifling my awe. The medieval grandeur of the place was stunning. Huge tapestries tumbled from stone walls, and religious statuary stood in every corner. The antique furnishings—some more than six hundred years old—gave me palpitations. A magnificent upper-level cloister overlooked a colonnaded courtyard of manicured boxwoods and ornamental trees. Oh my. I could barely contain myself.

I was shown my room and accepted it without making a big fuss. It was a spacious, high-ceilinged room with cream-colored walls, deep crimson bed coverings, a faux cream-and-crimson tapestry headboard, crimson-matted artwork, and hotel-stock mahogany furniture. A copy of *Don Quixote de la Mancha* rested on the bedside table. There was a bar fridge, a phone, a TV, a small, round glass-topped table, two armchairs, and a balcony with a view that wasn't awful but was no roaring hell, either. The bathroom contained a tub, bidet, toilet, and requisite plastic bottles of soaps and lotions. Also big, fluffy white towels.

The room itself was large enough to accommodate twelve bunk beds. There was, however, just one king-sized bed (which could have slept three pilgrims) all for me. I was thrilled beyond words.

Once the snooty bellhop left the room, I stripped off and upended my knapsack, sorting its contents into two piles: stuff that can be washed and stuff that cannot be washed. I did not care how much it cost. I searched for a fluffy white bathrobe, but it was not hanging in the bathroom or in the closet. Dare I call the front desk and complain? I made do with a fluffy white bath sheet.

The maid appeared at my door within minutes of my arrival.

"*Lavado, por favor,*" I told her, handing her the stinky pile. "*No planchado.*" Washing please. No ironing.

And then: "*Dos horas.*" Two hours.

She nodded sweetly and left.

I bolted the door, then rushed into the bathroom and ran the tub. Hot water on full throttle. I added the hotel's bath gel, which, to my horror, doubled as shampoo. I had been using Campsuds to do the same double duty all along the Camino and had hoped for a respite. What I wouldn't have given for my Vitabath.

I slipped into the bath and let out a moan as the hot water rushed over my skin—part orgasm, part baptism.

I picked up a facecloth, soaked it with water, and pressed it into my aching shoulders. The hair at the back of my head stood up. I scrubbed every inch of myself, and washed my hair three times to shock the lice into submission. I lingered in the tub for several minutes until I realized that the bathwater had turned brown. I was that filthy.

I toweled off—finally, big fluffy white towels!—and applied generous globs of body lotion. I brushed my teeth vigorously. Then I brushed them again.

As I stood naked before the full-length mirror to comb my hair, the fog of steam lifted, revealing someone I barely recognized. My cheekbones were more clearly defined; my neck appeared longer. My eyes wandered down the length of my body. At first I was horrified—my ribs and hipbones were visible—but then I let out a Homer Simpson "Woohoo!" It had to have been ten years since I had last seen my hipbones. Thirteen days and three hundred kilometers had whittled my waist and hips and toned my legs and arms. My shoulders were muscular and looked as if they could carry the world's burdens.

I wrapped myself in a plush bath sheet and slipped into bed between crisp layers of white linen. A room-service menu, the kind you hang on the door, announced that breakfast could be delivered to one's room if one preferred. One did. One checked off every box on the menu.

I flicked on the TV to see what was happening in the real world.

While I had been out for a long walk through a peaceful land of stunning beauty, acts of unspeakable brutality had been going on elsewhere in the world. An American had been beheaded in Iraq, and the footage was available on the Internet for all to see. Dr. Phil was talking to Larry King and advising people not to allow their children watch it. Even adults, said Dr. Phil, should not watch it. He admitted he had done so as part of his research, and his face wore the look of trauma. When the voluble and fearless Dr. Phil has trouble articulating something, you know a line has been crossed.

There was a knock at my door.

I pulled the bath sheet around me.

"*Hola?*"

I opened the door, and two maids filed in carrying large, flat wicker baskets. My clothes had been washed, dried, folded, and inserted into individual cellophane envelopes stamped with a large gold P. The P, dear reader, did not stand for Pilgrim.

Mountain Equipment Co-op clothing has never been treated so well. The hotel's dryer had failed the quick-dry towel and CoolMax quick-dry socks, however, and mystified the staff, who apologized over and over for not being able to get them dry within the promised two-hour period. No worry, I assured them. The room's radiator would fix them by morning.

One of the maids noticed my walking stick propped against the wall in a corner.

"*Peregrina?*"

"*Sí,*" I replied proudly, and told her I had started my journey in Saint-Jean-Pied-de-Port.

She grabbed my hands and implored me to deliver her prayers to Santiago himself. What was it about this James guy that had everyone begging for face time?

She examined my face and gently stroked it. "*Momento,*" she said, disappearing into the hall.

Seconds later she was back with both hands filled with small bottles of the hotel's body lotion. She told me to slather it on my face. I was thoroughly grateful.

I slipped into freshly laundered and pressed clothes—even my underwear had been carefully folded—and was reborn. I fluffed my hair, put on some lipstick, and took off to explore.

I glided down the stone staircase to the lobby and waltzed into the courtyard. I entertained the possibility of doing the Camino Parador to Parador.

The walled garden of the Parador San Marcos was an oasis of serenity, simplicity, and order (boxwoods hold a tremendous appeal for Type A personalities). I strolled through the colon-nade, drawing my hand across the cool stone columns, along a stone sarcophagus, on top of clipped shrubs. I wanted to touch everything, and I wanted it to touch me back.

I impulsively pushed on a plain-looking unmarked door in a corner of the colonnade and stepped over a high threshold. I sup-pose I should not have been surprised to find a chapel attached to the Parador San Marcos, but I was.

The Parador San Marcos began life as a monastery in the twelfth century with a mandate to provide lodging for pilgrims on the Camino. (In that sense, I had checked in to the right place but in the wrong century.) The original building, having outgrown its humble space, was demolished, and construction began in 1515 on the present building. Its hundred-meter-long Pla-teresque façade, decorated with carvings of hundreds of religious and historical figures, is one of the most recognized in Spain today, and the building itself is considered the country's most beautiful example of Renaissance architecture. What would you expect of a building that had housed the legendary Order of St. James, whose knights were the enforcers of the Camino?

I returned to the hotel lobby and flashed a smile and a bright "Hola!" at the desk clerk. Then I gave a wink—that was all he was going to get—to the snooty bellhop, who, with his mouth agape, rushed to hold the door open for me. Yup, I clean up real good.

The desk clerk had provided me with mapped instructions to get to an Internet café, but by the time I crossed the Plaza San Marco and the busy Paseo la Condesa de Sagastas, I had no clue where I was or where I was going. I asked a young woman for help, but she just smiled and shrugged her shoulders.

An elderly, well-dressed couple, arm in arm, approached me. "No Español," I confessed, then "Estoy perdido." I'm lost.

They studied the map in my hand, linked their arms through mine, and walked me toward the Internet café, despite the fact they weren't entirely sure what an Internet café was. On the way they stopped a couple of young men, who bowed respect-fully to them, and assisted with directions. Every so often, the elderly man turned me around and made me face the direction from which we had come so I would recognize landmarks—the crumbs that would ensure a safe and speedy return to the hotel.

When we arrived at the Internet café, the couple accompa-nied me inside to make sure it was a decent establishment. Satis-fied, they hugged and kissed me and then were gone. How nice was that?

I e-mailed a few friends, including Sharon, the organizer of the half-Camino expedition, and gave her a quick update. I had lost my group, the Camino was hard, I wanted to bail out, but in the interim I had managed to book myself into the most expen-sive hotel in Spain.

A few hours later, having returned to the hotel, tucked myself into a bed the size of a prairie, and turned out the light, the phone rang. It was Sharon herself.

"Stay in León till Sunday," she urged. "We'll finally be able to meet in person. You can join our group so that you don't have to walk alone."

It was a tempting offer, but I turned it down. I needed to keep moving, I told her, something was pushing me on, in spite of my frequent attempts to quit the Camino.

I turned the lights off again and whispered some prayerful words into the void. I thought of the distance I had covered that day and the contrast between where I had woken up that morn-ing and where I was now sleeping. I thought of the Three Ameri-can Boys and asked God to look after them.

THERE IS NO happier pilgrim than one who is clean, pressed, rested, and stuffed.

I crammed into my backpack what was left of the obscenely abundant continental breakfast while CNN continued its wall-to-wall coverage of the beheading of the American hostage.

Television has a way of replaying a story ad nauseam until viewers become desensitized. Meanwhile, another story was bubbling: U.S. troops had been discovered abusing Iraqi prisoners.

The rumble of an angry world vibrated inside me. I was suddenly homesick for my Camino cocoon. I gathered up my gear and checked out.

The total cost of my Parador splurge, including the laundry, was 172.53 euros (Can$240, US$300) excluding tips, which I only gave to the chambermaids. I rationalized the expense as the going rate for uninterrupted sleep, privacy, and a change of scenery.

The sun was shining, and everything sparkled. I felt as if I had stepped out of an ad for a household cleaning product.

At the bus station, the departure schedule indicated that a bus would be leaving for Villafranca in three hours. I glanced around. There was no way I was sitting in a bus station for three hours. I looked back at the departure board, and just then the name Ponferrada began to flash. I approached the ticket wicket, but instead of "Villafranca," the word "Ponferrada" came out of my mouth.

Lacking the language skills to have the ticket changed, I settled for Ponferrada. The bus didn't leave for an hour, so I sat down and consulted my trusty maps.

I had become obsessed with maps. I had walking maps, elevation maps, maps of northern Spain, a map of León. If I spied a map I didn't have, I would pick it up because, well, you never know. My obsession with maps was matched only by my obsession to go home. The latest variation on my plan would get me to Santiago by May 24, ten days hence. It was longer than I wanted to remain in Spain, and I kept checking and re-checking the maps for a shorter route. As much as I wanted to go home, I was now determined to conquer the Camino and get to Santiago. I wanted that piece of parchment as much as I wanted big, fluffy white towels.

A man sat down beside me and lit a cigarette. The smell was atrocious, and I glared at him for having ruined my Parador bath.

After I arrived in Ponferrada, a young man on the street drew me a map to the *refugio*: "Keep going along this street, up, up the hill [words I don't like to hear], turn the corner, and go past the castle ruins." It was not a long walk, perhaps two or three kilometers, but the shift from pilgrim to passenger had made my body lazy. Two kilometers suddenly felt like ten.

I had grown so blasé about my surroundings that the young man's mention of a castle had barely registered. But at the top of the hill, when I turned the corner, I saw it and stopped in my tracks. This wasn't just any castle; it was the Castillo de los Templarinos, headquarters of the mighty and feared Knights Templar.

Long-dormant fragments from high school and university history classes floated to the fore of my brain. Knights Templar, pilgrimages, the Holy Grail, the Crusades, the mysterious Masonic code. Along the Camino, I had noticed red stylized crosses, the Templar emblem known as the tau. Of course! It all began to make sense.

I forgot my sore back, my weary legs, the maps, and the carefully thought-out plans. I could not take my eyes off the castle. I practically ran to the *refugio*, signed in, dumped my gear on a spare bunk, showered, and took off to investigate.

In 1119, just after the First Crusade, a Cistercian monk named Bernard de Clairvaux came up with the idea of a holy army that sanctioned killing as long as it was done in the name of Christianity. By all accounts a convincing and persistent speaker, Clairvaux made his case before Pope Calixtus II, insisting that such an army was needed to defend the faith. The spoils of war from the Crusades had included the Temple of Jerusalem, and at the very least the site required fortification against the infidels.

Thus was born the Order of the Knights Templar, a monastic military machine whose adherents took vows of chastity, poverty, and service and patroled the realm with sweeping powers and a brand of religious devotion that was essentially fanaticism dressed up in a white tunic and a few pieces of armor.

Within a year of its founding, the order had attracted thousands of recruits from all walks of life and social classes. As their numbers grew, so did their influence. Templar strongholds sprang up across the continent.

Around the same time, the pilgrim trade was booming, and it opened up a convenient sideline for the knights. Pilgrims, whether headed for Jerusalem, Rome, or Santiago de Compostela, started depositing their cash with the knights of the order to avoid robbery. The order, in turn, developed a system that was the precursor to today's instant teller or credit card system. It worked like this:

Pilgrim cash was exchanged for a coded chit or "note of hand," not unlike a traveler's check or credit card. Each time a pilgrim stopped on his journey, the chit was presented to the local Templar rep, who deducted expenses and updated the chit. At the end of their journey, pilgrims took the chit to the Templar treasurer who had first issued it and received or paid back any funds owing.

The order's financial prowess brought it progressively closer to the epicenter of power. Knights became advisers to kings and popes, and although usury was forbidden by the order, its financial acumen and ability to keep the peace was rewarded with gifts of land and sometimes entire towns and villages.

Ponferrada was one such gift from the kings of León. It was little more than a minor outcrop at the time, but when the knights rolled into town they spun it into their most important Spanish base, and the place flourished exponentially.

What Ponferrada possessed in addition to its strategic location was a tradition of pilgrim traffic streaming toward Santiago. Osmundo, bishop of Astorga, had thoughtfully constructed an iron-railed bridge in the eleventh century for pilgrims to use while crossing the Rio Sil, and the bridge earned the settlement its name: Ponferrada, or "iron bridge."

Templar power spread across the continent, and the knights' presence on pilgrimage routes was pervasive. They were the cops of the Camino, and their success and influence had rock-star appeal.

Nothing breeds jealousy like success, however. Enter King Philippe iv of France, known as Philippe le Bel, or Philip the Fair. It was an ironic moniker that referred to his long blond hair and blue eyes, not to his character, as you will discover.

Philippe was having problems with cash flow and began to cast a covetous eye in the direction of the knights, who had bags of the stuff. Philippe decided the knights had outlived their usefulness. He made several attempts to shut down the order, kidnapping one pope (Boniface viii), blackmailing another (Clement v), and arresting the order's Grandmaster (Jacques de Molay) on grounds of corruption. Philippe also tried to infiltrate the order in an attempt to worm his way into its leadership, but when his plan was uncovered, he was blacklisted.

The burn of humiliation fueled Philippe's determination. Having filled his inner circle with ruthless men trained in civil law, he set about destroying the order. There was no accusation too false or outrageous for Philippe's legal team to concoct and no shortage of instruments of torture with which to extract confessions or produce witnesses to achieve the necessary results.

In a chilling covert operation, Philippe issued a sealed decree that was distributed throughout the realm in mid-September 1307 with strict instructions that the envelopes were not to be opened until the evening of October 12. The instructions were clear: on Friday, October 13, all the knights were to be rounded up and placed under arrest on charges that the order had been contaminated by greed, religious perversion, and sodomy. It was from this event that Friday the thirteenth is said to have earned its unlucky reputation.

More than four hundred knights were burned at the stake or otherwise tortured to death, along with hundreds of squires, foot soldiers, aides, and sympathizers. Given their power, wealth, and numbers (there were about fifteen thousand knights in France alone), how did the knights' military intelligence and vast influential network fail to tip them off to Philippe's devious plot?

I pondered this question while taking in the castle's hulking presence. It's the size of twelve football fields, and you have to climb the castle steps to one of its crenulated towers above the massive drawbridge to fully appreciate its place in the landscape. It looks west toward the Rio Sil and across a broad plain now occupied by the growing metropolis of Ponferrada, where trendy stores, Mercedes dealerships, and the sweet sound of power tools and heavy machinery attest to an economic boom. South of the castle was the second line of defense: the snow-capped Montes Aquilanos, which look so surreal they force a double take. As an aside, these mountains are home to the largest and therefore most significant gold mine in the Roman Empire; the Romans excavated an astounding 800,000-plus kilograms of gold from this site alone.

The castle wasn't always as impressive as it looks today, certainly not in the days of the Knights Templar. It began as a small Roman settlement, an enclosure made from pebbles and clay, which was later reinforced and expanded by the knights, who built a higher wall of lime and pebbles. When the order was forced to vacate the premises in 1307, the fortress was taken over by Pedro Fernández de Castro, who built a castle at one end of the enclosure. The next owners went one further: the Duke of Arjona, his sister Beatriz de Castro, and her husband Pedro Álvarez Osorio, Count of Lemos, built a bigger castle at the opposite end of the enclosure, turning it into the opulent digs portrayed in legend.

There's no evidence of any of that today. The site is a mishmash of styles, a complex layout of skeletal ruins from various incarnations. The European Union is trying to fix that. In 2003 it pledged more than eight million euros to stabilize and repair the castle.

Buildings in Spain were rarely completed in a lifetime; generations of families and tradesmen worked on a single building or were conscripted into service. Plaques around the castle attempt to explain this, illustrating the various building materials used in no fewer than thirteen stages over a nine-hundred-year period and pointing out the preserved crests of each lord who inhabited the castle that were affixed to the section for which said lord was responsible. .

But the castle's disjointed construction can't compete with the heady, romantic Templar legend. Visitors are helplessly seduced by the spiritual aroma of the place and a desire to reconstruct in their minds a Hollywood version. The Templar legend oozes from every chink, and fact and fantasy quickly mingle.

While I strolled through the ruins, I became aware of an unsettling presence. It became so strong and alarming that I moved closer to a young couple who were also taking a self-guided tour. Suddenly my imagination was off the rein. It does that sometimes when I let it merge with history.

A breeze picked up and hurled a babble of voices from the past toward me. In my mind's eye I saw a marauding horde, flags raised high, stampeding down the Montes Aquilanos and over the plains toward the castle. The dull sound of a gong resounded through the castle and tripped off a furious rush as soldiers girded for battle and with military precision wheeled munitions and armaments into position. Metal scraped against stone. The smells of fire, perspiration, fear, and adrenaline caused me to spin around and face the interior of the castle. People were moving in every direction, but with a practiced calm and sense of duty. In one room, above a fireplace mantel, something valuable was pulled from its perch, quickly wrapped in cloth, and spirited away to a safer hiding spot. What was it? I craned my neck for a better view, but the chaos was overwhelming. Panic mounted. My heart raced, my pupils dilated, my head pounded.

And then I snapped out of this dream state and became aware that I was the only person around. Yikes! How long had I stood there? Had the castle closed? The sun had dipped, and long shadows were moving in like knives toward a prey.

I ran along the parapet through a passageway and flitted down a flight of ancient steps. Someone or something was following me. Protecting me? Pursuing me? I ran until I heard voices—real, modern-day voices—and then I walked briskly under the castle arch, over the drawbridge, and onto the street. I have never been so grateful to see traffic.

I glanced back at the castle, which now looked menacing, and scampered back to the safety of the *refugio*. I arrived just in time for evening prayers. A lay mass was conducted in Spanish in the adorably simple Iglesia del Carmen attached to the *refugio*. Partway through the service the congregation—about fifteen of us—was invited to voice aloud its prayers in our respective languages. The weight of the Camino was once again upon me.

The Camino does that to you. It preys upon your conflicted self. It forces you to make decisions when your spirit is at its weakest. Touring castles and cathedrals is a pleasant diversion, but once that's over the reality and rigor of the Camino creep back into your psyche. You constantly think about quitting and going home. That single issue gets debated and rehashed by every pilgrim.

I bowed my head and stared into the cold stone floor. At this point in a relentless lonely journey, what would I pray for? Help? Forgiveness? Redemption? If I left the Camino now, would I be labeled a failure? Was that even something worth worrying about? Getting a piece of parchment for all this slogging no longer seemed attractive to me. I had already covered more than three hundred kilometers; was that in itself accomplishment enough? It obviously wasn't, because as much as I wanted to go home to my family, I could not. I felt as if I were being held against my will, a prisoner of the Camino.

And so I said as much.

I prayed for my family, which I missed to the aching point, and for my wayward group; I hoped they were safe and well.

"I also pray for the countless pilgrims like me who are broken— broken of body and spirit, who cannot imagine going another step on this Camino," I said aloud. "Please send me someone who will move me forward." I wanted to add, "And by that I don't mean a bus driver," but I had used enough of God's time.

I sulked back to my room no wiser or more enlightened about what to do next. When I opened the door to my room I was startled to see a woman about my age standing next to my bunk and folding some clothes.

We introduced ourselves. She was from France, she said, but had lived in Canada at one time. That single point made her practically my sister.

"Why are you walking?" I asked.

"Because I love to walk," she said almost dreamily.

I told her of my plan to bail, and this news prompted her to stop what she was doing.

"Well, you simply can't do that!" she said, holding a half-folded shirt against her chest.

"Why not?" I asked.

"Because you're walking with me tomorrow."

14

WE SET out bright and early the next morning, my new best friend—Brigitte—and I. We were headed for the bus station, which did not bode well for someone who had recommitted herself to the walking life, but Brigitte was insistent.

"I hate cities," she declared, "and the walk out of Ponferrada will be boring. We will take the bus to Villafranca—it is only twenty kilometers anyway—and we will walk from there."

I followed her through the maze of narrow residential laneways wending through Ponferrada's citadel toward the Rio Sil.

"I cannot see wasting our time on a city highway, risking our lives with all that traffic," said Brigitte as we stood in line at the bus station and purchased tickets for Villafranca. "Besides, we are pilgrims, not martyrs, right?"

She had a point. A pilgrimage is not about punishment but about making an intentional decision to look at the world with fresh awareness and to consider your place in it. A pilgrim defines her own pilgrimage; maps are guidelines, not prison sentences. If I walked every single step of the Camino's route, it would not make me a better pilgrim or a better person. It could make me a superhero, but I had already traveled that road and found it to be highly overrated.

The bus let us off on the outskirts of Villafranca. I felt mildly put out that we had to actually use our limbs to reach the town.

So this was Villafranca, I thought, as we followed the Camino's arrows and stylized shells through the town. It was a charming, prosperous little place of white stucco buildings, well-tended gardens, and a large central square bordered by residences, shops, and a theater, the sort of place that gives the impression of quiet sophistication and a comfortable lifestyle. Everyone we met greeted us with a smile.

We passed the Parador, and I was immediately glad I had stayed at the one in León. It was hard to know where to place Villafranca's Parador in the pantheon of Spain's grand architectural gems because it was so shockingly bland. Was it Spain's first example of unremarkable architecture? A failed attempt to introduce low-slung California styling to the Spanish masses? There wasn't a hint of grandeur to the place, and let's face it, nothing says pampering better than a level of opulence you can't afford.

Villafranca was over in a matter of minutes. We strode out of town, crossing the Rio Burbia along a bending road that ascended gently through leafy scenery. An older man who was walking toward us from the opposite direction removed his hat as he passed and nodded respectfully, "*Buenos días.*"

"Now *that* was a Spanish gentleman," smiled Brigitte with great satisfaction. "Did you notice? He carried himself like a true *caballero.*"

Brigitte had no *caballero* in her life. She was divorced—her daughter had just completed university—and she lived simply, eking out a living as a translator in French, English, and Spanish. Tall and slender with chestnut hair that fell neatly past her shoulders, she had a wide smile that showed lots of teeth. She carried herself with an ethereal calm; she had made peace with the uncomfortable decisions thrown her way and was living life on her own terms. She was more Earth Mother than soccer mom, at home around nature and horses. She had come on the Camino with some friends, but she had no idea where they were at that moment, and it did not concern her.

"They are adults. They will find their way," she said matter-of-factly. She was only walking for two weeks, the amount of time she could spare to be away from her clients.

Her clothing set her apart from other pilgrims: not for her the polyester cargo pants or the quick-dry shells, shirts, and jackets. She wore a pair of black denim jeans and a cotton T-shirt, which in most hiking circles is grounds for excommunication.

Slung diagonally across her chest was the smallest backpack I had seen on the Camino. It was like a postman's bag with a clear plastic compartment in the front where Brigitte kept her guide-book opened to the page *du jour*, which meant she had only to flip her bag over to read the map she needed for that day.

"Your pack is so tiny," I remarked. "What are you carrying in it?"

Such issues consume pilgrims, who are always on the lookout for something to ditch to lighten their load.

"Well," she began, "in the main central compartment, I have a pair of light cotton pants—African batik, which I bought at an ecological fair—plus two light cotton T-shirts—one that I wear only for a few hours after my shower and before going to bed, the other, quite old, that I alternate with another T-shirt when I'm walking. I also have a spare pair of sport socks, briefs and bra, as well as my hairbrush and a little plastic bag containing my tooth-brush and toothpaste, nail scissors, tweezers. I also have a pair of leather sandals—they are the heaviest thing in my bag. Next time I'm going to pack something lighter. In the two small compart-ments on the side, I have four tiny samples of foot cream that a chiropodist friend gave me. I don't know if it has helped, but at least my feet smell nice. I have a small pot of white grease [Vaseline] to put on my feet every morning, plus vitamins, a tiny bottle of shampoo, some cotton to use in case of blisters, and a small piece of natural soap for my body and my clothes. My sleeping bag—it weighs six hundred grams—is tied to my pack on the side. I also have a light rain jacket and rain pants and a bath towel. Around my waist, I have tied an old sweatshirt, which I can wear when it is cool, and a lighter cotton shirt, in case I need that. I have my usual waist bag—see?—that holds my papers, money, a knife, a pen, and some paper."

Granted, she was only walking for two weeks, but a pilgrim could make do with all that for a month and just replenish the shampoo and soap.

"What about face creams, moisturizers, cleansers, toners, sunscreen?" I asked. I mean, didn't every woman carry these?

"Oh, why would I use a face cream?" she asked as if she had never heard of such an idea and that my question had inadvertently hurt her feelings.

"Doesn't your face get dry or flaky?"

"No, not really. If it does I put a little nut oil on it in the winter."

I made a mental note to add nut oil to my dermatological arsenal.

We hiked on and on. Brigitte was a steady though leisurely hiker. Often she would stop and point out a shrub, a flower, or something else we saw along the way, and explain its origin.

"This is broom," she said, stroking a hardy unattractive bush. "It's called this because people can cut the branches off, tie them together, and make a broom! Now this flower—hmmm, I'm not sure what it is, but isn't it pretty? Look at how the tiny drops of dew stick to its petals."

At this rate, it would take three months to get to Santiago. Still, I was grateful for Brigitte. She reminded me that pilgrimages weren't races; if anything, they were meant to teach you to stop, observe, and reflect.

At a small park along the riverside we came upon a sign in Spanish. Brigitte paused and parsed it while I stood by faithfully and attentively as the teacher conducted her lesson.

"*Tramo libre sin muerte*," she read slowly. "Now *libre* means free; *sin muerte* means without death. Hmm. What does that mean?" She considered the sign in silence.

"Aha! This is a warning to fly-fishers that they can fish, but they must only use one hook, and then must throw the fish back. See? 'Freedom without murder.'"

The lesson over, we moved on to the next.

"See those cows over there," Brigitte said. "Those are *La Rubia de Galicia*." She stopped and made me repeat the term slowly. "*La Rubia de Galicia*."

"They are blonde, as you can see, and they are a special breed. Do you see that they still have their horns? That is a sign that they are raised naturally."

She smiled at the thought. She liked life in its natural state.

"Now this church bell," she said, pausing farther along in front of a small stone church and pointing to the tower. "That is called a *clocher mur*, as opposed to just a *clocher*. With a *clocher*, the bell is actually in the tower, whereas with a *clocher mur* the bell is located in a hole that has been cut into the wall specifically to accommodate it. I guess they did it that way for economical reasons; it's less expensive to build a wall than a whole tower just for a bell."

Occasionally our conversation veered toward a subject we were not keen to discuss: O Cebreiro, our destination that day.

O Cebreiro is a remote mountaintop village, and it has been a significant stop on the Camino since the ninth century. Reaching it involves a hideously steep climb, more than 1,200 meters above sea level. It is a mini-Pyrenees. Brigitte had started her Camino in Burgos and had therefore missed the Pyrenees.

"You're in for a treat," I said.

Faced with a daunting challenge, we did what most people do under such circumstances: we delayed it. We stopped for lunch, for *cafés con leche,* for beer and chocolate. We sought out places that sold real ice cream.

"I detest soft ice cream," Brigitte said. "It's plastic food."

We sauntered through villages festooned with RE/MAX signs, places where you would not expect to see a realtor's sign—Pereje, Trabadelo, La Portela, Ambasmestas, Ambascasas, Vega de Valcarce, Ruitelán. I pondered a dozen renovation possibilities.

The villages of northern Spain are an endangered species, and there was ample evidence of this all along the Camino, where homes were shuttered and there appeared to be no signs of life. When I first set out on the Camino with my group, we remarked at the absence of people in the villages and put it down to the fact that Spaniards left for work earlier than we pilgrims hit the road. Then we decided that perhaps pilgrims were the early birds. The shuttered windows we passed in the afternoons indicated it was *siesta* time, we surmised. Or the inhabitants were at church. Or away on holidays. As we progressed across Spain, it became apparent that we were witnessing the decline and fall of Spanish rural life. We were walking through ghost towns.

A recent census found that many of Spain's five thousand villages are sparser in population than the Sahara. Once-busy little burgs were reduced to a handful of inhabitants—some as few as twelve. Young people had fled these towns, seduced by better jobs and bigger money offered in the cities, leaving behind the elderly to fend for themselves without bus service, cafés, or stores. Nowadays village folk purchase groceries from the back of a van that rolls into town a few times a week, tooting its horn upon arrival. The isolation, especially in winter, was the worst form of deprivation. One woman told a newspaper reporter, "We can cope with the cold, [but] the hardest part is the loneliness."

It was just after noon, and probably not the best time to be walking on open asphalt roads under the Spanish sun, when the path around Herrerías took a steep downward turn toward the Rio Valcarce and brought Brigitte and me into some of the prettiest scenery I have ever seen—fresh spring foliage, moss-covered rocks, a small stone bridge—all the ingredients needed to recreate Eden or to illustrate a storybook.

Although this portion of the river was little more than a creek, the noise from the water spilling over rocks dominated everything around us. We had never seen water so clean. The riverside was sprinkled with small stucco and wood homes; an occasional car drove by. I considered what it must be like to wake up to this sort of life every day. As much as I wanted to go home, I was constantly looking for a new place to set down roots, or maybe I had been on the road so long that I just needed a place, any place, to call home.

Eden only lasts so long on the Camino before another punishing climb is handed to you.

The climbing began sharply and didn't let up for the next two hours. On the upside, the trail was largely in the shade. I remembered José's advice to take baby steps while going uphill and kept my head down so as not to be daunted by what lay ahead.

An hour and two hard kilometers later we arrived in La Faba, our faces flushed with exertion and dripping with sweat. O Cebreiro, we were told, was another two kilometers away—all of it uphill.

There was a sign for a café, so we plodded on. Ten minutes later on a very narrow path, we came across the "café"—a vending machine lashed to barbed-wire fencing that circled a barnyard on the right. A few steps to the left of the vending machine was a six-hundred-foot drop. We were so out of breath that we barely registered the absurdity of the sight.

We staggered into O Cebreiro to find the place jammed with tour buses. Worse, the Saturday crowd of boisterous day-trippers had snagged all the seats in the bars.

O Cebreiro is famous for a couple of things. One is its *pallozas*, circular rough-stone buildings with thatched roofs that date from the eleventh century. A respectful job has been done to integrate them into the fabric of modern life without debasing them; there were no gaudy Ye Olde Fudge Shoppe signs around. Still, given that this was the twenty-first century, I guess we shouldn't have been surprised to find the village's sanctity tainted by crass tourism, pricey B&Bs, and a proliferation of the religious equivalent of head shops with batik skirts and dresses hanging from outdoor racks, clay statues of dragons, faux silver jewelry—the sort of bric-a-brac favored by old hippies and weekend Christians.

Brigitte would not sanction so much as a browse.

We abandoned the crowds and moved toward the little pre-Romanesque church, where you could count the number of visitors on one hand. It was here that O Cebreiro's claim to fame—a miracle—occurred in the early fourteenth century. It goes something like this:

One winter evening while a snowstorm raged outside this church, a grumpy, disillusioned Benedictine monk who had lost his faith prepared to celebrate yet another communion to an empty house. Midway through the service a peasant entered the church, having struggled up the storm-ravaged hill (and trust me, it's a struggle in good weather). The monk continued to say Mass, barely masking his contempt for the peasant's audacious interruption. As he held up the Sacraments, the bread and wine turned literally into the flesh and blood of Christ. The monk's faith was instantly restored—and no doubt the peasant's spirits as well. Today the chalice and paten from this miraculous event are on display in the church in a glass safe.

Ancient artifacts could not distract me from the fact that I was desperately thirsty. Brigitte was, too, but she refused to enter any bar that held the slightest hint of trendiness, which pretty much meant all the bars in O Cebreiro.

"Let's get to the *refugio* first," she stubbornly suggested.

When we arrived, we were met by a tough, unsmiling young woman who crossed her legs and folded her arms the moment she saw us. No mistaking that body language!

There was no room, Hitler's Sister snapped at us.

Brigitte, who spoke Spanish, employed her best diplomatic skills, but Hitler's Sister would have none of it. She let loose a rapid-fire explanation that tested even Brigitte's natural civility and dignity.

"We are leaving," Brigitte said to me, turning on her heel.

"May we just get a drink of water?" I asked Hitler's Sister politely. She gestured wildly and snarled at me.

I matched her snarl with a bark: "*Agua!*"

I shoved past her into the adjoining kitchen, adding loudly, "You fat, lazy cow!" Truthfully, the Camino would have strained the patience of Job.

We failed to secure lodgings anywhere in O Cebreiro and were forced to walk to the next town.

Two kilometers later we arrived at a roadside diner that advertised rooms to let.

"The thing with the Spanish," Brigitte instructed me as we paused at the door of the diner, "is that you have to ease your way into your request. You don't just come in and ask for a room. You have to talk about the weather, ask them how they are. It is like flirting."

We entered a gloomy room that was part grocery store and part diner. The ceiling fan made a limp wop-wop-wop sound, and I knew in an instant that this setting would not yield a successful outcome.

Brigitte smiled at the woman behind the counter and launched into a laboriously long and ultimately fruitless dance to get us rooms. I stifled my urge to slug the two old geezers on the bar stools beside me who suggested we sleep with them. As I removed my backpack, one of them ogled my breasts and licked his lips.

"In your dreams, Grandpa," I smiled, as I slid onto the stool and ordered a beer.

A further three kilometers away, in Hospital da Condesa, we snagged the last two bunks.

Showered and grateful for a bed, I went outside to catch the last few rays of sun while I wrote in my journal. It was a warm, tranquil evening, and once again I felt optimistic about Santiago de Compostela. Earlier that day we had passed a marker saying that it was a mere 142 kilometers away. But most of all, I felt blessed to have the company of Brigitte and to be able to feed off her momentum. Sometimes it takes the energy of others to spur us on.

My good mood was jarred by a man circling me and caressing his chest while he stared at me. Only on the Camino could I win the lusty affections of two geezers and a nutcase in the space of a few hours. This guy was more my age, so I suppose things were looking up. I stayed resolutely focused on my journal and avoided eye contact.

When I returned to my room, the man followed me and stood at the foot of my upper bunk looking at me as he removed his shirt. Slowly. I slid into my sleeping bag and continued to ignore him. He then lay on the lower bunk kitty corner to mine so that if I looked down on him, I could see him stretched out caressing his chest.

Exasperated by my indifference he reached into his pants and pulled out the only attention-getting tool he had—his cell phone. He proceeded to dial a friend. "*Hola. Que pasa?*" he roared into the phone.

The audio volume on his cell phone was turned up so high that anyone within earshot could hear a male voice on the other end yammering back.

After a few minutes, the Lout with the Cell Phone made another call. I glanced across the room at a young couple who had also taken to their bunks. It was after 8 PM, and most pilgrims hit the hay early because, well, walking thirty-five kilometers uphill in the searing sun has a tendency to make you tired. The couple returned my look and rolled their eyes.

The Lout made another call. And another. And another.

Brigitte climbed into her bunk. The Lout had been vying for her affections that evening as well, she told me. Two-timing bastard. He continued looking up at us, making loud noises to attract our attention. We did not return his leers but shook our heads and laughed mockingly.

Someone turned off the lights, and we all prepared for blissful sleep.

The Lout's cell phone suddenly rang.

"*Hola?*"

"Oh, for Christ's sake!" someone in the room yelled.

THE NEXT MORNING I set off without Brigitte. She seemed uncharacteristically pokey, and I assumed it was her polite way of letting me know she wanted to walk alone.

"You go on ahead," she said. "I'll catch up."

But she never did, and it was the last time I saw her.

It made me a little sad, but I was sanguine about it; Brigitte was as much a free spirit as I was, and I had to let her go.

The morning dew spread a gauzy veil over the surroundings. Everything was lush and moist, the sky was cloudless, and the sun was edging its way toward the horizon. It was a peaceful morning, and the view was breathtaking.

I made my way along a narrow footpath that clung to a ridge. The sun snapped open like the eye of God, causing the shadows that cloaked the mountains to beat a hasty retreat. There is nothing more wondrous and operatic than a sunrise over a mountain range. The sun pulsated above the horizon—the heartbeat of a new day— and I spread my arms in welcome and let its heat energize me.

My goal that day was Sarria, a little more than thirty kilometers away. Once there, I would be about a hundred kilometers from Santiago. I fished out the maps from my backpack to double-check my route.

If nothing else, being on my own was making me more adept at reading a map.

While training for the Camino, Beth and I would get together on occasion to peruse the maps. One day, I casually mentioned to her that I was planning to pack my swimsuit for the Camino.

Beth looked puzzled.

"Do you really think we're going to have time to swim?" she asked patiently.

"Well, why not," I replied, pointing to the many red-ringed circular markings on the maps in front of us. "Look at all the pools of water."

She gave a worried smile but was polite enough not to question my ability to lead a herd of sheep, never mind a group of smart women.

"Oh, Jane," she said softly—and I think it's fair to say that probably many thoughts ran through her mind at that moment, chief among them whether she had cancellation insurance—"Those markings aren't pools; they indicate mountains."

The swimsuit stayed home.

As crowded as the Camino had been at the beginning of the journey, the pilgrim horde had noticeably thinned out. The solitude spooked me. The yellow arrows and stylized shells were the only indications that I was on the right path.

I did not encounter another soul on the twenty-kilometer footpath through a swath of forest that led to Triacastela. Not one. Desperate for companionship, and to erase the fear of walking alone, I had no choice but to create my own.

A man had momentarily appeared on the path a short distance ahead of me. From the back he looked exactly like the actor Steve Martin.

Wow, I thought, what would be the odds of finding Steve Martin on the Camino? The man evaporated and suddenly Steve Martin was right beside me.

"Hi," I said. "Do you speak English?"

"Why yes, I do," he replied. "Where are you from?"

"Canada," I answered. "You?"

"The States."

"Ahh, there are a lot of you on the Camino," I smiled.

"Really? I haven't met anyone from the U.S. They all seem to be Belgians."

After a few moments of awkward silence he spoke again:

"My name's Steve." He smiled in his aw-shucks way and extended his hand.

"Jane," I replied. "Nice to meet you, Steve."

I decided not to let on that I recognized him. I mean, why make us both uncomfortable?

My feigned ignorance appeared to irritate Steve, however. He dropped clues so that I would say, "Oh my God! You're Steve Martin!" But I refused to play the game. I'm not the star-struck type.

Besides, it wasn't important that it was Steve Martin; it was only important that he was another human being who spoke English. I was craving conversation, craving it more than *café con leche*. I was desperate to connect in a meaningful way with someone, even if it was fleeting, even if I had to make up the person.

Steve was a pleasant walking companion. We discussed Bush's foreign policy and debated whether weapons of mass destruction were merely a ruse for an attack on Iraq meant to divert attention away from a covert parallel operation to flush out Osama bin Laden.

"The whole thing seems so farfetched," said Steve. "I mean, c'mon, how does a guy in a cave manage to elude the world's superpower? Then again, maybe America isn't the superpower it says it is. So it goes after small fish like Iraq. I mean, Iraq. Give me a break. I'll bet Jamaica could take out Iraq."

We discussed the theological aspects of the Camino. Steve admitted he was wrestling with whether the spiritual component of the pilgrimage measured up to the physical task.

Our conversation was brief because the dirt path came to an end at the edge of a parking lot in Triacastela.

I gave a jaunty wave and a "*buen camino*" to Steve. He waved back and headed in another direction. What a nice man, I smiled to myself, and then worried whether it had been petty of me not to let on that I recognized him or to tell him how much I had enjoyed him in *The Lonely Guy.*

I walked into a café where a fat, greasy-looking lascivious old man asked my breasts what I wanted. I glanced down at my breasts because for a split second it occurred to me that if I was capable of having an imaginary conversation with Steve Martin, I was capable of leaving the *refugio* without my clothes on.

To my immense relief, I was fully clothed.

Behind the bar, on the wall facing me, was a pinup of a totally nude woman spread-eagled on a studio floor. If not for the red rose in her talonlike fingers—and I'll let your imagination determine what she was doing with the rose—the poster could have been a gynecological diagram for medical students.

The gruff bartender slammed down a *café con leche* in front of me, causing its contents to slop onto the saucer and the counter. He made no effort to clean it up.

Just then a little girl skipped into the café, resplendent in a pale pink dress tied at the waist with a huge pink bow. Her dark hair was divided into two pigtails that were festooned with pink ribbons. She wore dainty white leather Mary Janes, and her white-gloved hands carried a small white Bible. She ran up to the man, and gave him a kiss. This pig was her grandfather? Oy!

The girl's mother teetered in looking like a drunk slattern, a cigarette drooping from her red lips as she rummaged through her purse for a lighter.

I grabbed my gear and left. Sometimes the only way to take the high road is to walk it. And sometimes the metaphorical high road becomes a literal one.

Try as I might, I could not find my way out of Triacastela. I would walk a few hundred meters, then double back because the way did not feel right. I consulted my maps. I stood in the middle of the road trying to get my bearings, turning my maps every which way to glean a hint of direction. Without another pilgrim around—where the hell was Steve Martin when I needed him?—I was left to figure it out myself.

I chose one route and hiked along a paved road that led up and up. For four kilometers I climbed, and at the top of the road I arrived at—a garbage dump. A dead end.

"What a perfect metaphor for my life," I screamed. "I always take the long, hard way; always stick with difficult people, climb steadily toward what I think is a goal of resolution, and the pay-off? Garbage dumps!"

I stomped all the way down the hill.

I tried the other route and walked and walked. And walked some more. I recognized place names from my map, and realized with resignation that I would be taking the scenic route to Sarria.

I walked along footpaths and through villages that were so tiny they didn't even merit a sign displaying a place name. I passed farmyards and pastures. I paused to watch a lamb suckling its mom. There were cows everywhere. And dogs. Everyone seemed to own a German shepherd. The upside to walking in the noon-day sun was that the dogs were too hot and tired to bother strangers. In her account of the Camino, Shirley MacLaine wrote about masses of wild, ferocious dogs prowling for pilgrims, yet every dog I came across could barely muster a bark or a growl.

On and on I walked. Up steep hills and down through leafy glades. I did not see another human being.

I often like being in a place where there is absolute silence, where I feel like matter, where I feel as though I do matter.

Then there is the creepy type of silence, the type that puts me on the cusp of a panic attack. The internal dialogue goes from "Wow, how wonderful to have the place to myself" to "Gee, where is everyone?" to "Oh my God! Am I the last person on the planet?"

That last question was the one I was asking on the desolate but very charming stretch of road between Triacastela and Samos. Low stone enclosures bordered a narrow asphalt road that wound higgledy-piggledy through the verdant rural landscape. The air was fresh, the grass was tall, and the sky was blue and sunny. But there were no people and no sounds of activity. A few homes were scattered here and there, and I considered knocking on one of the doors just to check for signs of life.

I strained for a glimpse of someone—a farmer plowing a field, someone hanging laundry on the clothesline, a car whizzing by—but there was no one. Even the birds were silent.

I was both afraid and elated. Absolutely no one knew where I was. I could have simply walked off the face of the Earth—disappeared—right there, and no one would have had a clue where to begin looking for me. The idea was momentarily tantalizing.

Then again, what if I had a heart attack, a stroke, or an aneurysm? What if I twisted my ankle or dislocated my knee? Who would help me or even find me? No one. I willed myself not to get sick or hurt. If by an act of fate something did happen, I still had a few spare tabs of morphine in my pack.

I remained in this state for a very long time, perhaps five or six hours. It was thoroughly unsettling. Eventually I saw a café, and I made a slight detour toward it just to confirm the existence of human life. If no one was there, I decided I would steal a beer.

The café was a run-down joint under the proprietorship of equally run-down people, the type who wouldn't care if they were the last people on Earth. I inquired about the distance to Samos and was dismayed to learn I had four kilometers to go. Four kilometers feels like fourteen kilometers when you're hiking alone through high, dense vegetation along an infuriatingly winding path. Had the route been straightened, it would have shaved two kilometers off this particular stretch.

At the same time, it was an exciting route because you never knew what lay around the corner. The scenery inspired a deep and abiding reverence, but it could spook you, too.

Something rustled in the grassy border of the path, and out of the corner of my eye I saw a snake slither into the bushes. I hate snakes. It was the first time I had considered their existence in Spain. Suddenly I was panicked about what other wildlife was lurking about. Wolves? Poisonous vipers?

This is the sort of research more practical and intelligent people conduct when they embark on a hiking journey. I tend to take the blunder-in-with-staggering-ignorance approach.

With my faculties on high alert, I glanced back to allay my fears that the snake had not morphed into a massive, venom-drooling, red-eyed beast with a long, quick tongue. I pretty much ran down the path.

Under a blazing Spanish sun, I staggered into Samos to find that the *refugio*, which was attached to a monastery, did not open for another hour and a half. I sat down on a cold stone step and quietly wept—wept for the tiny blister that threatened to erupt on one of my toes, wept for my sore, aching legs, wept for my separation from all that was familiar, wept for my loneliness and fear.

By 5:30 the next morning, I was on the road once again. It was dark and frightening, but I no longer cared. I was fueled by the sort of anger and brazen courage that comes from sleep deprivation.

All night long, I had been kept awake by the woman in the next bunk. She snored. All. Friggin'. Night.

I had been forewarned. One of the woman's companions had thoughtfully told me that I might want to choose another bunk because his friend's snoring was bad—so bad that all her companions routinely slept at the opposite end of the *refugio*.

I thanked him but stubbornly stayed put, certain that I would be fast asleep before anyone else got to bed.

But I miscalculated the decibel level of the Incredible Snoring Woman. Not only did she snore, but she also farted constantly—big, noisy farts. She was still issuing loud bodily emissions from both ends when, in the too-early hours of the morning, I swung my pack into position and groped in the darkness for my walking stick. I considered whacking her with it, but had I started I would not have been able to stop.

I slipped through the *refugio*'s wooden doors onto the dark, ghostly street. I moved quietly, barely holding my resentment in check. Was it possible to return home from a pilgrimage more grumpy and sleep deprived than I was before I left? How can spiritual enlightenment be achieved amid farts and snorts and groans? Was this another one of God's test? C'mon God, throw me a bone here.

My grumbling stomach reminded me that it had been a few days since I had eaten a real meal. The night before I had seen a couple eating a steak dinner and almost dove on them. According to the waitress, I was five minutes too late to order the steak. I had to content myself with a beer and a bag of potato chips, which I munched on while trying to decipher my horoscope in a Spanish women's magazine. At the table next to mine, a couple of pilgrims were complaining about the erratic dinner schedule.

"If you speak Spanish," one grumbled, "you can somehow get a meal any time of the day; if you don't speak Spanish, you're out of luck."

With darkness blanketing the world, it would be hours before I found a café. I strained to make out the yellow arrows painted on the pavement leading out of Samos. The main road curved around the side of the monastery, whose spotlights illuminated an expanse of lawn and manicured gardens.

There had been a Mass the night before, but I had been too exhausted and too depressed to attend; now I regretted not making the effort, especially since the day before I had encountered one of its priests, who actually smiled at me—the first cleric to do so on the Camino—and who had gently warned me, in Spanish, not to sit too long in the sun.

The early-morning air was a chilly contrast to the late-afternoon heat. In the morning, everything was closed up tightly, including the flowers. By the time I reached Sarria, twelve kilometers away, the buttercups, forget-me-nots, and miniature daisies were wide awake.

I stopped at the first open café I found, threw back a *café con leche*, and carried on. Alone. I wondered how long a person could go without speaking before the ability to communicate ceased entirely.

I considered my feet and how the action of putting one foot in front of the other over and over and over again could induce a Zenlike hypnosis and an out-of-body experience simultaneously. I was mesmerized by the movement of my feet. I asked myself lunatic questions such as, "How does locomotion work? How do feet instinctively know how to walk? How do they know where to go?" This last question wasn't so insane; I often felt my feet were leading me on the Camino, not my head.

On the far side of Sarria, the trail descended steeply through a field and led into a forest.

Two men were on the path ahead of me. One was tying his shoelaces very slowly, and as they glanced at me they seemed to be purposely hanging back. They were Spanish; one was older than the other—a father and son, perhaps? It was obvious that they were day-hikers, because they carried no packs. Both of them smiled at me as I walked past, and I nonchalantly smiled back. But something about them spooked me.

Suddenly the rape dream I had had before setting off on my pilgrimage resurfaced. I felt a growing terror. I picked up my pace, but I could hear the two men close behind me. I moved as fast as I could without making it appear that I was running from them.

Farther along, a bunch of elderly Germans were negotiating their way across a stream. I offered to assist them but was rebuffed. The Germans, however, intercepted the two Spanish men and asked them to snap photos of the group, which the men graciously did. I sprinted quickly ahead.

The trail was a winding, pebbly one, edged with low stone walls covered in age and moss. In some places the vegetation was so dense that it formed an arbor over the path. Huge, ancient tree trunks protruded from the stone walls like enormous carbuncles. The numerous turns and unexpected shifts in the terrain kept me engaged and enchanted. I half expected Gandalf at the next bend.

I passed small, shantylike settlements, and then several minutes later passed grand homes. The contrasts were startling.

My initial plan had been to walk as far as Barbadelo and check in to the *refugio*, but a quick check of my maps showed that I had somehow missed Barbadelo and was well past it. Ferreiros was the next stop with a *refugio*, and I resolved to stop there for the night. I was hot, sweaty, parched, exhausted, dirty, and starved.

There were a number of places along the route where refreshment was available, but my legs inexplicably refused to stop. Something kept pushing me forward, and it was so strong at times that I stumbled under the pressure to move faster and faster. At a gorgeous café that seemed carved out of the forested surroundings, I looked longingly at a display of cold drinks, but my feet refused to pause, whisking me past a trough where I just managed to scoop up a handful of water and splash it on my overheated face.

The trail left the leafy, shaded sanctuary of the woods and delivered me to a dusty, dry, thoroughly unappealing road. The sun was intensely hot, there wasn't a stick of shade anywhere, and, adding insult to injury, the road led uphill.

"That's it," I screamed silently to my stubborn body. "I don't care what your hurry is, but I am stopping at the next place. I will die of heat if I don't get a drink."

At the crest of the hill, I found the *refugio*. Not surprisingly, it was closed. I rattled the door knob and tapped on the curtained windows, hoping to rouse someone, but there were no signs of life.

I looked up the road. A cluster of backpacks rested against a barbed wire fence. There had to be a café nearby.

As I approached the backpacks, my own felt suddenly lighter. The buckles mysteriously unlatched themselves, and the pack slid from my shoulders to the ground. I turned my head and noticed a café, its forecourt arranged with white plastic tables and colorful umbrellas.

Then I saw him: the fair-haired man.

15

HE WAS munching a sandwich when our eyes locked. Although he was seated, I could see that he was tall and slim. His fair hair was largely covered by a pale straw Panama hat. I gathered all this information within two seconds.

I looked away indifferently and pretended to be occupied with my backpack while I considered my next move.

I walked toward the café—I was getting a drink, man or no man—and debated whether to make eye contact again. As I passed his table, I heard people sitting with him speak English.

I'll go in and order a drink, I said to myself. If he's still there when I come out, I'll ask if I can join him.

He was still there when I returned with a cold beer.

"Mind if I join you?" I asked. I am never this forward.

"Of course not," he smiled. I detected an accent.

He rose slightly from his seat while I sat down across the table from him. I liked him immediately.

"What's that?" I asked, nodding toward the half-eaten sandwich he held in his hand. "It looks good. I haven't eaten in days."

"Not sure," he replied. "I think they call it a *bocadillo. Jamón*—ham. If you want to order one, you can take this in with you and show it to them."

"That's OK. I'll muddle through. Will you watch my beer and stuff while I go in and order one?"

"Sure. Mind if I look at your maps?"

I was certain I could trust him.

When I returned with my *bocadillo*—and I'm ashamed to say I devoured it ravenously—the man and I began talking.

"Are you Australian?" I asked.

"English," he corrected. "You? American?"

"Canadian. We don't like being lumped in with Americans."

"I am so sorry," he smiled, adding, "We don't like being lumped in with Australians."

His mouth moved into a grin. I wasn't sure whether it was a blush or the heat that made my face flush slightly. The brim of his hat shielded a fair complexion freckled by the sun. He had swimming-pool-blue eyes, a trim blond moustache, and a broad smile that showed off a straight line of teeth. I love a good set of teeth on a man. A tuft of gray chest hair sprouted from the neck of his T-shirt. I love chest hair, too.

An older blonde woman suddenly plopped down into the chair beside the Englishman and began complaining about her sore feet and blisters. She sounded Scandinavian. The Englishman looked very concerned as he listened to her tale of woe. Were they related? Friends? Lovers?

"Where are you two off to?" I asked eventually.

"Portomarín," the woman replied brightly. She struck me as a very kind soul.

"Any idea how far that is?" I asked. "And where are we anyway?"

The Englishman turned the maps around and pointed.

"Ferreiros," he said. "I think that's how you pronounce it."

"So, we're not far from Portomarín," I said. "It says it's about ten kilometers."

"More like twelve or fifteen," he said. "The maps are way off."

"Would it be OK if I walked with you guys?" I asked shyly.

They looked at one another, shrugged, and said, "Sure!"

I stuffed what was left of the sandwich into my mouth and belted back the beer. I was so excited to have people to walk with that I could barely contain myself.

We saddled up and returned to the dusty trail. I felt like Dorothy in the *Wizard of Oz.*

"To Portomarín?" I said, restraining myself from linking arms with the Scarecrow and the Tin Man and skipping off toward our destination.

"To Portomarín," the woman and the man smiled in unison.

We introduced ourselves. The Englishman was named Colin, and the woman was named Hannah; she was from Denmark.

"Where did you start from today?" Colin asked me.

"Samos," I replied.

"No!"

"Yes," I said. "Where did you start?"

"Sarria. My God, do you know how far you've walked?"

"Um, yes. A long way."

"Oh, you couldn't have walked that far," he continued, shaking his head.

"No, really, I did. I left at five-thirty."

I proceeded to tell them about the Incredible Snoring Woman.

It turned out I had already logged twenty-five kilometers and was now pumped to do another twelve. Chalking up nearly forty kilometers in a day would be some feat, and yet I no longer felt tired.

It never ceased to amaze me how far I could walk in an hour. Long before I hit the Camino's trail, the idea of walking five kilometers seemed a major undertaking. But I discovered that you can cover four or five kilometers easily in an hour. When I considered the short errands I do by car, I realized how much more fit, healthy, and relaxed I'd be if I used my feet rather than fossil fuels and took the world at a leisurely pace. Sadly, like many North American women, I have learned to pack a lot of chores into an hour, thanks to my car.

For all the benefits that walking creates, however, I can't say I jumped up each morning on the Camino and said, "Yippee! I'm walking today!" I almost always hated it until I passed a lovely view or the trail was easy or I had someone to walk with.

During our conversation I learned that Colin and Hannah did not know one another beyond casual recognition on the trail. They were part of the same tribe.

I told them about my lost group.

"It is hard when you don't know anyone," Hannah commiserated. Both she and Colin had arrived on the Camino alone.

They were lovely people, and it was a joy to listen to them. Especially Hannah; she was a talker. Colin was quieter.

As we walked I surreptitiously took in Colin's appearance. He was thin—really, really thin. He wore blue jeans and a cotton T-shirt, over which he wore a long-sleeved cotton shirt that floated on his rakelike frame. He carried a very large and heavy pack. I could not imagine how someone so thin could carry such a heavy load.

"Why are you wearing jeans?" I asked. "I thought we were supposed to wear polyester because it dries faster. And your tops are cotton, too?"

"I wasn't aware there was a dress code on the Camino," he smiled. I loved that smile.

We continued through a lush wooded landscape toward Portomarín. We were now in the province of Galicia (or as it is pronounced in these parts, "Galithia"; Galicians pronounce their *c*'s as *th*'s, which makes them sound as if they have a speech impediment).

We encountered more pilgrims along the way, none of whom I recognized. Strange, I thought, how I had walked alone for days without seeing anyone and now suddenly I was part of a pack.

Colin had decided to go beyond Portomarín to the next town. As much as I wished he would stay, there was no way I was walking farther than Portomarín. I had walked far enough for one day. Ditto for Hannah.

We crossed the vast brick bridge spanning the Rio Mino and arrived at a steep set of stone steps leading to Portomarín's center. We groaned in unison. To our immense dismay, we discovered at the top of the stairs that Portomarín's streets were all on an incline. More groans.

Although Portomarín has existed since the eighth century, the part we were walking through was all twentieth century. In the 1950s, while work was being done on a new reservoir, the town burghers decided to submerge the old village underwater and reconstruct it on higher and drier land. Historic buildings were dismantled and relocated in the new town. Even the Church of San Nicolás, a fortified Romanesque edifice, was taken down stone by stone and rebuilt on its new site.

As we climbed the last (we hoped) hill toward the *refugio*, a man yelled out to Colin and came running toward him.

"We have rented an apartment for the night," he told Colin breathlessly in a thick German accent. "We need one more person to make it more affordable. Please stay with us."

Colin and I looked at each other. I smiled good-bye and left him and the German to sort out their arrangements. I turned back to the road with Hannah.

At the *refugio* we were met with disappointment. There was no room. Hot and tired, and knowing that Hannah was having foot problems, I demanded that the *refugio* keeper find us accommodation.

He got on his cell phone.

"The girl, she will be here soon," he told us.

The "girl" arrived and walked us to a nearby apartment building and up two flights of stairs. Everything I did seemed to involve a climb.

The apartment was a three-bedroom suite with a gross kitchen, a living room/dining room combo that had seen better days, and a standard bathroom. In short, it was perfect. The bedrooms each had a double bed.

Hannah and I were prepared to share a bed until we learned that we could have separate rooms for fifteen euros each. The deal was done.

It seemed weird to be sharing an apartment with a woman I had met only hours earlier, but that was the Camino for you; it gave you what you needed when you needed it. A bed to myself and a bathroom. This was my reward for putting up with the Incredible Snoring Woman the night before.

"Let's get a drink and some food," I said to Hannah. She had removed her boots to reveal feet that looked truly painful. One toe was black.

"Yikes, you need to get that looked at," I said. "It looks infected."

"It does, doesn't it?" she mused with a dreamy attitude. "What do you think I should do?"

"We should find a doctor," I said. "C'mon."

"It doesn't really hurt," she said. "Let me see how it feels after a drink."

Around the corner from the apartment, the ubiquitous collection of white plastic tables and chairs heralded a bar. A man sitting at one of the tables was waving at us. It was Colin.

"We thought you were going on," I said.

"Gunther—the German guy—needed someone to share the apartment, so I decided to help them out," he said.

"That's great. Do you want to join us for dinner?"

"I promised to eat with Gunther and his friends, but why don't you join us?" he said. "I'm sure they won't mind."

"First, we have to find a doctor," I said, nodding to Hannah. "Her feet are really bad—infected bad."

"No, I'm fine now," said Hannah cheerfully. "I'll see how I am in the morning."

After a well-deserved libation, I left them and wandered off to find an Internet café.

To my utter surprise, there was an e-mail response to a message I had sent several days earlier to Theresa. My old group was still in Spain. As I suspected, they were about a week behind me.

"Is there any chance of you taking a bus back so we could all regroup and walk together?" Theresa implored in her e-mail. Dr. Dan the Massage Man was, she added, pining for me. "Oh, and Kate asked me to tell you something. She said, 'Fuck the Cad.' That's all. Said you'd know what it meant."

There was no way I could rejoin the group, not at this point, and I told her as much. It had been a hard enough slog to get this far, and now that I was closing in on Santiago, I could not imagine reversing my journey. I decided not to tell her about Colin.

That night the restaurant pushed together several tables as a bunch of nationalities exchanged tales from the trail. I could not believe my good fortune in having a real meal with real people. Colin and I sat side by side.

"What do you do?" I asked him as I helped myself to some salad and passed the bowl to him.

"I'm a policeman," he answered.

I never would have guessed; he seemed much too gentle, too fragile.

I tried to take an equal interest in others at the table, but I was smitten with Colin and only wanted to know about him.

We were leaving the restaurant after dinner when I noticed Barbara, an Australian woman I had encountered over the last few days, dining alone. She always walked slowly and often urged me to walk ahead so that she would not slow me down. I figured, like Brigitte, she had wanted to walk alone.

"Isn't this food shocking?" she now said. "Really awful stuff."

"It's one of the few decent meals I have had on the entire Camino," I replied. Chicken, vegetables, salad, and yogurt with honey may seem like an ordinary meal but when combined with the joyful buzz of conversation and the warmth of community it became a feast.

Hunched over her food at a table for one, Barbara was adamant, however. It was the worst food she had eaten.

SLEEP THAT NIGHT was delicious. I had a room and a large bed to myself. It was nowhere near as luxurious as the Parador, but it gave me the same amount of pleasure.

When I woke up the next morning, I could hear Hannah stirring.

"Good morning," I whispered at her door before pushing it open gently. She was almost ready. "How are your feet?"

"I need to bandage them," she said. "You go on ahead."

It seemed everyone was shooing me off.

I set off along the streets of Portomarín looking for signs of pilgrims. It was still dark. Echoing off the deserted plaza was the sound of chairs scraping across the floor of a nearby restaurant. The night before Colin had mentioned that everyone was going to meet there for breakfast. I considered joining them but changed my mind and headed in the opposite direction. I didn't want it to look as if I were stalking Colin. At dinner the night before I had caught a few of our tablemates smirking at us while we were locked in conversation.

Descending the narrow streets of Portomarín, I saw a solitary figure with a backpack far below, crossing the bridge out of the town, and I hurried to keep the pilgrim in sight as a guide.

But by the time I got to the bridge, the pilgrim had disappeared, and I resigned myself to another day of walking alone.

It was a spooky kind of morning. A shroud of fog had wrapped itself around the bridge, giving the Rio Mino the look of a cauldron with steam rising from it. I veered to the right after crossing the bridge, following the yellow arrows to Santiago. I was now less than a hundred kilometers from my destination.

Upon reaching the main road, I made out the ghostly shapes of pilgrims moving in and out of the fog, staggering like zombies from the *Thriller* video. To my left came the small roar of a thousand frogs croaking; to my right, a slight breeze made the leaves shudder like maracas.

One of the figures ahead looked vaguely familiar. You could usually recognize people from their backpack or their legs—that was all you could see of them from the rear anyway. A pair of tanned legs in slouchy socks could only be one person—Barbara.

"Hey, Australia!" I called out.

She turned around and smiled wearily. "Where did you sleep last night?"

"I shared an apartment with Hannah, the Danish woman. We had our own beds. Real bed linens. Our own rooms. It was great. How about you?"

"There was no room at the *refugio*; all they had left was a place on the floor of the gymnasium. Not even mattresses. It was shocking. I barely slept."

Everything was "shocking" to Barbara.

"Even street people get more dignity than that," I commiserated. "You traveled all the way from Australia to Spain so that you could walk eight hundred kilometers and sleep on a gym floor," I said. "That's money well spent, eh? How are your feet today?"

"Shocking," she said in her clipped Aussie twang. "Blood everywhere. Constant pain. My husband's going to kill me."

"What? Why?" Now this was truly shocking.

"My feet are wrecked," she said. "He likes me looking nice. I mean, look at me. I'm a fright."

Barbara was hardly a fright. Short, wavy, light brown hair, great tan, turned-up nose, pretty face sprinkled with freckles, a slim, athletic build. She did not strike me as the sort who would fret over something as petty as a pedicure.

"How are *your* feet?" she asked.

Mine were absolutely fine. Not a blister or a callous. Vaseline had proven to be a miracle ointment. My feet felt better and looked better than they had before I left for the Camino. I had prebooked a pedicure for my return but was now debating whether to skip it and save my money. But this was not a time to gloat, so I told Barbara about my sore toe. And my shoulder. Yeah, the shoulder was a legitimate area of pain. If she wanted more gloom, I could show her my nail-less finger.

"What brought you to the Camino?" I asked, changing the subject.

"I do this sort of thing all the time," she answered. "I take a holiday by myself every year, and I balance it out by taking another holiday with my husband."

"And he doesn't mind?"

"Nah, we've been married thirty-three years. Four kids. No one gives a shit that I'm gone."

"Yeah, my kids were practically packing my bags for me, too," I admitted. "Though, on second thought, I think I had my bag packed months ago."

"You married?" Barbara asked.

"Divorced. Twice. Three kids. I'm so used to being single that I don't know whether I could cope with being married again. So your husband doesn't like to walk?"

"God, no."

"If he knows you're walking eight hundred kilometers, surely he doesn't expect your feet to be pedicure-perfect when you get home. It's pretty gutsy to do this sort of thing on your own."

"They think I'm weird," she said. "My friends. Most of them believe a married woman should always travel with her husband. Many women are so dependent on their husbands, though, don't you think? What happened to liberation? Sure it's great being married, but people need time alone. The ones who constantly cling to their husbands are idiots. Then they complain about not having a life."

"Has this been as exciting for you as you thought?"

"Nah, it's been fucking awful. Feet are so sore."

"Maybe you should rent a bike."

She laughed. "I had a funny experience with the cyclists. I had arrived at a *refugio* and must have looked at fright. The woman sent me upstairs to a big room. Had the place all to myself, or so I thought. I took a shower, and when I came out there were all these blokes in the room. It was the bloody French cycling team! They all started stripping off. Guess they looked at me and figured I was harmless, eh? But there I was standing in front of about a dozen naked young men; and me with just a towel wrapped around myself! I tell you those blokes are in really good shape. I mean *really* good shape. I e-mailed my daughter, and she was killing herself. Couldn't imagine her mum with a pack of naked guys. Yeah, some of them had amazing bodies."

She mulled over this memory a little too long, I thought, then snapped out of her reverie self-consciously to add, "And they were really decent blokes, too."

We stopped for a *café con leche*. The sun had broken through the fog, but our hair was still damp from the morning dew.

"You got a perm, eh?" remarked Barbara.

"This?" I said with surprise. "It goes like this naturally. It's been days since I've looked in a mirror."

"You're lucky. It looks styled. Look at mine; it's shocking."

We were ready to strike out again when Hannah strode into the café. We ordered another *café con leche* and waited for her. With rocket fuel like this in our systems, we could finish the Camino in a day.

Coffee breaks were a pleasant treat along the way. Really, when you think of it, what better pastime is there than walking a few kilometers on a pretty trail, stopping for a cappuccino, walking another few kilometers, having another cappuccino—at times, the Camino was a thoroughly civilized affair.

Along the Camino the lack of litter was surprising. Occasionally you would come across a trash bin, but it was always so laughably small—well, small by North American standards—and yet it would hardly be filled. By comparison, North American bins overflow within minutes of being emptied of takeout containers and food wrappings, coffee cups, pop cans, water bottles, newspapers, and Slurpee vats. Spain does not appear to have such a disposable society. When you want a coffee, it is served in a china cup with a saucer, and you have no choice but to sit at a table and enjoy it. Such a concept! I never saw anyone walking with a coffee cup, and consequently there was no litter of that sort.

The three of us walked together. Barbara kept urging us to go on ahead because of her slowness, but I insisted on maintaining her pace.

"I tend to walk too fast," I said, "so I've decided to force myself to walk more slowly today."

Hannah was still having trouble with her feet—to look at them you wondered how she managed to walk at all—but she was a brisk walker anyway, and eventually she and I drifted ahead of Barbara.

Hannah was in her mid-sixties. She had chin-length blonde hair and was a hardy woman with a cheerful face. I asked her about what it was like growing up in Copenhagen, and she began to tell me about her childhood.

"We were not a wealthy family," she began. "Times were hard and money was scarce. This was in the 1940s. My mother stayed at home and looked after me and my sister, while our father went to work.

"One day my mother discovered she was pregnant. My parents could not afford another child, so my mother used a coat hanger to abort the baby. Abortion in those days was not as acceptable as it is today. My mother ended up with a terrible infection and got very sick. The priest came to visit us, and I remember listening at the door of my parents' bedroom as he spoke to my mother. He told her that she was dying and that she deserved to die—this was her punishment for displeasing God. I'll never forget it. My mother died, and my father, because he was working and had no one else to care for us, put my sister and me in an orphanage.

"My sister was younger than me, about two years younger—I was about six—and I kept trying to reassure her. She was so scared; she could not understand that our mother was dead. All she knew was that our mother was gone and we were in a strange place. A lot of the kids were crying. Some managed to get adopted. We did not.

"We lived there for about ten years. My father eventually remarried, and he got us out of the orphanage and took us with him and his new wife to New York to live. So we stayed there, and eventually I got a job and met my husband, and we moved back to Denmark. I had children—two boys—who have children of their own now. My husband was an alcoholic, and he beat me. We don't live together anymore."

"What a sad story," I said barely holding back tears and putting an arm around her shoulder.

"Sad?" Hannah was surprised at my reaction. "Why, it's not a sad story; it's a happy story. My sister and I were looked after. We ended up back with our father. I survived that. Can't you see? It gave me the courage to go on, to not be afraid when things were unfamiliar. I've traveled, I've had a good life. My marriage wasn't so great, but I have two sons who are wonderful. No, I feel very happy and very lucky. Blessed even."

Palas de Rei was our destination for that day, but judging by the swarm of pilgrims waiting for the *refugio* to open, we knew we would not have a chance of getting a bed.

I rested my rump on a stone ledge and took in the buildings and my surroundings—Palas de Rei was once the headquarters for the kings of the Visigoths—before scanning the pilgrim crowd. With visions of Visigoths running through my mind, my eyes paused on a beefy guy—the Lout with the Cell Phone. Our eyes met, and I quickly turned away and struck up a conversation with a young Canadian woman and young American man sitting next to me. Nice kids. Both had finished their first year at college and were walking the Camino as much for adventure as for self-discovery. It always surprises me when I meet young people who talk about self-discovery and spiritual balance. They get it, and they integrate it into their lives at an early age.

Meanwhile, the Lout had begun circling like a vulture. He moved to a perch within my range of vision and began unbuttoning his shirt and stroking his chest while looking at me. What was with this guy and his chest?

I conferred with Barbara and Hannah, both of whom were game to hike ahead to the next town. We had already walked twenty-four kilometers, and the next town, Melide, was another fifteen kilometers. I was willing to walk as far as I had to in order to ditch the Lout.

We were walking out of Palas de Rei when I saw a pay phone.

"I need to call my kids," I said. "I'll just be a second."

It had been days, maybe a week, since I had last spoken to them. I could hardly wait to hear their voices. I looked at my watch: they would just be getting ready for school.

"When are you coming home?" my son said tersely as soon as he heard my voice. "We need to *talk!*"

My daughter wrestled the phone away from him.

"Nana thinks *Saved by the Bell* is inappropriate," she whined. "And she's moved the drinking glasses to a different cupboard. Where are you?"

"Has the sink been installed?" I asked, changing the subject. Suddenly I was not missing home nearly as much as I expected.

"The sink . . ." my daughter started to say, and then my mother grabbed the phone. Using her everything's-under-control tone of voice that somehow conveys the opposite, she filled me in.

"The sink has arrived," she reported cheerfully, "but it's much too big for the space. The contractor had to take it out."

She proceeded to tell me that she had asked my ex-husband to make a decision about a replacement sink and to consult with the contractor about installing it.

Wait a minute—my ex-husband was being asked to make decisions with *my* contractor about *my* home? What the hell was going on? Before I could ask the question, I felt the sun warm my arms; I stared into the distance, where a grove of palm trees seemed to be beckoning me with their fronds. Bathroom sinks and TV shows—how did any of that relate to my Camino life?

I replaced the phone in its cradle, still staring ahead.

"Is everything OK?" asked Hannah with anxious concern. "It's so good to hear your children's voices, isn't it?"

I wasn't quite sure how to answer that.

A kilometer down the road, at a roadside hotel, Hannah announced she could not go another step and was packing it in for the day.

We said good-bye and promised to meet in Santiago.

Barbara and I left the steamy asphalt road, where waves of heat rose like a mirage in the middle distance, and followed the yellow arrows into a dense and leafy forest of dappled shade.

"Go on ahead," Barbara urged. "I'm just slowing you down."

I stayed with her, but half an hour later, as I was dying of thirst—even in the shade it was stinking hot—a breathtakingly beautiful stone inn set back from the road came into view.

"I'm going in to get a Coke," I told Barbara. "You want anything?"

"Nah, I'm fine. I'll keep walking. You'll catch up."

Two teenage girls served me behind the bar. I took my Coke into the empty dining room, slipped off my pack, and pressed my hot back into the cool stone walls. I tilted my sweat-soaked head against the wall and listened to Enya's ethereal voice float through the rooms.

She was singing about a pilgrim, about the curious irony of traveling a long distance just to find yourself. It was a haunting, seductive song, amplified by the soothing atmosphere. I glanced around and wondered whether I should ask for a room and spend the night.

Suddenly a harsh voice interrupted the dreamy moment, and the music came to an abrupt halt. A few seconds later I watched through an open window as a short bald man marched angrily— stereo system tucked under his arm—toward his white car parked in the grassy driveway. Within seconds he sped away, trailing an agitated cloud of dust.

"Well, that sucks!" I wanted to say to the girls behind the bar, but lacking the necessary words in Spanish to express myself, I took the interruption as my cue to leave.

The oaks and pines that bordered the gentle path produced an aroma of freshness and cleanliness. I ambled along contentedly, at peace with myself and the world.

The path crested slightly, and as I prepared for a gentle descent, I spotted a figure in the glade ahead of me—a tall thin man wearing a straw Panama hat.

It was Colin.

I called out. He turned around and walked toward me.

"Do you remember me from . . ."

"Of course I do." He laughed and embraced me with a friendly peck on the cheek. I'm never sure when I have made enough of an impression for people to remember me.

Like me, he was hiking to Melide.

We continued along this idyllic route, barely noticing the sign announcing that we had crossed the border between the provinces of Lugo and La Coruña. The yellow arrows had been largely replaced by stone markers half a kilometer apart that counted off the distance to Santiago. We were less than fifty kilometers from our Mecca.

We caught up to Barbara, who was resting on a rock, and I introduced her to Colin. She made a move to get up, but Colin suggested she stay put for a few more minutes to rest until she was ready. We weren't in any hurry, he said.

When we did return to the trail, Barbara urged us on.

"I'm such a slow walker," she said.

"She keeps telling me that," I told Colin when we were out of earshot. "I don't know whether she's being kind or whether she just wants to walk alone."

"We'll no doubt see her once we get to the *refugio* in Melide," he said.

"How was your night with your German friends?" I asked.

"Well, something really funny happened," he laughed. "There was this old German fellow—you met him last night, the one with the white hair? Anyway, he was all upset because someone had left their wet underpants on the apartment's radiator and hadn't properly wrung them out. By the time we got back from the restaurant, there was a large puddle of water on the floor. He started to scold me about it, because he assumed they were my underpants. I kept telling him they were not my underpants, but his. He seemed put out, and finally I held them up so that he could see for himself. I mean, there's no way you could mistake my underpants for his. His could hold a family of four!"

Indeed. Colin was a walking bone rack, whereas the German was, to put it kindly, a fleshy fellow.

"So, why are you doing the Camino?" Colin asked.

"To affirm my faith in God and to mark my fiftieth birthday," I said. Having been asked the question so many times, I had the answer down pat. Well, sort of. Pilgrims don't always know why they feel compelled to make a pilgrimage. Loss, trauma, a personal milestone, the desire to escape the world for a while—these were reasons that drew most people to the Camino, but it often took days if not weeks to work out precisely why you were there.

I casually turned the question back to him.

"I don't want to talk about it," he replied.

"Pardon?"

"I don't want to talk about it," he repeated.

Well, that was blunt.

"Can you give me a hint?"

"Nope."

"Tell me just a little bit," I said.

"Nope."

We walked on in silence as I tried to figure out how to deal with this situation. It was odd for someone not to share his or her reasons for being on the Camino. If anything, the Camino provided the most supportive environment you could imagine;

pilgrims were always generous about listening to and sympathizing with other pilgrims. I initially thought Colin's reluctance was a male thing, but then I remembered how open José had been.

"Is it a woman? Did someone die? Did you lose your job?"

"Nope."

"Ah, your marriage broke up," I said.

"I would have had to have been married to have a marriage break up." He smiled wanly.

"So maybe you were living with someone and you left her, or she left you."

"Nope."

"Did someone in your family die?"

"Look, I'm not talking about it, OK?"

"Just the gist of the problem."

"Nope."

We passed a marker: forty-seven kilometers to Santiago. Something told me that this would be the longest part of the Camino.

I asked less challenging questions, but Colin was reluctant to answer even those. He would not tell me about his family, though he repeated that he had never married and had no children.

As much as I tried to cajole answers from him, he would not budge. He folded his arms across his chest.

"OK, what about music and movies?" I asked in surrender. We had to talk about something, for God's sake. "What's your favorite movie?"

"*Apocalypse Now.*"

Was there a man alive who didn't name *Apocalypse Now* as his favorite movie? I asked about music, making a silent bet that his answer would be, *"Dark Side of the Moon."*

"Dark Side of the Moon," he said.

"What is it with you guys?" I said. "That album is so boring!"

"What about yours?" he asked.

"Gone with the Wind and *Back in Black,"* I answered.

"Gone with the Wind and AC/DC? What sort of a combination is that?"

"Eclectic," I replied haughtily. Two can play the evasive game.

We arrived in Melide and found the *refugio*, a handsome white stucco building surrounded by a lovely garden that was shaded by large palm trees.

There was no lineup when we arrived, and as a result there were plenty of empty bunks. We found two near an open window, where the palm fronds hung lazily in the late afternoon heat. I snagged the bottom bunk; Colin took the top.

It had been a scorcher of a day, so naturally there was no cold water in the shower; instead it was scalding hot. I had given up expecting anything more.

After we had freshened up, we found Barbara sitting on her bunk, massaging her blood-stained toes. They were shocking. I offered to get a doctor, but she refused. Would she like to join us for dinner? To this she agreed.

In a nearby restaurant, tall, frosty glasses of gin and tonic were delivered to our table as we perused the menu. I felt happily civilized.

"Are you going for the octopus?" asked Colin peering over the top of the menu. "This is what Melide is known for, after all."

Someone had obviously done his research.

Octopus wasn't the first thing I would have ordered, but then again neither was an eight-hundred-kilometer walk.

While the octopus was being fried, Barbara put Colin on the grill and asked him why he was walking the Camino.

Australians are far more direct than Americans. Whereas Americans will eventually back off when told, Australians are fearless. Had Colin said, "I don't want to talk about it," Barbara would have snapped back, "What are you, a fag? Did you murder someone?"

I played with the serviette on my lap and pretended to be engrossed in the menu. I learned more about Colin from Barbara's ten-minute interrogation than I had during the entire day I had walked with him. She didn't trifle with questions about favorite movies.

His answers were credible though vague—something about wanting a holiday—and then he expertly turned the conversation back to her.

I was a little hurt that he was more open with Barbara than he had been with me. Maybe the trick was to put a gin and tonic and a plate of food in front of him.

Barbara and Colin both worked in corrections; he was a cop, and she taught English to inmates at a maximum-security jail.

"Those blokes come strutting into the class thinking they can get away with things with me," said Barbara. "Some of them are murderers and rapists, but I make it clear to them right from the start that they can't fuck with me."

Colin and I exchanged nervous glances and took polite sips from our G&Ts.

On the way back to the *refugio*, our conversation turned to Santiago. We were two days away from it, and there was an air of excited anticipation. It was like the approach of Christmas Day. Other pilgrims were planning rendezvous points and times, and everyone seemed more upbeat and relaxed. Normally the *refugio* lights would be out by 8 PM, and the snoring would begin, but now the lights stayed on past 10 PM as people took the time to socialize. Even the morning routine had altered; the 5 AM hustle waned the closer we got to Santiago. Yet with the anticipation that the journey was almost over came a tinge of regret. I began to understand why people returned to the Camino year after year; the gypsy lifestyle was addictive.

But that was something to think about later. At the moment my mind had become fixated on the man in the bunk above me.

THE NEXT MORNING we passed Barbara's bunk. She had already cleared out.

"She walks slowly," I reminded Colin, "so I'm sure we'll catch up to her."

For the next two days, I walked with Colin. We shared a stride, a pace, a pattern of breathing. Our connection was as natural as putting one foot in front of the other. He wouldn't talk about the pain that had ripped into him but was receptive to hearing about mine.

He did throw me a few crumbs. He said he had lost fifty pounds in the aftermath of the Trauma That Could Not Be Mentioned and admitted that he had not discussed his distress with family, friends, or therapists. That's the irony of the Brits; they celebrate eccentricity but have a nationwide phobia about mental illness. Then again, I come from a culture that turns to therapy because of a bad hair day.

I did my very best to probe and prod my way into Colin's confidence, but he would not let me in. After a while my tenacity abated. I was afraid that if I pestered him too much about the Trauma That Could Not Be Mentioned, he might leave me, and I could not bear to be without his company. Santiago was closing in, I was almost at the finish line, and I did not want to arrive alone.

I dropped the subject and bit my lip.

At a café in Arzúa, while Colin was busy ordering a drink, I stole a quick peek at his passport to make sure he had given me his real name. He had.

"May I look at your passport?" he asked when he returned to the table with his drink. Maybe he thought I was lying, too.

I was delighted to show my passport; the photo was a particular source of pride, as it had taken four repeated attempts in various photo outlets to produce one that didn't make me look like a heroin addict or a middle-aged mother of three.

"Would you mind," he asked shyly, "if I had someone take our picture?"

"You want a picture of me?" I asked.

He ran a comb through his hair and smoothed the creases in his shirt. I engaged in no such fluffing; I had neither the tools nor the self-assurance that doing so would make an iota of difference.

Then, before we resumed our walk, Colin asked for my address and offered me his. This was getting serious.

At another café farther along the trail, one that had material-ized in the woods, we settled into a table beneath a sprawling shade tree. Colin's gentle nature drew me in; it was all I could do to restrain myself from leaning over and kissing him on the cheek, egotistically thinking that by doing so I could make his sorrow disappear. I wanted to throw my arms around him and hug him, run my hand through his thatch of ginger hair, stroke his back; I was falling hard for him, and yet I had the sense that if I overstepped the boundary of propriety he would disappear.

In a lapse in decorum, I put my hand on his shoulder, and he jerked it away as if he were unaccustomed to human touch.

At lunch that day I resorted to a devious prank.

We had finished our *bocadillos* and were about to take off, when I casually said, "You have something on your face."

He wiped his face and looked at me expectantly.

"No, it's still right there," I said, pointing but not touching.

Again, he wiped his face and looked at me.

"No, you haven't got it," I laughed. "It's right *there*."

"Where?" he asked.

With my finger, I stroked the soft area around his mouth. Of course there was nothing on his face at all; I just wanted to touch him.

"What was it?" he asked.

"Mustard, I think."

"But I didn't have mustard on my sandwich," he protested.

"Beats me," I said shrugging my shoulders indifferently and turning away from him to hide my smirk of victory.

In a noonday sun reserved for mad dogs and Englishmen (and hopelessly infatuated Canadians), we walked and walked. The Camino moved from gorgeous forested paths and leafy cano-pies to hard gravel roads and paved avenues taking us through a parched terrain that refused to make apologies for the lack of shade.

Despite the elements and the hardships, nothing broke Col-in's silence.

16

For a place that ranks number three in the Holy Hot Spots of Christendom, first impressions of Santiago inspire anything but reverence.

High atop Monte del Gozo, a broad hill on the outskirts of Santiago, you get the lay of the land. Behind you spans nearly eight hundred kilometers of largely peaceful trail that bends and meanders to Nature's mold; below you awaits several kilometers of complicated concrete and asphalt that spiral around Santiago like one of the circles of Hell, none of which had a pilgrims-only lane. To steal a phrase from Barbara, it was shocking.

You would think medieval spires would be fairly obvious from a vantage point like this—they were, once upon a time. Nowadays the horizon is clogged with the usual high-rise offenders of modern architecture.

What Colin and I saw—and it was not a pleasant sight—was a no-man's-land of construction zones, impatient traffic, incomprehensible street names and directional signs, and a population inured to a millennium's worth of pilgrims. How we were expected to find yellow arrows amid all that chaos was anybody's guess.

It put the "grim" in "pilgrimage": trucks spewing exhaust, jackhammers pounding impenetrable pavement, cranes swinging pallets of building materials through the air, monstrous dump trucks materializing out of nowhere and bearing down on you with their blaring horns as you try to sprint across multiple lanes of traffic with a twenty-pound pack lashed to your back. Then shouting voices, screeching brakes, cars kicking up dust and debris, turning the air into a dusty, choking cloud that stings your eyes and catches in your throat. A pilgrim's newly acquired traits of humility and tolerance are put to the test. Throw in Spain's searing sun, and you wonder whether the miracle of the Camino is the fact that pilgrims don't go berserk at this point.

The scene certainly bore no resemblance to my naïve expectations about arriving in Santiago. In my mind's eye I had pictured myself with the women in my group rushing down the grassy hillside of Monte del Gozo, holding hands as we sang, laughed, and skipped our way into Santiago. Think of the poster for *The Sound of Music*, and you get the idea.

The reality was a bit different. I dragged my bones through a grimy purgatory, sweat and dirt mingling on my skin, hair, and clothes. I never felt dirtier, and I never looked dirtier. I probably never smelled dirtier, but then I couldn't tell; my nasal passages were clogged with particulate emissions. Adding insult to injury was that my head was pounding with confused emotions and a major hangover.

The night before, in Arca, Colin got it into his head that we had to have a drink in every bar in the village. Arca had about ten bars. We started off with gin and tonics and ended with brandy. I have had three brandies in my life, all of them consumed within the last hour of our impromptu booze-up.

It had been a fine night of talking as long as the conversation did not stray into personal territory. Our main topic was our arrival in Santiago—specifically, the religious tribunal that pilgrims face at the end of the Camino. From what I had pieced together from conversations and advance research, pilgrims arrive in Santiago and file into a large hall, present their pilgrim passport, and speak with a priest or monk about what lessons have been learned from the Camino and how those lessons would be integrated into daily life. If the clerics were convinced of your pure heart and intentions, you were granted a parchment that signified completion of the Camino. I worried that the hall would thunder and shake when it was my turn to face the tribunal, wavering as I was between carnal thoughts and pious intentions.

"I don't want to arrive in Santiago alone," I had confided to Colin in Arca. "Can we walk together tomorrow? And since my group isn't with me, would you hold my hand when we enter the cathedral?"

He had smiled and nodded indulgently. Brits are like that; they seem almost too polite, and although they agree to your request, you can't help but wonder if, in the back of their minds, they're saying, "Bloody hell; that's a lot of cheek!"

By 10 PM, the bounds of my alcohol tolerance had been stretched.

"I have to go to bed," I told Colin, and we staggered back to the *refugio.*

At the entrance to our dorm he stopped, turned to me, and said, "Goodnight." Then he bent his head and kissed me. On the lips. A slow, full, divinely passionate kiss that seemed to swallow me whole, the sort of kiss that someone might regret the next morning.

"I love you," I whispered impulsively.

"No you don't," he smiled sadly. "You're being silly. There is no way you could love me."

"I know what I know," I said defiantly.

"Go to bed," he whispered, kissing me again, this time on the forehead. "I need to stay up a little longer. Go on."

I entered the dark dorm, stumbling past sleeping, snoring pilgrims, groping for my bed. I have no idea how I accomplished this under the influence of so much alcohol, but I managed to climb into my upper bunk without the assistance of a ladder.

Once I was inside my sleeping bag, my head swirled and my heart raced. Colin's words perplexed me. "There is no way you could love me."

I pulled my trousers back on and scrambled out of my bunk.

I found him sitting on a bench outside the *refugio* door.

"What is wrong?" I asked.

He turned his head to me and looked extremely sad. His face barely resembled the one I had come to know and love over the last two days. Just two days? It felt like weeks.

I put my hand on his arm, but he moved away.

"No," he said.

"Why won't you tell me what's wrong?"

"You wouldn't like me if you really knew me," he said staring up at a new moon.

"I can't make that decision unless you tell me what you're upset about, but really I can't imagine you doing something awful. You're just not like that."

"I'm not a nice person," he said softly. Then, turning to me, he added, "Really. I'm not. Trust me. Go off to bed. Now."

By morning the full effects of consuming cider, gin and tonic, four glasses of wine, and three brandies—and that was only the stuff I remembered—hit me. Oy. Were points deducted for being a hungover pilgrim?

A wave of disappointment washed over me (at least I think it was disappointment; it might have been nausea). I had embarked on the pilgrimage to seek resolution and insight away from the noise of the off-Camino life. Now I was on the cusp of finishing it with a major hangover and a heart in freefall. And I was hauling someone else's unnamed emotional baggage along with my own. This is what men do to me.

I rolled my head to one side. Colin was still there in the opposite bunk, and he was looking at me. Without a word, he stretched his arm toward me over the aisle; we grasped hands and lay staring at one another.

Our journey that day began on a path through a lush, moist forest of ancient trees with mottled white trunks. Ivy spilled over the embankments that framed the path, and dewy moss seemed to cover everything from rocks and tree trunks to the path itself. The air was fresh and new.

And then it was over. We exited Shangri-La and found ourselves on a dry, dull, dust-choked road that carried us through an industrial park and past a chain-link fence that separated the Camino from the runway of Aeropuerto Lavacolla, Santiago's airport.

We huddled in a sliver of shade at the concrete entrance to a hydro substation and gulped down water that had turned warm from the intense heat. The air felt like a dragon's breath.

Our conversation, like the route itself, was dry and parched. We had crossed an emotional border, and neither of us knew the language. We joked a bit, mainly about the amount we had drunk the night before, but not one word was said about The Kiss.

THE WALK TOWARD the Santiago cathedral seemed as long as the Camino itself. By now my feet and legs hurt so much that it was painful to stop walking. Waiting for the traffic lights to change put me in a level of agony I had never experienced before.

With the pilgrimage about to end, I faced the added confusion of not knowing where I would spend the night. I did not want to leave Colin, and yet I had no idea what was on his mind.

Of one thing I was certain—I was done with *refugios*. I was done with bunk beds and snoring companions and shared bathrooms and communal living.

We had passed the last *refugio* on the pilgrimage at Monte del Gozo, where more devout pilgrims than I rest up before making their way to the cathedral. It had all the warmth of a concentration camp—barbed wire and bland design. Apparently, a cairn existed nearby where pilgrims of yore placed a stone from home, and that act would net them one hundred days off their stint in purgatory. Nowadays, a night at the Monte del Gozo *refugio* confers the same benefit. Thanks, but I'll take my chances with purgatory: I had no desire to stay there, and, thankfully, neither did Colin. (Still, pilgrims were raving about Monte del Gozo like Pentacostals.)

While I struggled to come up with a way to broach the subject of accommodation, Santiago's asphalt streets changed to cobblestone. We had entered the medieval quarter and were taking the final steps of the Camino.

Then, before we knew what had hit us, there it stood: the grand Cathedral of Santiago de Compostela.

It hits you with its powerful presence immediately. Its immense girth and height dwarf everything and everyone around it. Once you get used to its size, it sucker-punches you with a dizzying display of Baroque decoration. And this, we discovered, was only the side entrance.

We passed an opened door as an angelic voice from inside the cathedral drifted out to us, luring us toward it. Impulsively I moved toward the sound—I had never heard such a clear, pure voice before—but Colin yanked me back.

"We can't go in yet," he said. "We can only enter through the Holy Door."

"Who said?" I asked.

"Well, no one, actually," he replied. "But I read that because it's a Holy Year, pilgrims get to enter through the Holy Door. If you enter the cathedral that way, all your sins are forgiven."

Poor man. It was so important for him to do the right thing, the ritual thing.

We had decided earlier that before entering the cathedral we would find the pilgrim office, face the daunting tribunal, and get our *credencials*. The lineup would probably be horrendous, we figured, but since it was relatively early in the day, there was a chance we might beat the rush.

I had seen medieval renderings of pilgrims queuing up for their *credencials* in a long line that snaked around the cathedral. At the height of its popularity in the late eleventh and twelfth centuries, the Camino and Santiago attracted about half a million pilgrims. If the line was like that in the 1300s, it would surely be twice that size in 2004.

Colin and I discussed strategy. We would get a space in line, and one would relieve the other for breaks. It would be a long, hot ordeal, but there was no alternative.

We found the pilgrim office on the quaint, cobblestoned Rúa do Vilar. A small sign pointed upstairs.

Aha, the lineup is upstairs.

"At least it can't be too long then," I said, afraid to voice aloud my worst fears. "And at least it will be inside, out of the sun."

We climbed two flights of stairs. Not a pilgrim in sight. Was the pilgrim office closed for lunch?

We walked into a large modern-looking room, outfitted with posters and tourist brochures. A couple of bored young women sat behind the counter.

"We're looking for the pilgrim office," Colin said tentatively.

"*Aquí está.*" Right here, said one of the women. She stretched her hand out wearily for his passport.

The other young woman did the same for me.

She glanced indifferently at my pilgrim passport and pulled from a well-stocked drawer a piece of 8" x 10" cream-colored paper decorated with a Latin inscription set inside an elaborate border of shells, garlands, and ribbons and topped by a cameo of St. James. She printed my name on it in Latin, stamped it, and handed it back.

"What do I do now?" I asked.

"That's it. You are done. Congratulations." She turned back to the fashion magazine she had been flipping through before we disturbed her.

"But what about..."

Anticipating my question, the other young woman interjected, "You can get the *credencial* laminated downstairs in the shop across the street."

That was not my question.

In stunned silence Colin and I walked slowly down the stairs to the Rúa do Vilar.

"It's rather anticlimactic, isn't it?" he finally said in that stoic yet understated way the Brits do so well.

"What about the tribunal?" I asked incredulously. "The questions about our journey? Probing our Christian souls to see whether we were true pilgrims? Whether we had grasped the holy lesson of the Camino? Whether we had deep questions about our faith that needed to be answered? Where's all that?"

"I guess this is all there is," he said, shrugging his shoulders. "We're done. Let's get a beer."

We were desperate for something to slake our thirst. We were also desperate for a shower. I wasn't going to walk into a cathedral looking this filthy.

It was the start of the Ascension Day weekend, a big deal in the Spanish calendar. On our way to find a beer, we stopped at a few small hotels to inquire about rooms, but most of the places were booked or hugely expensive. At one hotel someone was kind enough to draw us a map to another hotel in its chain that had a room available.

"You do know that we will need separate rooms," Colin said quietly but firmly.

"Of course," I said, as if insulted that he would think otherwise. But, I was hurt. What single man doesn't jump at the chance to spend the night with a woman?

We found a café and sat down. The town was so pretty and romantic—cafés spilling over the plazas, narrow streets devoid of cars except on the perimeter road, tons of shops, and a celebratory air. I wanted to smile and laugh, but I was afraid my enthusiasm would turn Colin off.

"*Enough of this,*" I thought to myself. "*I didn't walk eight hundred kilometers to suck up to someone and suppress my feelings. I'm getting a hotel, and if it means having to say good-bye to this guy, so be it.*" I recalled the incident in Logroño with Beth and Kate. Compromise was an option, but total abdication was not.

But before I could open my mouth and tell Colin what was on my mind, he said, "Let's get the room."

"What?"

"Let's get the hotel room. I think we deserve something nice after all—a nice bed and a real bath."

All right! Now he was coming around to my way of thinking.

"OK. We'll make sure it's not too expensive," I offered by way of compromise. "We'll check out the hotel that the lady at the last one told us about."

"Actually, I was thinking of taking a room in that expensive place," he said.

"That's a bit much for me," I answered prudently. "Besides, they said they didn't have single rooms."

Then, I added efficiently, "Even if we have to share a room, I don't mind. I mean, it's not like we're going to have sex or anything."

He laughed nervously.

We paid the bill and headed off in the direction of the hotel, yet another map in hand.

The Hotel Pombal was not far from where we were. When we arrived the clerk—a beautiful woman with luxurious long dark brown hair and smooth olive skin—said she had received a call from her counterpart at the other hotel alerting her to our arrival.

"However, I'm sorry to have to tell you," she said, "that we do not have any single rooms left. We do have a room with two separate beds."

I looked flatly at Colin. "Is that OK with you?"

He nodded.

"Good," the dark-haired beauty behind the desk smiled. "It's my favorite room."

"I'll bet you say that about all your rooms," joked Colin.

"No," she said seriously. "It's really a very nice room." Handing us the key, she added, "Just up the stairs. Top floor."

Another climb.

We reached the top floor and followed a skylit corridor to our room. Colin put the key in the door. Hotel rooms always make me nervous; there's such a desire to have something exotic and lovely.

Instantly I could see why it was the desk clerk's favorite room; it was now my favorite room, too. Three steps descended into a spacious, loftlike room with a vaulted timbered ceiling and a large dormer skylight giving an unobstructed view of the Cathedral of Santiago de Compostela. It was poetic, romantic, and decorated in a casually elegant way. It was like something out of *La Bohème* with cash thrown in. I pretended to take no notice of the two beds that had been pushed together.

"Look at the bathroom!" I exclaimed. "It's so clean, and so nice. There's a skylight in here, too!"

"It is beautiful," Colin smiled, appearing to enjoy my excitement. "Now let's get organized and cleaned up. I think we should attend Mass at the cathedral at five. They said they would read out our names at that one. You can have the bathroom first. I need a little rest."

WE ARRIVED EARLY at the cathedral. As we crossed the threshold of the Holy Door, Colin grabbed my hand and gave it a squeeze. I shot him a puzzled look and then realized that he had remembered the request I had made in Arca.

There are a number of rituals that pilgrims complete at the end of the pilgrimage. I was glad to learn that Colin didn't expect to observe all of them.

In earlier times a visit to the tomb of St. James was the first order of business, followed by attendance at Mass and an offering of oils and candles. Over time more elaborate rituals were added— all-night vigils in the cathedral, confession, special masses, and Holy Communion, each accompanied by an expectation of cash.

These practices have, in modern times, been adjusted, depending on the depth of your pockets and faith. Still, the cathedral
is the biggest show in town, and every effort is made to pack the
place and swell its coffers.

We joined the long line of people waiting to hug the Apostle, a grotesque-looking gold and bejeweled idol that has presided over the blindingly ornate main altar since the cathedral
was consecrated in 1211. The requests made by those I met along
the Camino to hug the Apostle on their behalf was a duty I was
honor-bound to fulfill. As the 22 *Miracles* asserts, James is ready
to help those who beseech his assistance with a "proper heart." I
did what had to be done, but it did not feel genuine.

Next we traipsed downstairs to the vault beneath the high altar
where James's bones and those of his disciples, Theodore and
Athanasius, are kept in a small silver coffin. It has been tucked
into a large stone niche, protected from the horde by a Plexiglas
plate. A high-intensity spotlight is positioned in such a way that
the reflected glare from the coffin makes you shield your eyes.

So this was it. This is what pilgrims from all over the world
and for a thousand years have traveled to see after enduring an
often treacherous journey. This is where pilgrims collapsed into
a weeping heap to beg St. James for a miracle.

Around me, old ladies genuflected repeatedly and covered
their mouths in awe. I bowed, more out of respect for the women
than for St. James, and said a quick prayer for an end to war and
world poverty and left it at that.

I couldn't help feeling scammed. Nothing felt authentic.
Although James's name was all over the Camino—he was its fig-
urehead and its spiritual guide—I felt indifferent toward him.

I had hoped that a month on the Camino would have given
me some insight into James, made me sympathetic toward him
despite what is often written about him, but it didn't. He was no
better known to me at the end of the pilgrimage than he had
been at the beginning of it. He had as much depth as a card-
board cutout. One statue depicts him as a humble, stooped-back

pilgrim; another portrays him astride a stallion, wild-eyed and brandishing a saber as Santiago Matamoros (St. James the Moor Killer). The portrayals of him were so inconsistent that you could not tell what was fact and what was fake.

Back upstairs, in the central arch of the Glory Portal, where the most popular likeness of him exists, in a seated pose atop an elaborately carved Tree of Jesse, I posed the question to him directly. Why, after all those kilometers, do I feel as if I don't know you, or, worse, that you don't matter to me?

James stared back with an alert yet bemused expression as if to say, "Hey, I can't understand what all the fuss is about, either. But just look at this—isn't it fantastic?"

"Are you feeling happier now?" I asked Colin as we settled into a pew, as if happiness could be switched on and off in a man so wracked by emotional pain.

He barely smiled.

"But you have to feel more unburdened," I said. "You walked through the Holy Door. All your sins are forgiven."

"Are they?" Then, with a wink, "You don't know what I've been thinking since I walked through the door."

The angelic voice we had heard earlier that day once again filled the cathedral. It came from a small, plain, expressionless, mortal nun, an unlikely source for such a magnificent voice.

My mind wandered during Mass as the previous three weeks came rushing back. Had it only been three weeks? It felt like a lifetime. In a way it had been; sometimes a journey is not measured by kilometers but by how much your soul absorbs. The lessons and their impact would take months and even years for me to process.

I had crossed a landscape like no other. It was a landscape I could smell and feel, one that permeated my skin and burrowed itself into my very soul to the extent that when I eventually returned home I could still feel it, my body yearned for it.

The physical distance, too, was hard to fathom. When you

think of it, walking eight hundred kilometers—largely alone—in a foreign land with only a backpack and map and arriving at your destination safely is a miracle in itself. It bears adding that to be able to say you walked across a country is a pretty big deal, too. Sure, Spain isn't Canada, but it's not exactly Liechtenstein, either.

Up to this point the Mass had been a solemn, passionless murmur of Spanish, but a surprise awaited the standing-room-only crowd. The priest turned away from the altar, made eye contact with the congregation (finally), and said, in English (with a theatrical flourish), "And now, the *botafumeiro!*"

The reason for the crowds quickly became apparent. They had not come for the pilgrimage (most of the people in the cathedral had not walked the Camino) or to hug the Apostle or to view James's reliquary. They had not come to attend Mass on a hot Friday afternoon. They had come to see the *botafumeiro*.

The *botafumeiro*, a huge, heavy silver incense burner— roughly the size of the nun with the angelic voice—takes four men to hoist into the air and launch through the cathedral's interior. Back in the day, the *botafumeiro* was used to dispense incense over foul-smelling pilgrims who humbly bowed in spite of the insult. Today the *botafumeiro* is not used over chastened pilgrims but over well-heeled tourists toting digital cameras and micro-sized camcorders.

To the oohs and aahs of the crowd, the *botafumeiro*, supported by a single cable hung from a rig within a cupola about a light-year above our heads, was swung out to the congregation. On cue, cameras were raised as if we were at a rock concert. The presence of so many cameras and flash bulbs was so mesmerizing that I found myself watching the proceedings through the tiny viewer on the camera held by the tourist in front of me. After a short eternity, the *botafumeiro* came to rest, and the congregation erupted in wild applause.

"I don't like clapping in church," Colin said disapprovingly. "It sounds cheap, doesn't it?"

The crowd quickly dispersed with the money-shot it had sought.

I passed the column where St. James was seated, his back to the tawdry spectacle we had just witnessed, and I shot him a look of disappointment. The simple and, by all accounts, moody fisherman from faraway Yaffa, son of Zebedee and Salome, apostle of Christ, evangelist, martyr, and saint, had become Spain's Mickey Mouse.

PILGRIM TRADITION holds that once you get your *credencial*, you are entitled to three free meals at the opulent Parador in Santiago. Here's the fine print: pilgrims take their *credencial* to the hotel's garage, where a security guard hands them a chit. Pilgrims then proceed through the garage to the staff kitchen, where they eat their meal.

Well, thanks, but excuse me. After schlepping nearly eight hundred kilometers, trudging up a few mountains, bunking down in lice-infested *refugios* without a shred of privacy, the idea of chowing down in the basement of a hotel holds little appeal for this pilgrim. I'd rather don a bra made of sackcloth than eat in a hotel kitchen.

Instead, Colin and I found a brightly decorated little restaurant where we had a real meal that night, a sumptuous five-course feast served on a kaleidoscope of dinnerware. The bold colors of the restaurant—periwinkle blue and terracotta—boosted my spirits to the stratosphere.

We forgot about the long, hot days, the sore muscles, the sweat, the dirt, and the loneliness that solitary walking can induce. For a moment we were a couple on holiday, and it felt good. I didn't care if it was transitory; I needed to feel I belonged to someone.

It had become chilly when we returned to the streets of Santiago. Rain splashed against the cobblestones, and we decided to head back to our hotel.

We reorganized our backpacks, threw out unnecessary papers, reread our maps (which we no longer needed but couldn't part with), washed out our clothing, counted our money—in short, we did everything to avoid the fact that we were a man and a woman attracted to one another in an unbelievably romantic hotel room anchored by a huge bed.

In the midst of our puttering, I glanced toward the skylight.

"Quick! Look!"

A rainbow. A perfect, clear, full arc had appeared over the cathedral.

We grabbed our cameras. The sun burst through the clouds.

"There's another one forming," said Colin excitedly. "It's a double rainbow!"

"You see," I said turning to him. "Miracles do happen. Maybe that's a sign."

"A sign of what?" he asked.

"A sign that, um, color is back in your life. God is wrapping His arms around your pilgrimage. We were meant to have this room so that you could witness a miracle of hope that would release you from your pain."

Well, perhaps that was a long shot.

Later on we crawled into our respective beds. The starched sheets were tucked as tightly as a straitjacket, especially on the side where our beds touched. There would be no chance of one person's foot straying into the other's territory, no likelihood that one of us would roll over into the arms of the other.

We faced each other and clasped hands as we waited for sleep. Occasionally I opened my eyes and saw Colin looking at me, but not a word was spoken.

IT WAS GRAY and chilly when the bus pulled out of the depot two days later. I was on my way to Finisterre, the End of the Earth, as it was known until a bright spark named Christopher Columbus discovered a big new world beyond the Spanish shores.

Colin was going to Finisterre, too, but he was making the 150-kilometer journey by foot. We had parted company that morning after a total of five chaste days together.

It had been an awkward good-bye. I was half crying, half impatient to get out the door so that I would not be late for the bus. We had delayed our good-byes until the last possible moment, and suddenly there was no time to do it properly.

As soon as we parted I felt as if a piece of me had been amputated. And I was also angry. It wasn't the sexual tension that had frustrated me but the emotional game-playing around the Trauma That Could Not Be Mentioned. Colin had not given so much as a hint about what was plaguing him, and I had begun to imagine worst-case scenarios. Had he committed a crime? Was he on the run? Hiding from the police? But he *was* the police! Had he skipped out on someone? Was he gay? Had he robbed a bank? Killed someone in the line of duty? Bounced bad checks? Was he a pedophile? A con artist? Had he jilted someone? Was he a Ted Bundy type—nice and civil on the outside, a cold-hearted murderer on the inside?

I was hurt that he had not confided in me, had not trusted me. His self-loathing had become a security blanket, and I was tired of it, tired of nurturing it and carrying it. Why did I take on people like that? What attracted me to emotionally and physically desiccated men?

From the bus seat in front of me, Barbara turned around.

"That English guy was a strange bloke, wasn't he?"

Barbara had asked me to join her and her friend Rose on a day trip to Finisterre. It offered me a convenient way to avoid a long good-bye with Colin.

Rose, who was also from Australia, had planned to walk the Camino with Barbara, but it had turned out quite differently.

"I got on the Camino," she explained in her thick accent heavy with cynicism, "and took about fifty steps, and then I said, "Screw this. I'm not doin' it. So I got on a bus and traveled through Spain and Portugal. Went to Madrid, Barcelona, Bilbao, the Algarve. 'Ad a blast."

She and Barbara had rendezvoused in Santiago.

It was easy to see why the Camino and Rose had not hit it off. With her high-styled flame-red hair, matching painted nails, and full makeup complete with bright red lipstick—which she insisted on wearing every day—Rose was too high-maintenance for the Camino. Bravo to her for realizing that. Bravo, too, to Barbara for not holding it against her.

By the time we reached Finisterre, the weather had brightened. The same could not be said for Finisterre itself.

"Attractive" is not an adjective I would attach to Finisterre, its long stretch of beaches notwithstanding.

Many pilgrims consider Finisterre—specifically, its lighthouse—to be the true end of the Camino. Despite the esteem in which it is held, Finisterre does not seem to have done anything to foster the sense of hospitality that characterized so many other stops along the Camino. I wondered how Colin would cope.

We found a bland café, quickly downed our lacklustre *cafés con leche*, and went off in search of a better establishment or at least one that sold croissants to satisfy Rose's craving. After the fifth place, we gave up and repaired to yet another crappy joint for another crappy *café con leche*.

Rose pulled out some Snickers bars. "This'll have to do."

That day was an auspicious one for Spain. Prince Felipe, the heir to the Spanish throne, was marrying Letizia Ortiz, a divorced TV anchor. Every television set in the kingdom was tuned to the royal wedding taking place in Madrid, and we eagerly succumbed to the addiction.

We sipped our coffees and scrutinized Felipe's humorless expression as he waited nervously and impatiently at the altar. Princes, like pilgrims, don't like to be kept waiting. We agreed to stay put to see if his bride would make an appearance.

The TV camera panned the guests and the rows upon rows of European royalty and pseudo-royalty until it settled on Britain's Prince Charles, tugging at his shirt cuffs, as is his unfortunate habit. In unison, the three of us muttered, "Bastard!"

"What he did to that poor woman was unthinkable," sneered Rose.

The cathedral organ thundered into action, and the happy bride came into view to begin her own Camino down the aisle.

Barbara, Rose, and I drained our cups and marched off to find Finisterre's cape and its lighthouse. We made a quick detour to the nearby supermarket on the off chance that it sold croissants. It did not, so we bought a bottle of champagne and plastic cups instead.

"So what do you suppose that English bloke is doing now?" Barbara asked me as we climbed the road to the lighthouse. "He was a weird one."

"He's walking to Finisterre," I replied nonchalantly. How many times was she going to ask me this question?

I adore lighthouses, but the one at Finisterre was a disappointment. Nothing of its original self had been preserved; it was a modern, square slab of cement blocks.

We walked to the edge of the cliff. I spotted a few familiar pilgrim faces from the Camino. A young man covered in tattoos had assumed the lotus position on a boulder and was staring into the mighty Atlantic, his blond dreadlocked hair whipping in the wind.

We snapped some photos and started to leave.

"Wait, there's something I have to do," I said.

My stone. Among the many pilgrim rituals is this: a pilgrim brings a stone from home, carries it on the journey, loading it with prayers, wishes, confessions, and dreams, and then flings it into the ocean at Finisterre.

I held the stone tightly in my fist and made some last-minute additions: I will not allow myself to get sucked into unhealthy relationships ever again. I will not play the "good girl." I will not hide my feelings when someone hurts me. I won't play nursemaid to needy men; let them pay for their own therapist. I am a whole person, and I am no longer going to barter away bits of my soul.

I threw the stone, hard and far, almost dislocating my shoulder in the process. I didn't feel any less burdened once it had left my hand.

Having pronounced the trip to Finisterre resoundingly anti-climactic, Barbara, Rose, and I walked back down the road toward the village, stopping midway at a picnic table to uncork the champagne and toast our respective Caminos.

"Men would never think of this," cracked Rose as she poured the champagne and doled out her stash of apricots and more Snickers bars. How many did this woman have?

It wasn't that Rose had anything against men; nor did any of us. Quite the contrary. But we had weathered our fair share of disappointment in the romance department, except for Barbara.

"But look at you," Barbara said to me. "This English bloke might work out. I knew someone who met a bloke on a trip, and they're still together twenty-five years later."

"I am *not* marrying anyone," I said. "I'll probably never see him again."

"Oh, you liked him," teased Barbara, and turning to Rose she added, "Should 'a seen the two of 'em, Rose, walking with me one minute, then taking off the next."

"You told us to go ahead because we walked faster than you," I protested. "You said you wouldn't mind."

Barbara's needling was starting to bug me.

"How about you?" I asked Rose. "Did you meet anyone interesting?"

"Nah, I saw a few cute ones but..."

"Well, you know what they say about men," I said. "They're like buses. If you miss the first one, another will be along in five minutes."

"Actually," said Rose, "men are like coffee. The best ones are warm and rich and keep you up all night. Or they're like floor tiles. If you lay them right the first time, you can walk over them for ever."

Rose let out a raspy, self-satisfied cackle and downed the last of her champagne.

"OK, let's clean up," she said.

THAT EVENING we were sitting at a table in a rather nice restaurant back in Santiago. "I want a big, fat steak," said Rose. "I need red meat."

It was hard to believe that less than a week earlier, we had been stomping along a hard, hypnotic path, consumed by various physical complaints. Now we were arranged politely around a mahogany table, smoothing out starched napkins on our laps and fidgeting with the silverware. We were Ladies Who Lunch. We had almost fully transformed into our pre-Camino states. I can't say I felt entirely comfortable about that.

Rose, Barbara, and I had been joined by Hannah. We recounted the highs and lows of our respective Caminos, and then Barbara brought the conversation back to—whom else—Colin.

"And there they were walking with me one minute, and then off in the distance the next," she recounted for the five hundredth time.

"You told me repeatedly that it wouldn't bother you if we walked on ahead because you were a slow walker," I said with undisguised exasperation.

"I know I did," she said.

"But it obviously did bother you, because you've brought it up at every possible opportunity," I said firmly but politely for the hundredth time. "I'm sorry I failed to read your mind. So let me get this clear: when you say, 'Walk ahead, I'm a slow walker,' you really mean, 'I'm a slow walker, so you'll have to bear with me'?"

"Now, that English guy was a weird bloke, wasn't he?" she said changing the subject and addressing the others.

I rolled my eyes. Here we go again.

"I ran into him just outside of Santiago," said Hannah.

My heart jumped.

"What time did you see him?" I asked, appearing unconcerned but privately wondering whether I had time to catch up to him.

"Oh, it was early in the afternoon," said Hannah.

But I already knew he was gone. When I had returned from Finisterre to the hotel, I had found a single long-stemmed red rose lying on my backpack.

"So what was his problem?" Barbara asked me pointedly.

"You liked him, didn't you?" I teased, turning the tables. "She had a crush on him, you know," I said to the others.

"He was a strange bloke," Barbara continued, ignoring me. "What do you think it was? Did he dump someone? Did someone commit suicide over him?"

"Maybe he had a drug habit," said Rose. "He was so skinny."

"No, I saw his bare arms," I said. "There were no track marks."

"Maybe he has AIDS?" said Hannah sadly.

I thought about The Kiss. Jesus.

"Maybe he murdered someone," said Rose, licking the steak blood off her knife.

"He could have accidentally killed someone in the line of duty," I suggested.

"He might have seen something on the job that traumatized him," said Barbara. "I know the sorts of things cops see on their beats."

"Maybe he's gay," whispered Rose.

"Did he touch you?" Barbara asked me, leaning in with narrowed eyes.

"We shared a hotel for a couple of nights, and no, he didn't come on to me," I replied.

"Definitely gay," she concluded.

After dinner, we bought ice cream cones and wandered leisurely through Santiago's maze of streets. We were all staying one more day before dispersing to our farflung homes.

We waved goodnight, confident that we would bump into one another the next day for final embraces and an exchange of addresses, but I never saw them again.

17

WHEN the come-ons from the restaurant hostesses and the street vendors begin to grate, when you find yourself constantly looking in vain for familiar faces, when the angelic voice of the nun in the cathedral sounds more like a wound-up tourist attraction than a paean to God, when you escape to your hotel room and can only find reruns of the Spanish royal wedding on the television, then you know it's time to go home.

I had been in Santiago for three days, and yet I could not extricate myself from it.

As I nursed a glass of *vino blanco* at an outdoor café, the cathedral bell tolled, and I felt the jab of pain that comes when you realize you will miss something that all along you thought you hated. I would miss it all—the small, ancient cities with their narrow roads and high, worn stone walls, the canopied path and dusty, punishing highways, the casual café society, the sound of gravel crunching beneath my feet, the church bells and cow bells.

Everything from my back-home life that I had come to love now seemed alien and pointless. I wasn't sure what I cared about.

All I knew was that I liked how I felt at that moment, and I wanted more of it.

I loved the fact that I knew Santiago like the back of my hand. I could navigate the place like a resident. From the Rúa da Virxe da Cerca, it was a quick trip through the Praza de Santo Agostiño into the Praza da Pescadería Vella, across the Rúa do Preguntoiro to the Rúa San Paio de Anteltares, around the corner to the Praza da Quintana, and then down the steps past the fountain at the Praza das Praterías to the Holy Door of the cathedral.

That was the other thing; everything started at the cathedral. Away from the cathedral there was a tomblike quality to the streets, but the closer you got to the cathedral the more the world seemed to come alive. The cathedral was the hub of city life; on our second night in Santiago, for example, the Praza da Quintana had been jammed with people of all ages, including Colin and me, for a rock concert. No one seemed concerned that a thousand-year-old cathedral, a Mecca of Christendom, was sharing a plaza with loud, throbbing rock music. I liked that.

From where I sat, a profusion of sculpted reliefs—fruit, shells, gargoyles, swags—festooned every building. No surface was deemed unfit for decoration; even the downspouts bore decorative flourishes. Design was imprinted on every facet of Spanish life and along with it the reminder that art was, and is, God's work.

I thought about some of the bigger architectural projects in my homeland. Oh sure, the boosters of the New Architecture talk a good game about "clean lines," "bold design," and "functionality," but let's face it, it's all a euphemism for cheap, stripped-down empire building. Once upon a time, grand visions were based not on how fast the project could be done, or for how much, but on the end product—even if it took several generations to complete. Today a lot of rich philanthropists seem more interested in scoring tax write-offs and name recognition than in erecting truly remarkable artistic creations.

I moseyed over to the Praza da Quintana and sat down with a glass of *vino tinto*. There was nothing left to do but sit, drink, and be mesmerized by the constant flow of pilgrims arriving in stunned realization that their Camino was over. And then there were the tourists, having just stepped off their coaches, loading themselves up with pilgrim staffs, water gourds, and humongous shells to hang around their necks.

A voice, *sotto voce*, asked, "Do you speak English?"

The question came from the man at the table next to mine.

He was from Belgium, he said, and this was his second time on the Camino.

"Why did you do it again?" I asked.

"After I finished it the first time—that was two years ago—I could not get it out of my mind. I had to come back."

The man went on to explain that he had tossed aside his marriage to satisfy his longing for the Camino. Now he was struggling under the weight of his addiction to it. He couldn't wait to walk it a third time.

His was one of several similar stories I encountered in my journey. Marriages broke up because of the Camino; some people couldn't stop dreaming about the Camino night after night, and they returned each year to walk the trail. I met a young woman who was on her fourth pilgrimage, and she cried with pain almost every step of the way. The Camino has its share of groupies and junkies, and sometimes it grips those who gravitate into its sphere a little too tightly.

I returned to my hotel, watched another rerun of the royal wedding, finished packing, and went to the hotel bar for a drink. I had an urge to return to the square in Santiago one more time, certain I would bump into Barbara, Rose, Hannah, maybe even Colin, but I knew that if I didn't cut the ties now, I might never go home.

The pilgrim life is a largely artificial one; you exist in a bubble of camaraderie, pain, and poverty, of shared purpose. Barbara

had said that the bond you forge with people on trips and vacations is transitory; rarely does anyone keep in touch, and it was
foolish to expect that such relationships could be maintained.

But then Barbara always struck me as a practical woman. I, in
contrast, have more passion than brains.

ARRIVING IN OPORTO, Portugal, I was so preoccupied with
where I was going—or rather, where I wasn't going—that I forgot
to say goodbye to my train mates, who were very nice people. One
of them was an American retiree who was traveling around the
world with nothing but a backpack. She had already been on the
road three months and still had Eastern Europe, India, and Asia
to cover. We had a fascinating conversation about being a traveler
as opposed to being a tourist, and in the end we exchanged e-mail
addresses. We still keep in touch from time to time.

I was in Oporto because it was where my flight home was
departing the next day.

I wandered though Oporto's majestic train station wondering
how I would even begin to find a place to spend the night, when
a young man who had traveled from Santiago in the same train
compartment appeared at my side.

"Do you have a place to stay?" he asked.

The man and I had not exchanged a word to one another in
the Santiago train station, where I first saw him, or on the train.
This was my decision, not his. He had looked open to striking up
a conversation, but my overcautious North American radar had
resurfaced, and so I avoided him. Now he was offering unsolic-
ited assistance. I was completely ashamed of myself.

No, I told him, I had no idea where to begin looking.

"See that building with a dome across the street?" he said,
pointing. "That's apparently a very nice *pensione*, and it's not
expensive. Then, up this street—do you see past those street
lights?—there's another *pensione*, again also very nice and clean.
It's on this side of the street."

With that, he wished me luck, gave me a friendly hug, and was gone.

I need to change my citizenship, I thought. North American society is killing my humanity.

The building with the dome was closer, so I headed there first. As luck would have it, a room was available. The desk clerk told me I was lucky I had arrived when I did; in a few days, he said, Oporto was hosting the European Cup. The upcoming game explained the flurry of construction taking place all around me.

That afternoon, I checked my e-mail and was ecstatic to find a message from Brigitte. She was back in France and wanted to apologize for dawdling that morning in Hospital da Condesa. Just as I suspected, she had done so because she wanted to walk alone. I e-mailed back immediately to tell her I had not been offended by her decision. We were all meant to trust our intuition and follow what felt right.

There was no e-mail from Colin. It had been exactly a week since we had met, a week since my life had shifted. Where was he? Would I ever hear from him again?

Then I did something really foolish. While wandering Rúa Santa Catarina in Oporto, I dropped into a hair salon and had my Botticelli-like curls snipped off. What was left was blow-dried into a smooth, characterless page-boy. I had been off the Camino only a few days, and already I was taming the gypsy within. I have no explanation for my actions.

That night, as I sat in bed against a headboard of black stained wood bearing a richly carved scallop shell, I removed both sets of earrings for the first time since the beginning of the Camino. The gold hoops didn't require much cleaning, so I just wiped them with a cloth and returned them to the holes in my earlobes. The diamond studs, however, had become clogged with gunk. As I worked at dislodging the accumulated dirt, I wondered why I continued to wear them. I never liked stud earrings, but I wore them, even had another set of holes punched in my ears to accommodate them, just to please the person who had given them to me. Someone who had deceived me and hurt me. If the earrings brought up such bitter reminders, why wear them? Were they a form of self-flagellation? I was not much different from Colin in stoking a painful memory, I was just better at hiding it. I placed the studs carefully on the night table, then settled into bed and turned out the light.

The next morning the plane roared down a wet runway and lifted off into overcast skies, swallowed up by clouds as thick as cotton candy. We climbed and climbed until we reached an atmosphere of blue skies and sunshine, the sort of conditions I had walked beneath just days earlier.

Walking. The very thought pinched something behind my eyes, and I turned my head toward the window. The shock to my body of not being in the damp, dewy forests of Spain made my skin tighten, a withdrawal symptom of being denied hourly injections of water and frequent stops for San Miguel beer.

I rooted around in my purse to retrieve the diamond studs in order to put them on, but they weren't there. They were still on the night table in my Oporto hotel room.

Score another one for the psychic, I chuckled to myself. I had thought I could defy at least one of her predictions, especially the one about jewelry. *"Don't take jewelry,"* she had warned. *"You'll definitely lose something."*

A FEW DAYS later I was gasping for air like a fish out of water.

I was at home—the place that I knew best of all but that felt completely foreign to me.

I dissolved into sobs whenever I thought of the Camino. I played Enya, and I cried some more. The thought of not seeing Colin induced spasms of grief I couldn't control. My heart ached and broke like a teenager's, and I wondered whether I had had the same effect on him. It felt as if my life would never return to "normal," whatever normal was.

My children tried to comfort me, unable to comprehend why their mother, safely back from an exciting trip, was so inexplicably silent, sitting in a chair staring out the window.

"Why are you crying, Mommy? Do you miss Spain?" they would ask, putting an awkward but comforting arm around my shoulder.

"Yes," I would barely whisper, unable to articulate the experience in a way they might understand. How do I explain that Spain means Colin, Barbara, Brigitte, Rose, the Three American Boys, José, even the Lout with the Cell Phone? How to explain to anyone the power and the glory of hot, sweltering paths without shade, mist-covered laneways weaving up a hill, a sunrise cracking the horizon and spilling out onto a landscape covered in a dozen shades of green? Or yellow arrows, shells, thousand-year-old towns that speak to your soul, and double rainbows arcing over a shrine? How do you tell someone that it's not the journey that's important, it's the company you keep? How do you explain any of this without sounding like a crazy person?

I tried to maintain some of my Camino self by donning hiking clothes and walking to the office with my work clothes in my backpack. It didn't last. Not only did I arrive at work sweaty and exhausted, people on the street viewed me as an oddity. One day an elderly woman pressed five dollars into my hand "to buy yourself a meal," and I knew then it was time to hang up my backpack and make friends with my car.

"GO BACK TO Spain!" my son snapped at me.

I had been home barely a week when I was back in the thick of the usual parent-teenage drama.

But his "Go back to Spain!" comment was a sharp jab that stung not because of the rejection it was intended to imply but because of the guilt it induced. "Go back to Spain" was exactly what I wanted to do.

I wanted to tell him that four weeks away had shown me what I have not wanted to admit to them or to anyone. As much as

I love my children, my best-before date as a mom had expired. I didn't feel I fit the mom mold anymore. Perhaps I never did. Backpacking for a month across Spain freed my gypsy soul and gave me options I had never thought possible. Maybe I have always been a gypsy, and what I was mourning was the loss of the complicated, crazy woman I had gotten to know for a month. Sure, she was a lot of work, but her unpredictable spirit ensured that there was never a dull moment.

Most North American women don't tramp through mud lugging a backpack. They're home baking cookies for their child's class party or volunteering their time for some useful humanitarian project or going to the gym or booking regular nail appointments. I'd never slag such women, but we can't all be like that. Some of us cross a line that makes us question absolutely everything about the life we have made for ourselves and why it takes us so long to wake up and accept our true selves.

"Go back to Spain!" rang in my ears.

I wished I could.

EPILOGUE

ABOUT a month after I returned home from Spain, I invited the women from the original group to my home to share photos and memories over a few glasses of wine. Everyone had made it to Santiago in some fashion, and everyone had received the *credencial*.

That's the *Reader's Digest* version.

The group that met at my home was very different from the one that started out in Saint-Jean-Pied-de-Port on May 1. For starters, getting a few of the women to attend the reunion took some work. Not all of them liked each other anymore, and some flatly refused to be in the same room.

Those who did attend brought wine and stories. Tales tumbled out about severe bitchiness and other unsavory behavior within the group after I had left them in Redecilla. One woman complained to another that she "didn't want to hear another story about your fucking cats." Another woman was reduced to tears when she was pointedly and repeatedly shunned by others in the group. Two women, one of whom was married, had one-night stands on the Camino, and one of those two women also tried to kindle a lesbian relationship with another group member who was married and did not swing that way. There were tales of pettiness, power trips, alcoholism, and emotional abuse.

As I listened to all this in stunned silence, four words came to mind: There. Is. A. God. I was so grateful to whatever divine Grace had intervened and spirited me away from the group.

I still keep in touch with some of the women. Occasionally a small group of us gets together for an anniversary hike in May, but no one has attempted an extended hike. There are occasional rumblings about doing the Camino again, though the unspoken caveat is "not as a group."

If nothing else the Camino instilled in me a love of walking and of exploring small towns and the countryside. I cannot visit a place now without taking a measure of it on foot. And I never walk anywhere without slathering Vaseline on my feet.

I'm sure you're dying to know what happened to my fingernail. The infection magically healed by the time I returned home—without any medication (though my fingers were always in Vaseline, and I'm happy to give credit where it's due). It took a while for the nail to grow back, but now you'd never know it had been damaged.

The psychic's predictions had all proved correct—the cat fights, the group dynamics, the search for profundity, the death, the loss of jewelry, the too-rustic aspect of the Camino, the fair-haired man, the fact that the adventure would not turn out exactly as planned. She was even right about meeting someone famous—I figured that was the Vancouver mother and her plus-size-model daughter, not Steve Martin's ghost. As for the possibility that I would overspend? She was probably right about that, too, but how do you put a price on such an adventure?

There have been many happy outcomes from my Camino pilgrimage.

I keep in touch via e-mail with Brigitte, and we hope one day to meet up again in person. In her notes I sense that she wishes for life to be easier, and I wish that for her too, with all my heart. She is happiest when she is telling me about horses, which she loves—the ones she has succeeded in breaking in and the ones she has taken on long trail rides through France.

José and I corresponded once or twice, but after his return home he was bitten by the Camino bug and within months had laced up his hiking boots and was off again, this time walking from his Brussels home all the way to Santiago. I'm not sure whether he managed to find the faith he was seeking.

I received a few e-mails from Dr. Dan the Massage Man, but his lengthy missives about himself couldn't hold my interest, so I didn't write back.

I tracked down the Three American Boys—Ben, Ian, and Peter—and one of them wrote to me, but then I lost the address. I suppose I could try to contact them again, but I'm content with the memory of our brief friendship.

By far the best outcome was this:

A few weeks after my return home, as I moped about in a daze of culture shock, the phone rang.

"Is that you?" an English-accented male voice asked from the other end of the line.

It was Colin. I was beyond ecstatic.

"Where are you? What time is it?" I fumbled with the telephone receiver as elation overtook coherence.

"I'm back home in London," he said. I could hear the smile in his voice. "It's about midnight here. When did you get home from Spain? I was trying to remember the exact day you said you were leaving."

He had made it to Finisterre—he didn't find it exciting, either, but then again that wasn't the reason he had trekked there. He had completed a ritual—there seem to be as many rituals as there are pilgrims—of taking his knapsack down to the Galician shores and burning all his pilgrim clothes on the beach.

We talked for an hour.

Not long after, he flew from England to Canada to see me and stayed a month. As I write this, three years later, we are still together. Well, as together as two people who live on opposite sides of the Atlantic can be. We have become frequent if not somewhat eccentric fliers. One cold, snowy night he appeared unannounced on my doorstep on the eve of my birthday and stayed just one night because he had to be back at work by Monday morning. I returned the gesture a couple of months later when I showed up at a surprise birthday party his family had thrown for him.

And yes, Colin did eventually tell me about the Trauma That Could Not Be Mentioned. It was nothing like the wild conjectures made around the dinner table that night in Santiago with Barbara, Rose, and Hannah; it was an overwhelmingly sad story that concerned the untimely death of his fiancée. Beyond that I will say no more.

Colin had allowed his grief to eat away at him for seven years, during which he refused to discuss the subject with anyone.

He has since mapped a way out of the labyrinth of sadness. His journey, though long and painful at times, has rewarded him with more sunny days than gray ones now. Turns out that perseverance and patience are as vital for coping with everyday life as they are for coping with the Camino.

Remarkably, Colin's decision to walk the Camino had been a spur-of-the-moment idea hatched just weeks before he left for Spain.

That's Impulse for you.

We still marvel at how the small actions of our lives altered our course, how two people from different parts of the world, each heeding their separate calls from Impulse, could meet on a lonely, dusty, parched road in the middle of a Spanish trail and be catapulted into a deliriously unexpected direction. And to think it all started with a tiny bottle of wine spirited aboard an airplane.

You can't be certain when or if it such serendipitous moments will happen, but it helps if you leave yourself open to the random nature of life unfolding. What you can stake your life on is this: there's an adventure waiting around every corner. Of that I am certain.